A Place in the Rain Forest

Settling the Costa Rican Frontier

by Darryl
Cole-Christensen

━━━━━━━

A Place in the Rain Forest

UNIVERSITY OF TEXAS PRESS, AUSTIN

Requests for permission to reproduce
material from this work should be sent to
Permissions, University of Texas Press,
P.O. Box 7819, Austin, TX 78713-7819.

⊗ The paper used in this publication meets
the minimum requirements of American
National Standard for Information Sciences—
Permanence of Paper for Printed Library
Materials, ANSI Z39.48-1984.

Library of Congress
Cataloging-in-Publication Data
Cole-Christensen, Darryl, 1934–
    A place in the rain forest :
settling the Costa Rican frontier /
by Darryl Cole-Christensen.
        p.   cm.

    ISBN 0-292-71191-3 (pbk.: alk. paper)
    1. Land settlement—Costa Rica—
    Coto Brus (Canton)—History.
    2. Frontier and pioneer life—Costa Rica—
    Coto Brus (Canton)
HD350.C68C65   1997
333.3′172867—dc20   96-32321

Contents

Foreword

*I*n a few years, probably, several books will have been written about Coto Brus and its settlement. This part of Costa Rica and its recent past lend themselves to a narrative of adventure as well as to disciplined scientific study. Other accounts of this story may take up its separate aspects.

In the present book I have combined the narrative of adventure with a framework of information about why and how the adventure occurred. Thus, the subjects of romance and pioneering may be looked at critically so that readers can draw their own conclusions about the outcome of the transformation of a natural world. The process by which the rain forest frontier was transformed into an agricultural community was not a simple one. It had many elements. I have tried to show them as they interacted, each part playing upon the other, all producing a new order of life systems and human relationships.

None of us who caused these changes must make an apology beyond what was possible at the time and within the scope of our understanding. We believed; we tried; we failed; we recovered and tried again; and we learned. In putting down this record I have endeavored to stay away from any rigid points of view. Many things came to bear upon the lives of those of us who came to this land. I have described them in a context of both their relevance at the time they occurred and their relevance to our present time.

This book makes frequent reference to Finca Loma Linda, my family's farm. Without the assistance, the vision, and the fortitude of my mother and father it would not have come into existence nor would it be what it is today. My wife and our three daughters have made not only this book possible but also the story which it tells. There have been many people who have worked on Finca Loma Linda over the years, their faces and names written in the pages of this farm. I want to particularly express my gratitude to the memory of Adolfo Montero; his work and loyalty made Finca Loma Linda a better place for many.

Finally, the people of Coto Brus have written with their hands and their hearts a large part of this story; in many respects this book is for them.

A
Place
in the
Rain
Forest

Introduction

Masters of the Earth

*A*mong the characteristics of our present time is the diminished opportunity to do something new on the face of the earth. I refer to the opportunity to initiate a sequence of events, causes and effects, which, separately and in combination, will transform an entire order of life systems—eliminate earlier orders, produce new orders, and compel countless species, individuals, and generations, human and animal, to adjust, or seek to adjust, to the results of the actions taken by a few persons. I am not referring to the cataclysm of a nuclear holocaust or the decisions taken by leaders of powerful nations or the sweeping effects of warfare but rather to the acts taken by humbler people, the settlers of new lands in the tropical rain forest. These settlers, the farmers, have in their power the ability to exterminate life systems; to reduce or wipe out ecological orders; to alter the resources of air, water, and soil; and to intervene in the processes of the life-sustaining capacities of lands in such a way that these may be impaired over successive generations of men and women and their children on the earth. Having the power to wreak such mischief, these farmers may go on to produce and sell "poisoned" food, further contaminate resources that have been impaired, and arrive at a position of near despair in personal and professional impoverishment.

In many respects these "masters of the earth" hold far greater power over the chain of consequences ensuing from their use and misuse of resources than do the leaders of nations. For the masters of small or larger segments of the land do not recognize a system of checks and balances in political and institutional form. They are accustomed to answering to none but themselves, and when they do recognize a system of checks and balances which is far more comprehensive than any that may be applied by society, they are circumscribed by its effects even while they do not understand its mechanisms or recognize its apparently endless scope of consequence. They face within themselves the knowledge that they cannot know the end result of processes they have set in motion, even while acknowledging that they themselves may be among the most immediate victims of their initiatives for change.

The men and women I describe, the settlers and farmers of new lands, do not see themselves as abusing their powers. Without exception, they look upon themselves as builders. Many dream of, and spend a lifetime of tireless work seeking to accomplish, fine things. They become the pawns of an appalling ignorance, that which, only faintly glimpsed, conceals behind its indefinite facade an ageless dimension of the unknown.

I am a member of the group of persons I describe. In 1954 my family and I undertook to settle on a previously unexplored and unknown section of rain forest in southeastern Costa Rica. We shared an opportunity and a responsibility which have become by now part of an almost vanished past. But the consequences of what we, and others, have done will remain well into the future.

The South Frontier

The region of land referred to during the 1950s and 1960s in
Costa Rica as the South Frontier was a relatively small land area in
a small country. Situated between the Pacific slopes of the Cordi-
llera Talamanca, the central mountain range dividing the Pacific and
Caribbean watersheds in southeastern Costa Rica, and the lowland
Pacific flood plains, it occupied a mid–elevational range of 800 to
1,400 meters, subject to annual rainfall of from 3,000 to 4,000 milli-
meters. This unpopulated and partly unexplored region was entirely
covered by unbroken primary rain forest. To the east was Panama,
lands adjoining the South Frontier which had seen some settlement
by the mid-1950s, albeit sparse; in Panama, too, in the province of
Chiriquí, there were large integral tracts of rain forest occupying
the higher elevations. Temperatures were cool, for this was a land
of deep forest shade under multistoried canopies of vegetation. The
surface of the area itself, not easily discerned, certainly from the
air in flights over the region, and also not easily measured within
the forest because perspectives were foreshortened by the trees
and understory, was steep and broken, with few areas that might
be called flat or level. Everywhere were sharp gradients, abrupt cleav-
ages in the surface of the land, small streams running in deep seams.
The sky, as seen from the forest floor, was visible only in fragments,
always through the branches of trees or, occasionally, where wind-
falls had opened a somewhat larger space overhead. The earth itself
was crowded with life, covered by mold and leaves, always wet or
moist, harboring in every nook and interstice countless mysteries.
This land knew two seasons, the wet and the dry, the first beginning
in May and running to December, the latter occupying the balance
of the year.

The first explorers who came to this region in our time (shards
and artifacts found throughout this region give evidence of habi-
tation by indigenous people at a much earlier period) did so afoot.

They came from both the Panamanian and Costa Rican sides of a border between the two countries which had not been completely defined during the period of exploration. Following these explorers, in the decade of the 1940s, a few pioneers took up landholdings at scattered sites throughout the frontier. These men and women with their children had established such outposts by the time an Italian – Costa Rican colonization project was initiated in 1952. At this point an organized thrust toward settlement of the new land was begun.

This thrust was conceived by *Comandante* Vito Sansonetti, who, on a visit to Costa Rica from Italy in 1949, was captivated by the vision of Italian colonization in the remote but seemingly fertile rain forest frontier in southeastern Costa Rica, the prospect of a new life for war-stricken rural families, especially those from the south of Italy. The idea found a favorable response in Costa Rican government agencies, and the colonization project, to include the settlement of 250 families, 20 percent of whom would be Costa Ricans, received an endorsement for financial assistance from private and public sources, including the Instituto Nacional de Crédito para Trabajadores Italianos en Tierra Extranjera.

To the west of the land which was to become the site of this spearhead of colonization, and at an elevation only a little above sea level, were the coastal flood plains, planted in large tracts in bananas by the United Fruit Company. These plantations were linked to the coastal port of Golfito by a railroad, and the South Frontier was connected to this railroad, the plantations, and the port by a tenuous road built during the Second World War along a limestone rampart of cliffs dividing the highland from the lowland. The road, rock surfaced, narrow, and in many places clinging to the cliffs, had not been completed into the highland frontier area by the end of the war and existed in this segment only as a path through the forest at the time the Italian colonization venture was begun. Following some work by the first colonists, this path could be negotiated during the dry season by four-wheel-drive vehicles, winding their way among the trees, traveling at little better than walking speed. During the wet season this road became impassable to wheeled vehicles, and supplies for the colony and the settlers were packed by horses and mules. Under the wettest of conditions, the pack animals themselves would founder in the mud, and packs would have to be off-loaded, carried by hand, and retied on the pack animals several times during the trek, the mule drivers and their pack train arriving at their destination exhausted and covered with mud.

A market for farm produce from the frontier did exist in the banana plantations' many commissaries, general stores set up throughout the plantations to supply the needs of the hundreds of banana workers. Vegetables, fruit, meat, eggs, milk, cheese and other products might all find buyers were producers able to grow or raise such foodstuffs and transport them to market. Beyond this potential market, however, there was no practical or economical way of transporting such goods from the frontier either to Panama or to the interior of Costa Rica. There were no roads in either direction, so travel by land to either destination would perforce be by foot or by horse. Swollen rivers on both sides of the frontier at times made even such travel impossible, there being no way of fording the rivers during the heaviest rains. One airstrip did afford a link with the outside world for people living on the frontier; but this airfield, at an outpost called Agua Buena, was so enclosed at both ends by high mountains that only light, single-engine planes could carry passengers and some light cargo off it.

Shortwave radio connected the frontier with the world beyond its confines, and mail service was dependent on the flights of the small planes. There were, of course, at the beginning of the settlement, no schools, no medical facilities, no doctors or nurses, and only a few general stores offering limited and basic supplies. Life for the settlers during these early years was marked by solitude, isolation, and enclosure. Silence, in the absence of the normal sounds associated with humanity, was usually all-pervasive; battery-operated radios did not pick up any stations, or one or two only badly, and outside of the center of the Italian colony itself, there was no electricity or any of the services dependent on it.

For most of the settlers the rain forest was a threat, a danger. It was home to poisonous snakes: the fer-de-lance, the *mano de piedra,* the coral. Many tales were told of the jaguar; it was universally feared and rarely, if ever, seen. The forest housed peccaries, tapirs, anteaters, monkeys, a few macaws, many parrots and toucans, and at morning and evening settlers could hear the babble of guans. Each of the tall trees was, in its outspread branches, a world apart, the domain of amphibians and reptiles, epiphytic plants, insects and birds. Lianas drooped from many of these trees, the vines themselves encrusted with epiphytic life; and in the forest understory were many ferns, palms, philodendrons, and delicate, shade-loving plants. In the streams and springs which welled from the ground could be found aquatic insects and the habitat of aquatic birds.

The wildlife, in terms of the larger mammals, was mostly unseen; even many of the birds were secluded within the shadows. In the wet season the forest was ever wet, drops of rain clinging within the moss on trees and leaves, a silence in footfalls over the moldering humus on the forest floor; in the dry season the northeast trade winds would sweep over the forest, awakening a response in every leaf and twig, with a clattering of branches, a snapping and shearing of the crowns of trees, a crash and roar in passage.

The frontier was generally seen at this time in two ways by its settlers: there was the land, and there was the forest. On the land homes could be raised, communities would rise, isolation and a sense of loneliness would be banished by the acquisition of space; it would be possible to see from here to there, and there, beyond the confines of one's own plot of terrain, would be a neighbor and other people; a sense of commonality and community would exist. The land could provide food, an income, a garden, amenities even of leisure.

The forest, on the other hand, restricted, enclosed, almost suffocated one upon weeks and months within it. It allowed no light. Within it the land was useless; it was the great obstacle and antagonist to be overcome. No one had demonstrated that anything useful could be done with the forest. At another time and in a different place the timber in the forest might have held some considerable value, but here it was worthless; there were no roads over which to transport logs, no accessible markets for sawed lumber. The mills set up in the Italian colony and, later, elsewhere sawed only what

A PLACE IN THE RAIN FOREST

was needed for the settlers themselves. The timber from the felled forest would be left to decay on the land.

Most of the settlers saw no aesthetic value in the forest. All might agree that it was, indeed, impressive, even beautiful; but such considerations were superfluous; what mattered was an economic and practicable framework to sustain people on the land. That the forest was the habitat of many forms of life was obvious; but it was not clear why these forms of life might be useful for human needs or purposes in the future, and it was not even certain that the elimination of the forest here in the frontier might endanger species and populations. At that time there was much primary forest in Costa Rica, and settlers labored under the assumption, never actually ascertained with much thought, that while they found it expedient to disrupt the rain forest's natural state, in other places the forest would be left undisturbed.

There were other reasons to see the primary rain forest as the single most imposing and difficult obstacle to progress in settlement and eventual well-being. Most of the land in the South Frontier at the beginning of the 1950s was untitled. To qualify for a title to land, a settler had to "prove up" his holding. The key word in Spanish was *mejoras,* improvements. The initiation of improvements always started with the felling of the forest. To establish ownership of land, even though it was untitled, a settler needed to cut down the forest, and to the extent that he cut down more forest, he saw himself as becoming entitled to own that much more land. The most negotiable and evident credential of ownership during those early years in the frontier was the cut-down forest. Once a settler had cut the forest, he had demonstrated that he and his family were the owners of that land, and it would not be easy for someone else to dispute such entitlement or to lay claim to the land.

An attitude that "the land is for those who work it" prevailed, and certainly it was work to cut down the forest. That the land might stand idle and unused thereafter, and in fact did for many years in many instances, did not matter much, because ownership had been demonstrated by the work invested in the felling. As always is the case when something can apparently be had for almost nothing, there were many instances in the early years of settlement in which would-be landowners cut immense tracts of forest to establish ownership with the intention of later subdividing this land and selling it with its improvements. Thus it was that over a period of a few years light invaded huge areas of the South Frontier, the sky could be seen, distances and perspectives were established, and under a tangle of broken trees and apparent rubble the actual features of the surface of the land could be seen. In many respects they were intimidating; the topography of this region certainly was not the kind which would lend itself to any conventional kind of modern farming practice.

At this point in the settlement of the South Frontier, two worlds characterized this portion of the earth's surface. One was that of the disappearing forest and the emerging land, and the other was that of the visions, individually and collectively held by the men and women who had come here, of what the future would be. In reality these men and women would make the future. Whereas it seems paradoxical that two such opposite conditions should exist under the same canopy—for who could possibly be more destructive than those of us who propose to open up such a frontier?—these men and women saw themselves as builders, even as creators who would make good and useful things on the earth. And they considered themselves to be both fortunate and even privileged.

It was also an anomaly that such a primitive and difficult way of life should exist, and persist over a few decades, in what otherwise was a modern world with all the conveniences the settlers were denied. For this was the midpoint of the twentieth century—not a time when men and women and children faced without option such rigors because pioneering and settlement were a normal way of life. In many respects the South Frontier of the mid–twentieth century was an anachronism; it did not seem to really belong in a modern context. Yet the land was there, the people both wanted and needed it, and there was no other way of acquiring it than by going to it and working on it.

My family and I were among the persons and subject to the conditions I describe. For twenty-five years on our farm, Finca Loma

Linda, we lived without electricity, reading at night by candles and kerosene lamps. We knew the isolation and the struggle, but we knew the joy of working together and creating, as well. We also learned to face the outcome of our ignorance. My family now lives in the United States and has been there for many years. Finca Loma Linda has become the site for scientific research carried out by students and faculty from many universities, investigations into the ecology, the agriculture, the biology of land forming part of the humid tropics. We are studying ways to restore and provide a basis of knowledge to orient the future of those acts which here altered an entire world. This book is about what we are learning. It is also about what we have done.

ONE

Planning the Farm

The primary rain forest on the South Frontier was cut by men working with three tools: the axe, the machete, and the *garabato,* a stick, usually cut from a sapling, having a branch at somewhat less than 90 degrees and used along with the machete to clear understory. Chainsaws were only being introduced in Costa Rica at the beginning of the settlement of the South Frontier, and they did not play an important role in the early cutting of the forest. The men who worked with the axe, the machete, and the *garabato* were often barefoot or in shoes that were without laces, open and broken, nearly worn out. These men wore baggy pants tied at the waist with a cord or heavy twine, and their shirts were frequently without buttons, open across the chest. Each carried a file at the waist in a sheath for sharpening the axe or machete. A gourd of drinking water, taken from a stream, accompanied the men, and if they brought food into the forest, it was wrapped in banana or heliconia leaves and eaten with a spoon.

Often the men had the lean, wiry frame which seemed to draw its strength from no apparent reserve of muscularity; sometimes they looked almost frail. They were neither exceptionally tall nor exceptionally heavy. They worked with axes with long straight handles cut from the hardwoods of the forest and planed and fit by the worker. The preferred axe had a 3½- or 4-pound head, ground to an edge on sandstones. Workers devoted many hours to this task over a period of weeks. The men were divided about equally in their preferences regarding double- versus single-bit axes.

Some of the men lived with women and had children; by this I mean that they did not recognize the obligations or responsibilities of husbands or fathers beyond a transient relationship because they were not married and had no firm commitment to a family, a home, or the land. Others were married, or recognized a union with their female partner and children as having all the strength of the bonds of marriage, and these men believed that the purpose of their work on the land was to build a home.

There were other men who were single, with no woman or home, and might not even wish to have the permanency of land. These men worked for hire, and on Saturdays of some weeks they took their small earnings to the brothels and cantinas in a shanty town at the periphery of the United Fruit Company banana plantations, returning to work in the frontier, if indeed they did return, without any money.

The women who shared homes with the frontiersmen lived in thatched, earth-floor structures called *ranchos,* cooked on open hearths, washed clothes with their daughters in the streams, and bore or tended to babies. The women and girls usually were barefoot, and while working and tending to daily life in the *rancho* they wore loose, shapeless dresses which did not conceal the contours of bodies that looked exhausted in youth. At an early age, almost in infancy, the boys in the family learned to use the machete and the girls learned to tend the babies and wash clothes.

These men and women and their children initiated farms.

They had many options, some of which I shall discuss here; however, they did not, nor did I when I was starting as they did on the new land, recognize all of these options.

First, we might consider ourselves as architects in reverse, and by this I mean that we would disassemble and dismantle before we would build. Our structure was the primary rain forest and the land upon which it stood. We might see ourselves as building with light.

No settler was unaware that light, the light of the sun, was a motivating force in all that would ensue on the land. However, in starting on a frontier, each settler had within his power the ability to alter and shape an entire realm of existing light relationships and to devise new ones. The energy of the sun would, of course, be influenced by cloud cover, season, and climate. But within the canopy of trees it would also be influenced by relative shade and open space. Shade within the forest was already established, and it varied in terms of elevation from the ground surface up to the highest forest canopy. A farmer, anywhere in the world, is aware that an ability to influence the effects of solar exposure and solar energy is an important tool in agriculture.

This understanding is illustrated by a recent experiment on Finca Loma Linda which was adversely affected by what the research scientists referred to as an unwelcome "confound," a condition complicating the evaluation of the experimental data. The experiment was carried out in an open field with only one-year-old secondary vegetation covering the ground. However, at a distance of about 80 meters across the land to the southeast, some standing primary forest trees cast a long shadow in the mornings. This shadow, the researchers think, affected one half of the experimental site, causing it to respond differently than the less shaded side.

The point is: light is a fundamental factor in our management and use of the land, and the settlers of a new frontier have a unique opportunity to work with it. By manipulating the felling of the trees, leaving forest standing in relationship to sectors of land which were clean-cut, by anticipating the nature and stature of the successional growth and staggering the elevations represented by the primary forest's upper canopies and understory growth left intact at the edges of clear-cut clearings, the settlers might have engaged in an opportunity to work creatively with light.

A second element that the settlement of the new lands would alter and that might be managed by the prospective farmers was moisture—the relative humidity in the atmosphere at any given hour in the day or night and its corresponding counterpart, the moisture in the earth and that which sustains life on the earth and covers the surfaces of plants and tissues. The interactions of light and moisture with all else in the rain forest are subjects which may be studied but will never be fully understood either by scientists or those who manage the land. They are fleeting, never static; no sooner have we arrested a concept of them—and this indeed is all that can be arrested—than they are part of a nonrecurrent past, a condition that only might have existed and will never exist again.

We must understand these dynamics of life and energy systems as a component of our thinking, but more fundamentally, as a component of our attitude relative to what we perceive as our environment. It is never possible to halt and examine these processes with which we ourselves are integrated, but to the degree that we recognize their relevance to us, we may be able to relate action with action, stroke with stroke, in an orchestration which responds to our intercession. All who work with natural elements in environments have this opportunity. But those who initiate settlement on new land are inundated by the forces of primitive and intensely impressionable phenomena. It is not impossible to perceive the tap and beat of ever exigent life and energy systems. It is within the reach of the human whose bare feet are secured to the earth through labor and in whose hands are the implements of change—the axe and machete—to touch the inertia of a world in unfoldment and respond with heart and mind.

But certain principles can be drawn from our observations, and these can be useful in planning the farm. Moisture, like other conditions we encounter in the rain forest at the beginning of the settlement of this land, is a given set of conditions; it is only when we have intervened and altered or destroyed those conditions that we recognize the value they represented. Moisture, converted into deluges of rain or floods, or its absence, seen as prolonged droughts, calls immediately the attention of everyone. When it is nicely adjusted, as is so often the prevailing condition in the rain forest, we may tend to take it for granted. Yet the classroom in the primary forest is not always there; our opportunity to study the intricate life systems and the relationships upon which these depend in the rain forest is lost to succeeding generations of land users. It is no exaggeration, however, to say that the first generation of land users on a frontier have an opportunity to influence life-systems relationships and the balance of the environment in ways that will not be available after the forest is destroyed.

Another condition within the control, to some extent, of the settlers was relative temperature. One has only to walk on a hot day from an open field into the primary forest to appreciate this—that is, if the primary forest is there. Because the open fields surely will be there, and they will be hot and, during the dry season, brilliantly exposed to the sun. In the forest the temperature will be moderated; it will be cool at elevations such as these in Coto Brus, and the moisture in the air will be felt on the skin.

But what are the relationships between the periphery of the rain forest, if some of it has been left standing, and these open fields? Are there predatory birds in the forest, taking refuge there during the hours of intense heat, which venture out at other hours to feed on insects which have become crop pests? What are the relationships between forest-dwelling insects and the insects in the field? Are there plant disease–vector relationships that the proximity of the forest to cultivated fields, and thus different temperature relationships, may affect? These and similar questions have been touched upon at different times in research projects here at the farm, but we have no answers to any of them. Few doubt, however, that temperature relationships and a fuller understanding of them can have far-reaching importance in farming.

As always is the case with what we recognize as separate components of phenomena within an environment, temperature, like moisture and sunlight, is not a separate unit of being; it exists as a condition and a function of all else in the environment. Yet we focus our attention and concern on this single element in a composite in order to fix in our thinking what we may learn of it. We—those of us who caused the rain forest to yield and recede—must repeatedly recognize that our best opportunity for understanding these separate components of the environment and their composite relationships also withdrew and separated themselves from us as we reduced and eliminated the forest. The important role that soil temperature plays under ground-covering mulch, as exemplified in the primary forest, might alert the settler, any settler, in such new lands to soil temperature considerations for crop production at later times. It might be honestly supposed, from our personal perspective of need, that the forest, at any moment in its term of integrity, was there to instruct; it remained for the settlers to recognize the opportunity to learn.

Another condition within the control of the settlers was that of the circulation and currents of air. Depending on how and where the forest was cut, air currents, and all that they influence, would be affected. All planters, particularly in the tropics, know the effects of a stultifying stagnancy of air around plants. Pockets of unmoving air are not good for crop development. The opposite condition, strong winds buffeting plants, is not good either. Not only could the existing forest be used in moderating these conditions at the outset of settlement, but the entire layout and subsequent management of the farms could be related to them. Topography, the features of the land surface, would be a factor influencing the relationship of plants and animals subject to changes in the currents of air. At this point in the initiation of farms, the long-term objectives could be envisioned. These would unavoidably have to include consideration of the interaction between the farmer's management scheme and the factors of light, moisture, temperature, and air currents. These are only four of the hundreds of natural relationship conditions the would-be farmer and settler might have under his or her partial control. And each of these four conditions could be subdivided and further subdivided. But this did not happen and would not happen in the settlement of a frontier.

The four conditions I've referred to as falling partly under the control of those who plan and implement planning in farming are particularly important in their relationships to crop diseases. Here in Coto Brus (this is the name given today to the region earlier known as the South Frontier, and these names are used interchangeably in this book), as in similar areas in the tropics, plant diseases are a

A PLACE IN THE RAIN FOREST

major limitation in farming and, in terms of the measures taken to combat them, one of the principal causes of the contamination of the environment. The rain forest might have taught us, had we been astute enough to recognize its instructive posture, that environmentally acceptable adjustments in our quest to raise food and produce would probably be the result of our awareness of a variety of interactions and relationships, all of which, taken in their whole, lead to better practices in land management. In repairing an intricate machine or an electronic device, a mechanic or technician is careful to observe how it is put together before taking it apart. If we attempt to carry the analogy to the area of land settlement, two important differences stand out: (1) we never really understand the workings of life relationships within an environment, and (2) once we disassemble these life relationships, we have no means of restoring them to their original condition. There are no blueprints in such work. An awareness of ignorance is the first step in learning, for until we become aware that we do not know something, we are probably unaware that the opportunity for the acquisition of learning even exists.

The settlement of the South Frontier was rooted in actions by men and women. But let us speak of *acts* rather than actions. By association these men and women will find themselves moving and working in a stream of gigantic currents of energies within the environment, this environment which permeates even the smallest moments of their lives. The power of these energies, with their raw aspects of direct confrontation expressed in a multitude of adversities opposed to the needs and wishes of the settlers, will cause them to search for ways of expressing themselves by the dimensions of these forces. *These acts, produced by my hand, are the forthright expression of my strength measured by this greater strength. I shall awake in the morning and cast upon the day the scope of my daring. And by night I shall render account to none but the greatest scheme.*

The settlers I described at the outset of this chapter were the Costa Rican settlers who were engaged in the expansion of the geographical frontiers of their native land. It was they who trod the earth, their feet unclad, in their hands the tools of a subsistence in paucity. There were also other settlers, the Italians and a few other nationalities. These individuals were often imbued with visions, but the visions did not always find the strength of a culture rooted in the legacy of the native Costa Rican family. All worked and made sacrifices; all believed in something represented by a future, a future to be reached and won. But the men and women who converted the South Frontier into the community of Coto Brus were its native settlers, the Costa Ricans; to them goes the major part of the credit for what has been accomplished; they too must share in the major portion of the responsibility for the future they have gained.

All of the settlers of the frontier believed in their ability to overcome problems and find solutions by decisive action. And they saw ample evidence of the proof of this principle: to act was to overcome and prevail. If a stream needed to be bridged, trees were cut and logs made to answer the need of passage; if a road had to be laid, men took stone in hand and laid one by another until thousands and hundreds of thousands were so laid; if a school was needed, a hut became a classroom and this eventually a school. None of this happened either quickly or easily or without great hardship, but it did happen through the acts of people who placed their hands on tools and brought therefrom a new order. The point is this: the frontier was not settled by contemplation, reflection, or introspection; it was settled—and planned—in one fluid thrust. It is important to remember that through their actions the settlers believed they would find the answers to many things they did not know or felt they would someday need to know.

Two years ago we had a group of students from the School for Field Studies with us here on the farm for a five-day land settlement workshop. The students were undergraduates at the university level, mostly juniors and seniors. They were in Costa Rica to study sustainable development.

In planning the workshop for the students, I wanted them to touch firsthand this element of action in the settlement of a frontier. I had seen many students come to Coto Brus and contemplate and try through contemplation and observation to understand what they were seeing in terms of land management and how it might have

A PLACE IN THE RAIN FOREST

started. For many people, understanding and learning are enhanced by acting and thinking as they are acting. I wanted the students to simulate the settlement of land on a frontier by building a *rancho,* a shelter such as those first shelters made by the settlers, planting a pasture and subsistence crops, digging a well—doing some of the things that settlers do, and doing these things by taking tools in hand and working with them. My reason for this was fundamental: to understand how settlers deal with the land and the environment and how their children and grandchildren continue to do so, one must touch and experience the relationship of work.

The settler (if he were a man, and he usually was) would place both feet firmly on the earth, and, thus braced, take the long-handle axe and cut down an immense tree. While he was doing this his wife and children would be making things take place in the *rancho.* The settler would think as he cut down the tree and other trees: *Here I will make a pen for the calves and there a pasture, and my children will run there on a road made with this arm and this hand with a shovel, and there my wife and I will plant and harvest coffee.* And in time it came to happen. But the planning and the action were integral, for the settlers did not see themselves as separate from their work. They were aware that a time would come when their actions would stand and they themselves would no longer be present to answer for them, but they were people who thought as they worked, as they saw the realization of their plans as a product of what they did.

With these credentials, with the knowledge that the fruit of a settler's labor one morning becomes the reality of the new order of the day, a frontier was settled, the rain forest destroyed. A man and woman might stand on the land and look out and see nothing but what had been done by them, for none had been here before them in recent time. They felt a sense of closeness and identity with all that they saw. As long as their children remained on the farm and worked with the father and mother, this continuity was preserved, and the work of one generation merged with that of another. And the errors of the fathers might yet be ameliorated by their children.

But when the errors of the fathers became such that the children could no longer stay on the land, then the time of planning through action began to yield to a time of retrospection and reevaluation. A whole tide of uncertainties began to arise. Where it had required no more than forthright labor to span the stream, lay the road or build the school, it now required study and analysis to untangle so much that had become confused. Action alone no longer seemed to be the formula for everything.

Plans made by the individual settlers for their respective farms had many elements in common. A first requirement for all was the provision of basics in food supply. This condition, the ability to meet as many of the food needs of the family as the land and the skill of the new farmers might merit, came to be known as *subsistence:* no cash income was expected from this work of food production.

The rain forest itself provided very little food for the settlers. Settlers did some hunting during the early years, but wildlife populations, with the cutting of the forest, were swift to diminish. Fishing was of no use, as the settlers never found fish in adequate quantity in the streams. Vegetative food from the forest was very limited, palm hearts being among the most plentiful of a very few edible things that might be found there.

So the home-grown food for the settlers would depend on bringing into the frontier seed and livestock, pasture grass, fencing, tools. Here we touch on another element in land settlement that I was interested in having the students from the School for Field Studies experience: most of what is needed for daily life on a frontier must be brought in from some outside source, usually packed in by men and women over difficult trails and long distances. It is simple enough in planning the food supply for a family on the new land to think of raising chickens in order to have some meat and eggs. But chickens do not lay well without some supplemental feed beyond what they may pick up in the way of insects and grubs from the earth. This suggests the need for corn, and to plant corn in the tangle of the cut-down forest is not an easy thing. Cows would represent another important source of food in milk and meat, but pasture in the cut forest is also difficult. Just to find a cow on the frontier or the periphery of the frontier was a challenge, and the same might have been said of horses and mules. Without bulls, cows do not multiply and produce, and even when a bull and a cow and the pasture are on the land, it will be years before they can produce a herd.

Bananas, plantains, cassava, chayote, and some kinds of squash could be planted immediately and were. Common kidney beans could be grown after some experimentation and exploration of practices in the new land. A vegetable garden could have been planted, but few actually were during the beginning years.

Planning and implementation took place simultaneously with respect to these projects. It was clear that food was a first requirement for the settlers, and it took no analysis on their part to recognize this.

A balanced diet and a varied food supply were not foremost in the minds of the early Costa Rican settlers. The land could produce some food, and some food it could not; so it was seen from the first plantings. If a family had money it might fill in the shortcomings of the farm production by buying and bringing in nonperishable staples, such as canned goods. But most of the settlers had no money when they started, and so the shortcomings in food supply simply were not met. The problem was a matter of nutrition rather than actual quantity of food, and the health of the early settlers was reflected in many and advanced medical conditions caused by nutritional deficiencies. Later planning for the future of the farm would aim to overcome this problem.

After basic food necessities were met by some production from the land—subsistence provided—it remained to produce a cash income, for subsistence, by its nature, is not a satisfactory way of life. Here, too, in terms of cash income, settlers made plans to meet their own needs and those of others who came to the frontier. In these plans, as well as those taken for subsistence, there was a common focus in thinking about what was needed and what would have to be done.

A frontier such as that of Coto Brus has only two main options for cash income at the outset of its settlement. These are determined by what happens when the rain forest is felled; the land can be used over a period of many years only in very limited ways. On the South Frontier grass could be planted following the felling of the forest, and cattle, either dairy or beef, might be raised; or coffee could be grown. Either of these options would require years of development costs, without any income whatsoever, before initial income could be reached. During that interval, settlers would have to be content with subsistence.

We settlers were better planners in terms of production than we were in terms of marketing. We could see ourselves contending with the challenges of making the land produce; these translated often into hard physical work. We did not have as clear a view of how to market what we could—or expected to be able to—produce. This limit on foresight hinged upon our not having a means of reaching markets which we believed existed or had been assured existed but with which we had never acquired firsthand experience. We had only a limited concept of the nature of the market mechanisms we proposed to deal with and plenty of familiarity with the difficulty, or initial impossibility, of reaching them. Successful coffee production requires the transport of hundreds of tons of both the ripe coffee berries and the processed, export coffee bean. The single airfield in the South Frontier, allowing only single-engine craft to take limited-weight loads off it, could in no way meet such a shipping need. The cattle could not be driven overland to markets because, as I have said, the trail out from the South Frontier was too long, there were too many rivers to ford, it was too steep and difficult, and, above all else, if a farmer were disposed to subject himself and the livestock to such trouble, the outcome could not be profitable because other cattle raisers were closer to the distant market and could market steers at lower prices. The settlers might have tried to make cheese and market it by air, but it takes quite a long time to build up a good dairy herd. And no one had yet demonstrated that dairying would work on the South Frontier. In fact, no one had demonstrated that anything would work there.

So the settlers reached a further planning stage early in the development of farms. This was collective, community planning. It was initiated long before communities were established. This planning proposed that most of the settlers' production and marketing problems would be solved by the building of roads, roads that would connect the frontier with markets, which were sources, too, of supply. As a matter of fact, this single requirement, the need for roads, became the common scapegoat for much that was faulty in all of the early planning. I might add that for many years now the roads, and relatively good ones, have existed; yet many of the production and marketing problems have not been solved.

Concurrent with the conviction that roads would lead to eventual well-being in farming and food production in new lands was the belief that developments and improvements such as schools, electrical power, health care, and centers of supply within what was once the frontier would lead to financial success in agriculture. They do lead to a more educated citizenry, a citizenry with higher expectations and a determination to reach a better standard of living than that characterizing the recent past or that of the preceding generation. Often these developments help to lead an entire generation of young people to the cities to search for opportunities which cannot be found on the land at home.

Much of the planning during the years of early settlement of the South Frontier was really only a pursuit of different courses of expediency. It was necessary to have food, and so all things that could be raised or produced on the land were tried. A cash income was needed, and one or more of the two or three options in this realm were attempted and approached from many perspectives. Roads, schools, and medical facilities were needed, and plans were made to have them.

But the lessons which needed to be learned to reach an ecologically sound balance within the environment and secure a successful livelihood from the land are still with us today and have been both elucidated and complicated by what we have done.

Planning in most walks of life is the outgrowth of an application of a certain amount of vision established upon a foundation of experience and acquired knowledge. In the settlement of the South

Frontier there was no such foundation of prior knowledge or experi-ence. It is characteristic of frontiers that such prior information will be absent. It is interesting that, considering the long history we have accumulated as users and managers of the earth and its resources, we should find ourselves in such short supply of knowledge on how to do this in the humid tropics.

TWO

The Elimination of Perfection

The earth within the forest—the forest floor—was a lacework of roots, tiny plants, many insects, a diversity of forms of life. It smelled always of moisture, of mold, of many aromas of plant tissues, of gums and resins. In the wet season it was a dark earth; in the dry season it lost some of its dark cast; but always it was loose and friable, crumbling into many small particles of undecomposed organic matter. This earth, in the wet season, was soft and respondent to the passage of men or animals, absorbing the sound of footfalls, so one might walk over the earth in the forest almost soundlessly.

Associated with this soundless texture of moist and yielding earth was the dusk, the absence of bright light, in the forest. These conditions of dampness, resilience, and twilight created a strange softening effect within the trees and understory. Mosquitos hovered soundlessly in the motionless air; birds moved in almost soundless flight; sunrays fell muted and diffused among shadows.

Would you care to live in such an environment? Mornings would be darker, midday somewhat lighter with rays of light breaking through the forest canopy in occasional shafts of brilliance; evenings would fade swiftly from dusk to night, a close, surrounding, clinging night. As a settler on this frontier you would be aware of this closeness of the forest, of its multitude forms of implied life—for you would see only a small part of all that was there—and of your own apparent irrelevance in this scheme. Certain aspects of your relationship with the forest would begin to stand out. Let's look at some of these early relationships between the settlers and their land.

In the unseeable places, those enclosed in deep shadows, within the forest understory, beyond the outlined forms of trees, along the stream banks, overgrown with foliage and almost silent, were (or were expected to be) the big snakes, the fer-de-lance, the bushmaster, the *mano de piedra* with its thick body and huge head. Bent within the wet foliage, working with machete and *garabato,* you, as a settler, would see within this tangle of understory the coiled, fluid form, the gray and dark diamonds, along the length of the snake. Only a moment more, your bare feet on the wet ground, and just one further movement made by you, the snake would strike, now just a hair's breadth short of its range. A shudder of recognition would pass through your body as you drew back, the silence of this instant weighing like an eternity, your eyes and the snake's fixed. You would kill such snakes if you could, striking them with a cut sapling. But the image of the snake in the thick foliage would remain in your imagination. And if you didn't kill the snake, the thought that it would appear again would always be with you.

Thus the ground itself, the earthen forest floor, became a subject of apprehension. On the ground were the tarantulas, sometimes the scorpions, a host of biting and stinging insects, the clinging wet of the rain on decaying leaves, the coldness of an alien condition. Across the ground roamed the bands of peccaries, reputed to attack, impossible to escape if one were surrounded. There could be no home for the settler in the forest under these conditions of alienation from human needs. It required no analysis or philosophy to define this reality, the reality of the inimical nature of the forest: steps must be taken to overcome its hostility.

To the extent possible, the settlers, in making their first shelters within the rain forest, would rise above the ground. A first shelter, a *rancho*, was made by cutting small trees with an axe, trimming the branches, and cutting poles from the trunks. Hardwoods with smooth bark, the moss having been rubbed off, dropped into holes dug with a shovel, made good corner posts. Each stroke of the axe was like a brick in a growing edifice of security, and a sense of security in the rain forest is not unlike a sense of security in any other walk of life—it is a requisite for well-being. To be subject to the overwhelming compass of and forces within the rain forest is one thing; to take steps to liberate oneself from these forces is another. Thus, we build a *rancho*, beside the standing forest, within our first clearing with its fallen trees, logs, stumps, in a small opening to the sky. There is light, the wind touches the scope and stature of our little shelter; we have raised the corner posts, laid saplings for the floor of a loft and tied these saplings with vines, built a thatched roof using palm leaves. On the earth floor below the loft we build a fire for cooking and warmth. At every step we have demonstrated a mastery over the limitations of an environment which threatens us. Here, as elsewhere in human endeavor, we have needed to feel that we are in control of, exercising dominance over, the circumstances around us.

We had made the initial clearing in the forest for this *rancho* with our own hands. We had taken the axe and the machete and with these cut the trees and opened a space in the forest. It did not seem wrong or a violation of integrity that we should do this as settlers; we were looking for a home and a place to make a living and raise a family, and a long history of human effort over time supported our decision. From the shadows we had created light, for we knew that we could not live within shadows. From the cold and wet we had caused warmth and evaporation to apply, for these are needed for life as we know it. Where danger and possible death waited we had taken the logical steps to overcome them. We did not feel that it was necessary to make an apology for our reasoning. Each nation must make a part of its land available to its people, else the people will have no means of expressing themselves and their values within families and upon farms.

Let's return to the clearing and remember the settler experience. Even before our work with the axe is the *zocola,* a cutting of the understory with the machete and *garabato.* For this we use a 28-inch-blade machete and learn to cut with sweeping strokes, using the *garabato* to clear and collect what we cut. We advance over the land with these tools, encountering poisonous snakes, protecting ourselves as we move within the understory. Hours of this work bring on taut, tired muscles in the back and arms and legs, but also a sense of accomplishment.

Here, with our hands on the tools, there is more than an apparent response to a day's work. There is also an identification with many of the forces of life. Most men and women who accept the hardship and limitations of life on a frontier do so because they wish to plant and see a yield from their labors. At the outset of the work the settlers see two worlds: one that is present and another that will be. As I have said at the beginning of this book, few people are so privileged to create a world; few also have such ability to destroy. These two apparently opposite conditions become one as the rain forest is being cleared and the land prepared for planting. As we move through the understory of the forest, machete in hand, several things are taking place with each sweep of the blade. Space is expanding around us, there is greater freedom in the range of sight, and we can now see more clearly the contours and profiles of the land. As yet it is a little daunting to suppose that we may acquire authority over this segment of earth—there are a million things we do not know—and as we stand, machete in hand, and survey what we have done with this cutting of the understory, the thought comes: where will it all lead? This marriage may tie a lasting knot; indeed, it seems that it must. And no one relinquishes his or her freedom carelessly. Many men have walked away from the land they have despoiled (and, certainly, to clear the forest and later abandon the land is to despoil). It is not likely that they have ever been the better for it. There is a price for everything, and to wrest an unwon dividend from the virgin land and then flee in the cowardice of defeat is no honor to the soul.

We may feel as we see the results of our initial work, *Surely this is no small thing which my hand has now undone.* As we move on through the forest, with the *zocola* the terrain expands, and with it we must seek to grow, for our work has unbound an act of ages.

The *zocola* leaves the forest in a parklike condition, with shafts of sunlight slanting now everywhere through the high canopy of the treetops. Still, the sky is mostly unseen as the trees make an effective ceiling above us, but now there is open space between the ground and the treetops far above. The primary rain forest, such as it grows here in Coto Brus, does not have low lateral branches. The competition for light has been too severe. The trees have grown with straight boles, reaching well toward the sky before sending out heavy branches near the very uppermost levels of growth. Younger trees have lower branches, but all are reaching for the vital source of light. If again we take the machete and *garabato* and make a *repica,* a recutting of the understory foliage we have just cut down in the *zocola,* we will chop this into finer pieces until at length we have a carpetlike condition covering all of the forest floor. Let's decide to go further with this work and continue making the *zocola,* cutting saplings and small understory growth with the machete and axe at ground level, leaving no standing stumps, and follow this work again with the *repica.* Then we can walk through our forest, huge, towering trees all around us; there is a cathedral-like effect because we have made long, crisscrossing corridors of space within it.

Here is a good point at which to stop and plan the future of the farm; indeed, this is a good place to pause and decide to leave some parts of the forest, the trees, standing. Not many settlers did it in Coto Brus, for land clearing was one flowing sweep of devastation— but it *might* have been done.

As we walk within this "cathedral," we find a spring welling with limpid water from a quiet swale in the ground, and from this point issues a stream. It would be wise to leave the forest intact along its banks. The threats of the forest, snakes, peccaries, other hobgoblins, seem far removed at this point in our work, there is a serenity here now, and it may have been created by us. Long vines trail down from the upper canopies of the trees. It is easy to grab one and swing, Tarzanlike, from a hillside well out into space. Some of the strangler fig trees, having strangled their host trees, now have hollow cores;

that is, the fig remains standing and majestic while the host tree, once the core and mainstay of the fig, has decayed. The fig's trunk is made up of a latticework of crisscrossed, vinelike trunk, and this lattice can be climbed from either outside the tree or within the hollow core, as up the rungs of a ladder. We enter the core of the fig and climb well up within, looking out through the lattice as through windows, startling some bats living in the tree as we do so.

What do we see? Many things, depending on the person. A promise, perhaps a challenge, a long future of sustained effort, maybe a quick reward of making some improvements on this land and then moving on.

When it rains the rain falls like curtains through our forest, open now at its understory. The drops can be seen falling, but many have been shattered and broken into droplets and then into mist by having struck the upper forest leaves and branches. As we stand below the trees in what seems complete silence, despite the overwhelming sound of rain, we see this rain falling in ever descending veils that slant and dance on small currents of wind. So must the rain have fallen in the past, making a pact with the forest. Now we have altered this, and suddenly it becomes apparent that time has opened before us and we, an instant on its stage, must somehow meet an expectation: ours? something else? possibly something in this rain.

This is not poetry I am contriving; the men and women who experience the conditions of this work experience also some of these feelings. These conditions are gone now from much of our world of concrete streets and masonry landscapes, but they did exist in the rain forest and still do. What they represent is the presence of many kinds of life and natural forces. As people, as the human form of life, we are not unaffected by their presence.

Toucans and guans are more readily seen now in the upper forest canopy; although no howlers live at this elevation, whiteface, capuchin monkeys can be observed. However, elusive as always, much of the forest wildlife is seldom seen. Each clearing at this point in the settlement of the South Frontier is a small island in a sea of forest, and it is likely that the tapirs, peccaries, deer, jaguars, and other animals are retreating from our incursion. The machete and axe strokes here sound a knell of finality for many species. This is one of the great tragedies of our work on this earth.

We see grace and beauty in the forest with its understory cleared; all of the trees stand out clearly, their majesty apparent. But once the work of felling the trees with the axe begins, all beauty is destroyed and the true magnitude of what we are attempting becomes obvious.

Chainsaws are not yet in use in the felling of this forest; we work with the axe. There is inertia in the swing and stroke of this tool. The axe is an extension of balance, of purpose, an expression of coordination. The impact of the axe stroke springs from several points within the body; many impulses combine for fluid, rhythmic strokes. The work of felling a tree is, indeed, a fluid expression originating in the earth itself, with one's boots planted on the ground, and up from the ground flows a pivotal energy, through the legs and into the arms and hands and through the handle of the axe. It is impossible not to be aware of the earth underfoot when felling with an axe, for the source of strength in each stroke originates in the feet. The woods are often dense and hard here, and a poorly made stroke rebounds, leaving the arms and hands tingling and numb. We learn to use a line of vision to target the axe, the eyes fixing a striking point, the blade following, shearing cleanly. The fragrance of many resins fills the air as does the prevalent smell of moss in the rain forest. Moisture touches the skin ever in this environment, and without some moisture on the hands the axe could not be controlled.

The upper canopy of the tropical rain forest is often interlocked, the branches of one tree tangled with those of another. Vines will grow from one tree to a neighboring tree, often tying the two together. Here in the tropics death and decay overtake portions of trees more readily than in other climes. Part of the crown of a tree may be dead, the dead branches ready to break and fall. Some trees have not grown straight but lean well over on sloping land; these are always difficult and dangerous to fell. The hearts of many trees are hollow and infested with termites. There is no certainty of safety in this work of cutting trees.

Dawn brings us to the forest, the sunlight lying flat in bands across the forest floor. Measuring with our eyes the height of a tree, we look for the dead branches, the tangled branches, or the interlaced vines which can spell trouble, possibly death. Today if we were felling the forest—and I hope that none of us will—we would look carefully for the Africanized bees. There are many hives in the forest on the farm today; axe strokes against the trunk of a tree housing a hive would bring the bees swarming in attack long before the trees were felled. During the years of land clearing in the South Frontier, however, the killer bees were not a problem.

The first strokes of the undercut begin, then the backcut a little higher. A skillful axeman can work quickly and seemingly tirelessly, yet the minutes in the forest wear on. There is the sweat, then the little black, stingless bees clinging to sweaty arms and shirt, perhaps for the salt. A stillness now seems to infuse our thoughts, a stillness and solitude, expanse in the sky, the towering stature above us, the shrinking identity of self. Is there any scale by which this that we attempt can be placed beside this majesty? There can never be a moment which reaches quite like this, fluttering sound in whispers, the hesitancy; the rhythm, the measured blows, the chips flying from the axe. The leaves of this tree far above us, an azure sky, speak across dimensions in our striving, and yet this fragment of trust we plant must not waste or fade. The tree trembles; we have brought about its end. There is an escaping moan; then an eternal interval of sadness. The huge structure of symmetry begins to fall. A rush, the tremendous displacement of air, then the shuddering impact of the tree against the ground, its vibrations never ceasing. Coming forward from where we have withdrawn from the falling tree, we drive the axe into the bleeding stump and stand, breathing deeply, a coarse prayer written on the raw, respondent ground. There will be other days, other years; other forests will rise from the season of this regret. We will plant and bring forth new life.

We have seen—all of us who worked in the clearing of the land with the axe and machete—a tree leaning on a hillside suddenly snap apart and split along its entire length, the whole tree trunk springing like a bow, rising above us, then flinging back as though shot from a sling. We have trembled to the rush of air as a tree, seeming to be falling in its intended path, became lodged upon the trunk of another tree and was thrown back by that tree so that the entire mass of the cut trunk flew by us with the momentum of tons of force. We have seen an entire area of forest canopy at once disintegrate in broken branches and entangled vines and fall in a mass to the ground. Some men saw these things only for an instant and then were buried near the ground on which they would have made a home.

Nothing is more shattered and chaotic than the felled forest. If indeed these were green edifices, they have now become rubble. Everywhere wood is splintered and broken. The ground is laden with recumbent forms, apparently never to yield in their immobility. Stumps stand with splintered points pointing to the sky, a sky now open, brilliant, blue, bearing the low, tropic clouds. A song might spring upon the wind over this land, even as the whisper of the past relinquishes and withdraws in sadness, the song of a bird to be followed in time by a thousand more such voices heralding a new era of light and space, the songbirds which will eventually populate this land. Life has not been halted; its flow has been but altered in new channels, passages of which we are yet unaware.

Our clearing in the forest now, as I have said, is an island; all around us the rain forest continues to stand. That the tangle of stumps, logs, branches, leaves in this island can one day become a farm seems hard to accept. We cannot walk over the earth now; we must climb across and run along logs. We negotiate our way over this land, rising and falling, going up on the higher branches fifteen or more feet above the ground, dropping down to the big logs and running along them, then jumping to another. The texture of the wood is rough, the moss and lichens still clinging to the bark; lizards, frogs, a riot of orchids and epiphytes abound in a tangled array. Snakes which lived in the treetops are now found on the ground.

The early clearing of the forest in the South Frontier was made as often as possible toward the end of the wet season, under the heavy, rain-laden skies of the months of September, October, and November. Forest felled during these months would await the coming of the dry season, usually in late December.

There would steal upon the land a deep fastness; an arrested state of expectancy, a fading remoteness in the sky. One night the temperature would dip to 58° or 56° Fahrenheit. The stars would shine like a million eyes in a perfectly black and cloudless emptiness. Where clouds had dominated for weeks, now there were none. Then, as a great, sentient creature arising in the northeast, the winds would stir, a deep reverberation throughout the darkness and the cold, almost as if some irrepressible spirit had awaited this moment. The winds would be borne over the land. They came with a deep-throated muttering. The standing forest would bend; moans escaped into the night. In waves and pulses the wind would press, great impoundments of air expanding, breathing. Branches were snapped and broken in the forest; some trees were uprooted and fell. Over the clearing the leaves from the fallen branches and those wrested from the living trees blew in harried haste. Dryness came into the air and the smell of resins grew stronger. By day, at midday, the sun burned upon a land which had never before known its rigor. Plants which had grown in the delicate ambient of moisture and shade shriveled and died. In the season of moisture and shaded retreat there had been a certain restfulness, imposed perhaps by the hours of implied constraint in rain. Now, with the wind, the unrequited sky with its brilliant light, there seemed no release from energy; all was driven and flown in haste.

Because many hours could not be devoted to outside work during the wet season, the settlers would hurry now to make each day of the dry season produce a maximum of productive work. They dug wells, built shelters and *ranchos,* and made preparations to burn the land.

A common misunderstanding about burning land following the felling of the rain forest is that the cut forest will be burned and eliminated. On the South Frontier this was not the case; it was impossible to remove the cut forest from the land by burning. Yet, all of us did burn, and it should be asked, What did we expect to accomplish and what *did* we accomplish in subjecting the land to fire?

The cut forest left the land almost impossible to use. Anyone with conventional experience in farming would see this land as being unfit for food or commodity production. The earth itself was almost inaccessible, there being few patches of its surface actually uncluttered by the debris of the fallen forest. Certainly, some quick and easy way to clear all this rubble away would be welcome. All would hope that burning might accomplish this, but it took only a little thought to realize that it would not. The logs, many 2½ and some 3 feet in diameter, would not burn. The stumps were even more impervious to fire. The reason, of course, was that they were impregnated with water. The same was true of all but the lightest branches. What would burn following this felling of the forest would be the leaves and twigs and part of the leaf litter covering the ground. Following burning, the land would continue to be about as unfit for farming as before because of its incumbent obstructions. However, even the elimination of light branches and leaves would make some progress on the road to bringing this land into productive condition. So the fires were started.

Throughout the dry season, beginning in December and stretching to March, the wind continues to blow. At length the litter and light forest debris in the clearing are converted to dry, crackling tinder. In the early days of March the sunlight becomes intense; the world of the clearing has become very different from that of the surrounding forest. The forest around the clearing continues to be moist, dark, cool, impregnable to fire. Temperatures in the clearing are higher, the surfaces of all that we touch there feel rough, powdery; there is a sense of dust in the nostrils.

On a day when the wind is moderate, the sun in an azure sky, we take bottles of kerosene and matches into the clearing to the lowest point on the sloping land with the wind behind us. Much of our work is done on hands and knees, crawling among the logs, in and around the branches. We scrape up small piles of the dry forest litter covering the ground, sprinkle them with kerosene, and light them with matches. The flames leap into the leaves on branches bent above and over the litter; there is the smell of burning leaves, a rush of fire. Quickly we move from point to point along the slope. As the fire is fanned by the wind, the whole slope begins to dance with flames. Plumes of smoke rise, sparks lift on heat waves, carry across the slope and well into the sky. Far above the clearing, seen from various points and at many miles distance, this smoke tells the story of our work this day.

With greater speed now we jump and run from point to point, a dash of kerosene, a quick stroke of the match; the heat comes from around us, the heat now not just of the midday sun but also of the flames rising and racing among the upper branches, lifted where fallen trees seem to be supplicating with gaunt arms an implacable fury. Our bodies are drenched in sweat; the smell of smoke is every-where. Sudden air currents spring up across the clearing, generated by the heat.

There is no time to be careful in scrambling and moving over and around the logs and branches when starting such fires, and more than once we encounter snakes as we crawl and tunnel through the debris.

Then we withdraw, retreating from this thing we have released on the land. The great plumes of smoke and heat and sparks rise, and there is a cacophony from the release of energy and the rush of flames.

Smoke and the smell of charcoal and smoldering wood will hover over this clearing for weeks. None of the green timber will have caught fire, but many trees and stumps will have decayed, dead wood within them, and some of this dead wood, having dried during the dry weeks, will continue to smolder in coals long after the initial fire is out. All across the clearing now at night, feathers of sparks, occa-sional bursts of flames, lift upon gusts of air. There is a sense of loneliness here; as yet there are but a few of us on the frontier. We feel the loneliness in the emptiness of the heavens and the myriad sparks rising. Now, by night, seated on a log in our clearing, we lis-ten to the wind, watch the sparks fingering heavenward and bend in currents, hear the deeper sounds of solitude and silence. And we wonder how all this—ever!—could happen and if we ever could know or can tell what this moment has done, may bring—if ever there is a morning and a dawn. And deeply, in the distance, the wind speaks.

Around us the forest is not mute; tinamous, kinkajous, sloths, an occasional owl echo the darkness. Often there is the voice of the wind in the trees, but there are times when it too is perfectly still, an immense stillness emanating from the very nature of this time. We look into the eyes of the pockets of fire, the stars in infinity, and gaze upon this clearing. This place is ours; already we have begun to earn it—have we not sweated and endured some of its transition to a new order? We will meet its anguish and its trials; here will be born a crucible of our days without respite. The message is spoken this night on the wind. What will it all become, and what will our years here bring? The small secrets which bind life now infiltrate our thoughts and link us with this beginning.

Behind us this night is the well we have dug by hand. Delving deep in this earth we have tapped its water. There is a purity in it; all here is new, somehow clean and untainted in ways that only a place such as this can be. We have made a structure upon the land. This is not a *rancho;* it is a dirt-floor, aluminum-sided cabin with corrugated aluminum roofing, all hauled in to this land by us. Within the cabin there is a kerosene lamp, a wood-burning cooking stove, some books, rude beds, some provisions—and already it is home. Here we are safe from the rain; here the wind comes, but we are protected from it too.

One night the wind is a torrent in the darkness, sweeping, seemingly unsated. Within our cabin we listen to the tumult and pain in the nearby forest. The voices of a thousand trees are speaking. Then there is the wrenching sound of a tree being uprooted, a moment of breathless expectation, and the fallen tree crashes into the earth near our cabin. We snatch our bedding from the wooden beds and race into the night, across the logs, under the stars, feeling the force of the wind, rushing, reaching. We spread our bedding on the ground at a site out of reach of trees, where we will build our permanent home.

As the dry season continues, this home, the lumber sawed from timber cut in our clearing, rises and takes form. It will be two-storied, raised on posts above the ground. It will be strong, for the wind has taught us to build with strength. As the posts and structure of our home rise above the land, a new dimension comes into our days in the clearing, a dimension that rises like the forest we have felled, but a dimension created now by us. Yet, always there is the wind, and at night in the clearing the sparks are fanned and dance.

One day, with the passage of weeks, the wind has abated and a stillness comes to the forest. In the sky, partly filled with cumulus clouds, swallow-tail kites circle, riding currents of air which do not touch the ground with any perceptible motion. Across the forest there is a softened tone; the leaves, which have been so buffeted, are now still and there is a sense in the air of change. Over successive days, clouds rise, forming shapes and figures. From a distance comes a rumble of thunder. The clouds gather—it begins to grow dark. Moving quickly now, the thunderheads close, thickening, combining in mountains and chasms. Lightning breaks through the hastening darkness and the thunder is sonorous, shuddering, causing the ground to tremble. Now, almost as if it had been orchestrated, comes the rain. It does not fall at once where we wait at the clearing; it can be heard approaching in the distance, drops coming like millions of tiny feet treading above the forest. It approaches more swiftly until it spatters on the roof of our new home, proudly surveying the clearing. The sheets of rain, swaying in bodies and shapes, cross the land, and the sound of the marching feet is borne on.

Now from the clearing arise the smells of wet charcoal, still some smoke, and wet burnt wood. The rain continues in following days. A new season has come. The days of rush harried by the wind have withdrawn; a season for renewal is at hand. Now is a season for planting.

This is what the settlers are meant to do, for few who settle on the frontier do so merely to engage in the destruction of the forest; all await a time of planting, now to prove the worth of their individual ideas with seed in hand.

We have seen that the land is unfit for farming, the stumps and logs blackened somewhat now from the flames of our burn; but there they remain, all these logs, branches, stumps, and under them the land is only a patchwork, hardly an area big enough to lay out a single straight row. Still, this land is ours to sow, and now that the rain has come we will plant.

Early on a morning following a rain, we take a sack of molasses grass seed—the seeds are very small and each has an elongated hair—and we broadcast, throw by hand, this seed over the blackened earth in part of the clearing. The seeds fly out lightly as we cast them, making a fine gray, sparse mantle on the ground where they have landed. Each seed comes to rest upon the earth's surface or falls upon some part of the debris of the forest. And with the rains which fall in the afternoons now, this seed becomes lodged and ready to germinate. Within days it bursts open, a single, small leaf blade, in all a delicate green carpet just faintly changing the blackened hue of the land. This is the first crop we have caused to grow.

Many other plantings will follow, for where there is even a small space among logs, stumps, branches we will plant. And as we work, our clothes, hands, arms continue to carry the dark streaks of the charcoal from the days when the season was written in the strong characters of the wind.

Scientists and students studying ecology, biology, and agronomy look upon the tropical rain forest as a condition of life relationships approaching a kind of perfection in balance and adjustments. The complexity of these relationships is beyond our understanding; to decipher even a fragment of one such relationship may be the work of a lifetime. It is correct to look upon the destruction of such an intricate and delicate fabric as a general outrage; no one knows how to restore what is lost, no one even knows the scope of significance of what is lost. We don't seek justification for our misdeeds; as life, one in many kinds of life, we tread heavily upon this earth. However, it is likely that we will continue to do so—in many ways. So we must try to understand what we have done, some of its consequences, and what we can do to sustain those things we consider to be right. Let's look at what some of us have done to the rain forest.

The land which has been cleared is, of course, not clear. It will be twenty years before it is free of all its stumps, roots, and the biggest logs. Burning, dynamite, bulldozers, chainsaws, teams of horses, yokes of oxen, shovels, axes, machetes—all may be tried to clear it, but none will be economically practical over extended areas. The rain forest felled has transferred its burden to us. Decades of labor will be added to our lives. However ephemeral may have been our poetry at the outset, it is now converted to demands for responses to a thousand exigencies.

So one of the first things we must understand when we consider the consequences of the elimination of perfection, the destruction of the rain forest, is that there is a strong tendency for men and women to walk away from what they have done. To clear the forest and move on was a tendency among many settlers in Coto Brus. It remains to some extent in the shifting agriculture of today. Sustained food production on a given piece of land is very difficult here in the tropics, and, when possible, farmers will move from one piece of land to another, as migrants might do in seasonal work, never owning much land but farming little rented plots here and there until any one of them becomes unfit for the crops being grown, then moving on to some fresh piece of land and starting over.

We may learn from the destruction of the rain forest that it bequeaths a heritage of diversity and defies an imposition of monoculture. Every fragment of land in the rain forest is truly different from every other. The plants and other forms of life which adapted themselves to that particular stratum of sustenance did so over a very long period of time, and, whereas they may grow well in one square meter of ground, at several meters' distance from that point, they may not grow well at all.

The rain forest nurtured countless light and moisture and temperature relationships, varying, no particular segment being just like another at any given time. With the felling of the forest, all of these relationships perished and were replaced by a tendency to uniformity, relative uniformity, which was alien in degree to all that preceded it.

The soil itself was not a separate component in this scheme of relationships. It did not exist independently of moisture, light or shade, temperature, or the biota it sustained and which in turn composed it. Divested of these other attributes, the soil is no longer the same; indeed, we might say that were we to imbue it with a personality, it would not know itself. It must seek a new identity, a new *modus* of existence.

With the cutting of the rain forest an order in time vanished and a new one had to be established in its place. Many things had happened, slowly or swiftly, in the rain forest, and now that change had been introduced, a new sequence of time relationships would, of necessity, have to emerge. Some of the changes which would have to emerge and mature would seem tediously slow to the prospective farmer. His lifetime might not suffice to see them develop and stabilize, even were he to start as a young man.

The elimination of the rain forest is a process of interaction between people and this world of existent relationships. It is a fluid, ever-changing, never inert combination of things in which the perceptions, reactions, and attitudes of people will change from moment to moment the circumstances over which they exert some control. This is why I have dealt with the way settlers think, work, and feel in their relationship with the land in this chapter. I have referred to "balance" in the rain forest; I would not want this term to become confused with harmony. To the extent that I understand what I have worked with, harmony may be a principle in the rain forest, but it probably is not dominant. The forest is full of contention, strife, and struggle. People, the settlers, introduce new components of these elements. If we accept this, we see that we may have indeed eliminated a state of relative perfection in destroying this edifice of established relationships but that our presence is no less relevant on this earth than that of the others we have displaced. We stand now where they were, and the gradual realization of this is what the settler must accept. To reduce and eliminate the rain forest, to stand in its place and assume the responsibilities for some conduct of life relationships, is an act of continuity. It is easier to lament the passage of something than to accept that it has not passed at all but simply acquired a new form. With this latter recognition comes the awareness that we have not relinquished an opportunity but that, indeed, it has been always with us. The tropical rain forest is gone from much of the face of the earth. Where what remains can be preserved, it must be. But we must understand that, where it is gone, the life forces that created it are still with us and that we must deal with them today just as forthrightly as we should have hoped to avoid having to do had we left all unchanged. We as humans do exist as one segment of life in this world; we have needs, avarice, dreams. We must have the courage to accept that these are our burden.

We have made our clearing in the rain forest and we live now within its chaos. To the eyes of visitors it must seem that this pile of rubble and debris, once a beautiful standing forest, cannot possibly become more than a confusion and a regret. But to the eyes of the settlers there is the emergence of order and a future of practical worth. In time women and men and children will walk over this land and never suppose that a forest once stood here. There will be pastures, roads, towns, many farms with coffee. Will the image of the forest entirely vanish, then, from this region, an entire segment of mountainous terrain? It may, but it is in our interest to see that it does not; its disappearance would demonstrate that we had not acquired the skill to manage this environment so that it would continue to support life, diversity, balance.

The elimination of the rain forest does not mean that the principles it embodied are gone. It does mean that those principles are no longer as clearly defined, as magnificently expressed, as before. Can these principles be applied in farming, food production, environmental management? In the next chapter we will follow the steps in the settlement of the South Frontier and see what has emerged from the forest.

Isolation and the King's Highway

One afternoon in June, several weeks after the beginning of the wet season, when the rain had been falling for hours over much of southeastern Costa Rica, several horseback riders were making their way over a narrow trail toward the close of day. They were riding from a settlement, Volcán, in the El General Valley to the outpost of Agua Buena, in the South Frontier, a journey of several days. The riders, wearing raincoats, were leading pack horses, their pack saddles covered with light tarps. For hours the rainwater had sluiced along the trail, the horses' hoofs splattering in mud. The afternoon was sunless, the clouds low; on both sides of the trail the rain forest lifted and fell across uneven land. The riders were coming to the settlement of Potrero Grande, where they planned to spend the night. Ahead of them was the Cabagra River, which they would need to ford before reaching the settlement. The horses were tired from the hours on the trail, the riders wet in spite of their raincoats.

The rain had been falling in gray sheets throughout the day. It was not a cold rain; this was the lowlands—temperatures here were either warm or hot. The sound of rain had filled the day, its endless patter on the leaves of surrounding foliage, the drops spattering in puddles on the trail. Steam rose from the horses' withers and mixed with the smell of wet hair and sweat. The trail descended, snaking through narrow cuts made by erosion from earlier rains, in many places hardly wide enough to accommodate a single horse and rider. In these narrow places the riders lifted their feet from the stirrups to keep from having their legs jammed between the horses and the clay sides of the banks.

Well up on the slopes of the Talamanca Mountains to the east and north of this trail, the clouds, having banked against the mountains during earlier hours, had released the rain, and, the water, finding its way into many rivers, was causing flash floods. Surging through watersheds in the partly unexplored forest, these rivers brought turbulent water crests to the lowlands. As the fading light of the afternoon grew weaker, the riders descended the last slope before reaching the ford at the Cabagra River. Ahead of them was a flat thicket of successional forest, the river, and beyond, a steep climb to the *sabanas,* small plains of sparse grass growing on poor soil, around Potrero Grande.

Above the sound of the rain now, a rumble, the sound of moving rocks, came from the river. This sound conveyed an ominous feeling in the late afternoon, as though there, just beyond the trees ahead on the trail, a sentient creature waited. The first rider emerged from the thicket at the river's edge, his hand holding the reins, pale from hours in the rain, the reins and saddle sodden, creaking with the movements of horse and rider. The rider's wide-brimmed hat had fallen over his face, the brim bent shapeless; the horse dropped its head to crop some forage at the river's edge.

Across the width of the Cabagra River the water moved in muddy currents, rising and falling in swift serpentlike figures, dark loops racing over unseen rocks, intertwining and meshing, hurrying on below the ford to a point of rapids. The riders heard the grinding sound of rocks on the river bed being shifted by the force of the currents. No horse could keep its footing in such a current; it would be swept downstream where the rapids churned the white of froth and foam.

Night followed swiftly on this dark afternoon; well up the reaches of the Cabagra River the shadows deepened under the thick foliage of overhanging trees. The other riders approached and stopped; one element dominated this interval: the river, its force, its surge brought to concentrate at the ford. The riders unsaddled, turned out the pack horses to find some grass along the river bank, picketed the saddle horses, and slung jungle hammocks between trees in the thicket somewhat back and above the river. It was a wet camp: rain continued to pelt; with no fire, nothing dried; dinner was a cold one of rolled oats and some condensed milk. Throughout the night the Cabagra's deep voice rumbled in the darkness. About midnight the patter of raindrops on the canopies of the hammocks eased and stopped, and a heavy, wet stillness came over the land, interdicted by the rush of water, the shifting of rocks, in the ford.

By day the scene appeared less chaotic. The clouds began to part and the water level in the river dropped, its crests receding. By midmorning the riders had loaded the pack horses, resaddled, and moved into the ford. Seized in the current—it seemed a living thing—the horses found themselves caught by the force of water. There was a dizziness in this water, and each horse inched forward, the riders holding them angled upstream into the current. The riders lifted their legs free of the stirrups, these now swaying and flowing against the horses' flanks. The water inched up the horses' chests; muscles trembled. As the water reached the withers, the horses' ears pointed directly ahead, the eyes widened, fixed on the opposite bank of the river. The horses' footing tottered, uncertain on the smooth and slippery rocks of the river bed—a step and then a shifting of weight and the ever flowing and downward sweep of water. At midstream was a point where the water was dark and deeper; a step forward, the wavelets lapped fiercely, coming higher. Then a step on. One by one the riders bent over their horses' necks, urging them, feeling in their own bodies the taut muscles struggling to hold, and then another step.

By noon the riders had made the ford. Some pack animals, having turned back in mid-river, had been made to cross again.

On then to Potrero Grande and a couple of days' rest while the rain continued during the afternoons. Then to the ford on the Coto River, just beyond Potrero Grande, where there was no chance of riding the horses across. Packs and saddles had to be ferried across the river in a dugout canoe, the horses led into the river and made to swim.

The trail ride in June of that beginning wet season between Volcán and the South Frontier was made in 1954. The events I'm describing were those encountered by my mother and father, my wife, and me. We were on our way to the South Frontier to look for land, land which eventually became our home and our farm, and we were riding on the trail known as *El Camino Real*—roughly translated, The King's Highway.

The trail, believed to date from pre-Columbian times and to have acquired its name at a later date from the Spanish conquistadores, was the only link by land connecting the South Frontier with the populated and developed areas of Costa Rica to the northwest. In the midpart of this century there were only a few scattered and sparsely populated settlements between the South Frontier and the town of San Isidro del General, which at this time was connected by a rough, rock-surfaced road with San José.

I had first become acquainted with the Camino Real when my friend Gonzalo Guerra and I walked from the province of Chiriquí in Panama through the South Frontier and on to Potrero Grande and the settlements in the El General Valley as far as San Isidro. That was a journey of several weeks, and we had used a pack mule to carry our gear. Gonzalo and I had done some exploring of the lands we passed through, and it was during our days in the South Frontier that I became captivated by this region of mountains and rain forest which, I believed, held a promise for a family, a home, and a farm. My parents, then at our home in California, and my wife to be, who was with them, agreed with this selection of a new home site.

While in the South Frontier, Gonzalo and I had spent a night in the Italian colony, joining a group of the Italian directors and engi-

neers that evening for supper. Electric light burned, the current supplied by a diesel-powered generating plant. Several new structures
built within a site crowded with the stumps of the felled forest occupied the colony central site, many of the logs having been drawn
to a sawmill located here at the center of the outpost, an adjacent
machine shop, and the power plant. By day Gonzalo and I had seen
this beginning in the heartland of a wilderness. Here was a brave
gamble: men and a few women and children trusting to making
homes in a new land.

That evening the light burned in the second-floor office of the
newly built headquarters, a wood-frame structure, its timbers taken
from the forest. Even in this remote post on the frontier, our Italian
hosts had at hand after-dinner wine. As the bottle was opened and
the wine served 'round, those of us gathered around the wood table,
boots muddy, clothes bearing the marks of a day on the raw land,
joined in song, sung mostly in Italian (Gonzalo and I were listeners
more often than singers). An entire fabric of culture, past and future,
seemed to be woven that evening by the voices and in the faces, eyes
misty at times for the sunny skies of Italy, at other times expressing
a resolute pledge to the future of this Costa Rican venture.

I wrote to my parents and my betrothed of this place, these people,
and when they arrived in Costa Rica some months later we decided
to go to the South Frontier. It was because of these circumstances
that the rainy days of June 1954 found us on the trail on our way to
the outpost at Agua Buena. Gonzalo and I had forded these same
rivers on our trek over the Camino Real in 1953, and in the next few
years I came to know the trail well. In 1956 my father and I brought
six Percheron draft horses over the Camino Real.

Today segments of the Inter-American Highway (also known as
the Pan-American Highway) follow this same route, once known
only to indigenous peoples. During the early settlement of the South
Frontier, settlers used this trail to bring livestock and some supplies
on pack horses to the new region. As is characteristic of so many
of the mountainous areas of Costa Rica, the topography the trail
crossed was very broken, seldom flat for more than two or three
hundred meters, often quite steep and, in the wet season, slippery

and eroded. Between Potrero Grande and the Frontier the trail was not wide enough to be used by oxen with carts and remained over most of its length a foot or horse trail. During the latter part of the wet season it was impassable for days and even weeks because of heavy rains and flooded rivers. A problem with handling livestock on the Camino Real in the section immediately to the northwest of the Frontier was that it passed through uninterrupted rain forest and there was no forage or grass for the horses or cattle being brought overland save one small planting of grass in the middle of the rain forest at a place called Sabanillas. There was no water along this section, as the trail followed a long, high spur of land where there were no streams or springs nearby.

I have used the word *impassable* in describing conditions sometimes met on the Camino Real. The term was a frequently used word during the first two decades of settlement because it characterized and qualified life in many ways. It is difficult today to imagine how restricted and hazardous life can be when it is hard, or impossible, to go from one place to another in order to satisfy some of the needs of daily life. These limitations came into sharp focus on this same trip over the Camino Real in 1954.

After leaving Potrero Grande and crossing the Coto River by dugout canoe, we went on with the horses through the lowland to a point name *La Cuesta de la Pita*. This was a long and very steep climb into the highlands and the rain forest leading from there all the way to the Italian colony. Surmounting this escarpment, we went on into the highland, gradually gaining elevation. We were nearing the end of this stretch of trail with some tired horses—and some tired riders—in the afternoon when, having led the horses down a steep mountain slope, we found that the trail had been washed out by rains, just above a stream running through the forest. Our horses had been sliding and skidding down the trail on the way to the stream and had dislodged so much loose dirt that we could not turn back and look for another route around the cut bank. In effect, the trail had become impassable at this point. The location was lightless, with heavy foliage above us and on all sides, shadows darkly saturated with earlier rain. We unsaddled, off-loaded packs and pack

A PLACE IN THE RAIN FOREST

saddles, and, after doing some work with the machetes, prepared a landing place in soft clay at the foot of the bank. We would make the horses jump down over the bank into the loose soil at its foot. The saddle and pack animals shied and reared at the small precipice as we worked with ropes to force them to jump. None of the animals was hurt in the jump, but the sweat, the anxious eyes, the struggling, drove a message of fear and desperation in the moments above the stream. We were still smeared with the red clay, the lines of muddy ropes drawn across pants legs, when, wet and tired, we reached Agua Buena a few hours later at the end of the overland trail.

Not all of the settlers traveled on the Camino Real, nor did we when we did not have to move livestock and some heavy gear. We had the dubious option of flying. The airfield in Agua Buena, a grass strip that was used, when it wasn't serving for the infrequent flights in or out of the Frontier, as a pasture for horses and cattle, was limited by high mountains at both ends and only light, single-engine planes could lift limited weights off it. DC-3s and C-46s could land at the field, but they had to take off completely unloaded, without any passengers or cargo. Air travel during those early years was sometimes dangerous, occasionally involving accidents or near accidents.

One such close call happened on a flight in a single-engine Cessna 180 I made during the end of the wet season of 1953 from San José to Agua Buena. The plane was new and the turn-and-bank indicator was yet to be installed in a vacant space in the instrument panel. There were three passengers, quite a lot of cargo, and the pilot, a lean, tall man with somber features. As the heaviest of the passengers, I was seated next to the pilot in front.

When we came over the field at San Isidro del General, the first stop from San José to Agua Buena, there was no sign of the ground; everything was covered by low clouds. We could see some features of the settlement in patches, but nothing of the grass airfield itself. The pilot circled, and at length a hole in the clouds appeared under one wing and through this hole we could see a road which led to the field. The pilot dropped the plane's nose and wingtip, and we went through the hole, coming out under the clouds a little above the ground. With the increase in airspeed, we were no sooner over the field than we had passed it, and the pilot throttled the engine to full power.

As the engine, which had made a peculiarly quiet and lapping sound as the plane had been descending, reached full power and the nose of the plane tilted steeply upward, contrails of mist swept back against the windshield, making beads that flew off in small streaks. Now we saw nothing but the mist, completely enveloping us, its fine gossamer lit by the light from the sun above the clouds. There are mountains around the airfield at San Isidro, forested in those years. The plane was banking and climbing steeply, but there was an unreal feeling about our motion; in one instant it seemed that we were sliding through the mist, in another almost motionless. The propeller, whirring, threw back moisture.

Suddenly, directly ahead of us and reaching above the nose of the plane, trees emerged from the mountainside where the forest grew. They rushed at us; the pilot drew the wheel back sharply. Immediately the plane's stall warner sounded. The trees had disappeared, their place filled by cloud. The pilot shoved the wheel forward and in a moment the trees flew at us again. Again the wheel came back followed at the same moment by the stall signal. The wheel went forward, the nose dipped, and we were surrounded by cloud. Fernando, the pilot, jammed his right hand into his pants pocket and pulled out a key chain, a bunch of keys at its end. He shoved this at me, and I held it in front of us, like a plumb bob. Seen against the horizontal lines across the plane's instrument panel, the key chain took the place of a turn-and-bank indicator. Fernando eased the angle of climb, and in a moment the plane emerged above the clouds into the bright light of the morning sky. We went on to land at the airfield at Palmar and then to Agua Buena. I glanced at the two passengers behind me, who were en route to Palmar. Their faces were probably as pale as mine. There was a stony silence, interrupted once only by Fernando when he reached for the key chain I still held. "That was hard," he said, and returned the keys to his pocket.

Such experiences were not uncommon in those early years when pilots took chances to get their passengers and cargo to their destinations. Over the early years in the South Frontier many of the pilots the settlers came to know were lost with their passengers in accidents while flying in difficult weather and over mountainous terrain.

My purpose in relating these incidents is not to chronicle a few separate events in the settlement of the Frontier. Experiences such as these are part of the general history of the settlement of a new land. More importantly, they have an influence, and a lasting one, on the people concerned. Since those of us who lived on the Frontier during those years did encounter such experiences, we were shaped by them: the way we thought, the things we did, how we made our decisions. Recently, I read in a report by a visiting sociologist who had done some writing about land settlement in Costa Rica the remark that some of the recollections made by the settlers were "highly romanticized." Possibly so; but on the other hand, accuracy can actually suffer when we try to view the past with strict scientific objectivity. People are affected by the experiences they live with; sometimes the "romance" of struggle, of being at times close to danger, great risk, great loss, has a lot to do with what they do with their lives and the land and environment which these mold.

This aspect of the settlement experience is illustrated in the following account, which is adapted from a paper I presented some years ago for students and faculty visiting the Organization for Tropical Studies (OTS) field station at the Wilson Botanical Garden here in Coto Brus.

Three Flights for Survival

The year was 1954, and I had walked to Las Cruces from the settlement at Agua Buena on that morning because the owner of the land that is now a botanical garden as well as the land to the east and west was then offering that tract of forest for sale, and my family and I were in the South Frontier looking for a home and place to make our farm. It was a sunless morning and a light rain was falling. During the rainy season there was sometimes a feeling of loneliness and isolation, the raindrops pattering on a million leaves, the light a liquid green in a dark, enclosed realm of silence held ever, it seemed, in the grip of this rain. But on that particular morning, the silence was broken by the sound of the engine of an approaching plane flying low, I thought, under the clouds, just above the tops of the trees. I moved to a place where there was a small opening in the canopy of the forest above me. The plane would pass directly overhead, I guessed from its approaching sound; it would have just taken off from the airfield in Agua Buena and probably would be heading to San José. In a moment the silver wings of the single-engine craft did pass just above me, glinting even in the weakened half-light, another instance in the life of the frontier of that link with the other world—the world beyond this enclosure—that link which was so vital to those of us who had come here to make homes. I waved, hoping the pilot might see me as the plane passed overhead. Of course he would not, but it established a sense of contact for me just to know that I had seen and felt what the plane had meant. My family and I knew all of the pilots who flew the single-engine planes to the South Frontier then; they were all known to the settlers as friends, partners in this venture in the frontier. My thoughts went ahead, probing the route the plane would follow to find its way through the bad weather to San José. But Chale, as the pilot was affectionately known to us, did not reach San José that day. The wreckage of his plane was found some days later in a mountainous section somewhat to the southeast of San José, where he had apparently been trying to break under the clouds and reach the airport at La Sabana. The young woman with him, his only passenger, the daughter of a settler in Agua Buena, who was expecting her first baby, died with him on the flight that had passed over Las Cruces that morning.

Occasionally, in those years of lightless forest and rain, the very wings which brought us hope and a knowledge that beyond this

A PLACE IN THE RAIN FOREST

place there were others that might provide perspective for our dream of a time to come on the frontier—those wings crumpled and dropped from the sky, and the silence they left was numbing. For not all of the settlers were impassioned idealists. The women who came with the men to this frontier knew that they would be mothers in a frontier that was harsh and hostile to mothers. These women listened as the rain fell in the night and spoke with its huge scorn for the efforts being made by the men. And the women wondered if their men were not romantic fools to pit themselves in this way against a place so indifferent and so withdrawn. For what if that specter should come in darkness, in the night, which all knew must come and must be confronted when the rain turned the only trail to mud, where the mules sank and slopped hour after weary hour in the abysmal forest? Then indeed that thief and bearer of shattered expectations did steal through the night—and the Italian colony faced one of its first emergencies.

At about midnight on a night when the rain fell constantly and had so fallen, it seemed, for days, a young woman in the colony had a miscarriage and needed to be moved at once to a hospital in San José. The engine of a great crawler tractor, a bulldozer, started then, its exhaust making little flurries and clouds in the rain and vapor, its lights shot into the night, and behind the bulldozer was a large four-wheel-drive Mercedes-Benz truck, drawn by a cable; in the bed of the truck, under a canvas tarpaulin, was the young woman on a stretcher, her husband, and an Italian doctor. This strange, small caravan of bulldozer and truck started over the trail in the rain from the colony to see if it might reach the airstrip at Agua Buena. Beside the tractor and the truck walked Italian and Costa Rican men; they needed to believe that they could help, even if it meant walking for hours by the machines through the mud.

At dawn in Agua Buena, where my family and I were then staying in the barracks while we were looking for land for our home on the frontier, Álvaro Acosta, who operated the shortwave radio and was administrator for the Agua Buena outpost, called in an emergency flight to the airline that at that time flew its single-engine planes to the only airstrip on the frontier, the field in Agua Buena. The shortwave radio operator at the Italian colony had called both Álvaro and the headquarters of the Italian colonization agency in San José. All operators were also in communication with the airline headquarters at San Isidro del General. As light came through the clouded sky, all attention at the airstrip at Agua Buena was turned toward these clouds, pressing low over the mountains, the mountain summits obscured, the rain easing, then resuming.

Hours after they had left the colony, the men and the machines appeared in Agua Buena, streaked with mud, the men with drawn faces, the truck having been pulled most of the distance by the bull-dozer. The truck stopped by the edge of the airfield and remained parked there for some time. Occasionally someone walked to it and pulled aside the folds of the tarpaulin, and the face of the doctor looked out.

Somewhere beyond our sight and out of the range of sound, a plane was approaching the mountains at Agua Buena. The voice of the pilot came over the radio receiver on Álvaro's radio. The pilot was checking on weather conditions. Álvaro would walk out on the sodden grass of the airfield, look at the clouds dropping over the horizons, then report: conditions were worsening.

At length the sound of a plane's engine could be heard well above us in the clouds. The doctor left the truck and came to stand with the others of us at the edge of the field. The sound of the plane's engine drew nearer but then became weaker and was lost. Our eyes searched the sky unceasingly. Then, well to the east where the clouds met the mountains over Las Cruces, a speck of light detached itself from the clouds and began to bob and weave over the uneven ground, rising and falling with the terrain, just below the clouds. The sound of the plane's engine was at last audible; it came nearer, and in a moment the silver craft flashed by us, setting its wheels down, vapor and mist whirling back from its propeller.

The plane turned and taxied to a stop opposite the truck. The pilot opened the door, stepped down, and looked critically at the lowering sky and rain flurries. The truck's engine started as its driver prepared to move to the plane. Then a curious conference took place beside the plane. The doctor said that his patient must make the flight lying down and that he must make the flight with her. The pilot pointed out that such an arrangement would place too much weight on the rear of the plane and that with the grass as wet as it was, the plane would not clear the mountains at the end of the airfield on its takeoff. In 1952, on another rainy day such as this, a single-engine plane had failed to clear the mountains to the east of the airfield at Agua Buena and had crashed after struggling off from the sodden field, carrying the pilot and his passengers (among them Giulio Cesar Sansonetti, the young director of the Italian colony who had just taken up his post) to their deaths.

Urgently now, messages went by radio, crisscrossing from Agua Buena to the Italian colony, to San José, to San Isidro. The rain fell and the sky grew more somber. For Ugo Sansonetti, director now of the colony in San Vito, and Vito Sansonetti, general director for the colonization project with its headquarters in San José, the decision to be made while the plane and the truck waited at the airfield in Agua Buena brought back a painful image from the past. Now, only two years after the loss of Giulio, the elder Sansonetti brothers and their fellow Italians faced yet another life-or-death emergency at the airfield at Agua Buena.

Finally, the pilot returned to his plane and took off without his passenger or her doctor. The doctor and the husband returned to the truck, the truck and tractor started their engines, and the men who had walked beside these machines took up their stations to walk again. The caravan left Agua Buena and headed farther along the muddy track toward the rock-surfaced road several kilometers to the west which led, at length, to the banana plantations on the Pacific flood plains, where a railroad spur awaited them at the road's end. Hours after leaving Agua Buena, the woman, who had been thrown and bounced in the back of the truck, was placed on a special motor-car and taken by rail to Golfito and from the hospital there flown later to San José. She recovered from the miscarriage and the effects of this ordeal. But she and her husband did not return to live in the colony; they went back to Italy and took with them the memories of the night when a dream had died.

At this point in our review of such experiences it would be well to recall what I have noted earlier: The settlement of the South Frontier took place within a context of a modern world; it was unusual, possibly even rash, for men to bring their wives to such a frontier, for husbands and wives to raise children under such hardships. Those of us who made decisions to do so felt a personal and sometimes intimidating responsibility over the possible outcome of what we were attempting. It is normal under such conditions—those which threaten the lives of the ones we love in ways that come into being because of the decisions we make—to respond with more emotion and less intellect than we might under less stressful circumstances. In some respects this strong emphasis on emotion was a means of disguising what was felt by the individual as a lack of good judgment.

The men who experienced such emergencies as I have just described, those of us who saw lives threatened in such ways, were made angry and afraid. We were angry because we recognized that we had failed to protect our wives and children, and we were afraid because we suspected that this would happen again. I say *men*, rather than *men* and *women*, because during those first years of settlement there were more men, many more, than women in the frontier and because some of these men did want to provide a safe environment for wives and children. As the women came to the frontier and families were started, a new pioneer began to emerge from within the group of settlers. This person was a leader; he or she would speak whenever settlers were gathered to face the needs which all felt and which all knew must be overcome to establish a safe and secure future. These leaders would speak in impassioned voices—because they knew the nature of the men and women to whom they spoke—and they would say:

We must have roads! for our sick and our injured cannot be left in isolation! We must have a hospital! and nurses and doctors! We must have schools! because our children must be educated! And our nights must not dawn upon a day when it shall be said that we failed to extend the mantle of our love.

The people who heard these words, the settlers, were mostly illiterate; their intelligence was second to none, but their lives had been denied the opportunities of education. Very few had access to radios, and, of course, none saw television. Yet they were people who were moved by words, and the speakers, the new pioneers, knew this. They spoke with passion because they felt deeply the convictions of what they said, and they communicated with the people in terms that the people understood.

Such community leaders, such new pioneers, were Ernesto Araya and his wife, Zoraida.

Toño came to me one Sunday afternoon to tell me that his grand-daughter, Cecilia, had been hurt when the oxcart she had been riding in overturned and pinned her under it. I had just returned that morning from taking my wife and our daughters in our four-wheel-drive pickup truck to Villa Neily, where a bus service was just starting, carrying passengers from Villa Neily, at the edge of the banana plantations on the coastal flood plains, to San José. The trip by bus was a grueling twelve hours, as many of the bridges that exist today had not yet been built and rivers needed to be forded. Maria and our daughters and I had left the farm a little after midnight to reach the lowlands for the 4:00 a.m. departure of the bus. I had then loaded sand and gravel on the truck (we were building on Loma Linda) and after picking up some supplies had returned to the farm in the early afternoon.

Now, in the little chicken house which we had converted to an office on Loma Linda, Toño stood, a plain man in his plain Sunday clothes, his face speaking in emotion. He said, "Can you please do something for Cecilia? A stake in the cart broke off when it turned on her. Its point went through Cecilia's side and made a hole. An intestine has come out."

My first thought was of Ernesto and Zoraida Araya as Toño and I threw the sand and gravel off the pickup and prepared to go to Cañas Gordas, where Cecilia had been carried on a stretcher. As often as there was an emergency in the South Frontier, it was Ernesto and Zoraida who were called upon to help meet it. At that time there was no doctor in the Italian colony in San Vito, no hospital, no nurse. There was no doctor or nurse or medical facility any-where in the South Frontier. There were no roads which could be driven over with certainty during the wet season; often they were impassable because of deep mud, even for four-wheel-drive vehicles equipped with tire chains. There were log bridges over streams on which the logs had become rotten and could not be trusted. There was the airstrip in Agua Buena and a second which had been built at the Italian colony but no reliable radio communication from either. There was no electrical power, save a few privately owned diesel-powered generating plants. There was so much of what there was not that it was unwise to dwell on it. But there were people who would not tolerate this inadequacy, and these became the pioneers of the new frontier.

I found Cecilia lying on the counter of the general store in Cañas Gordas. A cluster of men and women stood nearby and outside under plastic hoods in the rain. In the store I looked down at the pale face that looked back at me bravely. Cecilia had sometimes come to Loma Linda to play with Juliet and Elizabeth, our daughters, as they were about the same age, so she recognized me.

"Cecilia," I said, "what has happened to you; may I see?" Cecilia's mother pulled open the simple white dress, exposing one side of the nine-year-old girl's abdomen. An intestine protruded from a small hole in the smooth flesh. Surely such a small injury cannot endanger life, I prayed.

Cecilia's father and Toño and other men lifted her on the stretcher and held it in the back of the truck while we drove to Agua Buena. "She cannot be carried in the truck over the road to Villa Neily," I explained to Cecilia's mother, who rode beside me in the cab. "I have just come from there. We were almost three hours traveling the thirteen miles this morning in the truck. I will go to Villa Neily to see if there is a plane at the airfield there and, if not, call one to come to Agua Buena for Cecilia."

I left Cecilia at the Arayas' home in Agua Buena. Ernesto was at the Italian colony and Zoraida had just gone to San José. But a worker at the farm said that Ernesto would return soon.

An airfield had just been built in Villa Neily. The shortwave radio which Álvaro Acosta had operated at Agua Buena was not there now, and no radio communication was possible from the airstrip.

I had not exaggerated the condition of the road to Villa Neily when speaking to Cecilia's mother. The track along the cliffs fell in switchback upon switchback. Each hole projected its emptiness upon a protruding rock, each rock meant a slower pace, a lower gear, a possible gutting of a differential; a tedium of near futility.

Toño, who had come with me, and I asked for a doctor when we reached the village. A young Cuban doctor had just been stationed there, we were told. When we found the doctor and I told him what had happened he said: "Ah! We must get her to a hospital immediately!"

We drove to the airfield; there were no planes there, and the radio had just broken that day. However, we knew that there was a ham radio operator in Villa Neily and we went to him.

"My set is useless," he said. "The generating plant has broken down in the village and there is no power for my transmitter."

It was late; darkness was but an hour away—and yet the rain fell. There was nothing more we could do in Villa Neily. The doctor and I looked at the mountains rising so steeply above Villa Neily, the road a ribbon in the distance, clinging to cliffs it skirted. This was the road to the South Frontier. "Take me to Agua Buena," the doctor said reluctantly.

The lights of the pickup probed through the rain, picking out the holes, the rocks, the shear drop-off into space at the edge of the road where it bordered the cliffs. Only infrequently did the doctor or Toño speak.

Ernesto had started his generating plant after returning from the colony. When we finally made it back to Agua Buena, we found people gathered in the light on the porch of the Araya home. At one corner of the room in which Cecilia lay on a table, her father and mother stood among friends whose faces were distant.

Cecilia's eyes were closed, but she opened them and smiled when she saw the doctor and me. I looked as he uncovered the injury, and a great sigh was wrenched from the doctor. The intestine was a fire-like red and had swollen in size. I left that room and Cecilia and walked into the pasture beyond the house, my thoughts bitter, my eyes unseeing. Gradually I became aware that it was light. The sky had cleared; the rain had stopped and a full moon shone. I thought that night as I stood outside the Arayas' home: there is enough light from the moon for a plane to land in Agua Buena.

When I told this to the doctor, he said: "We must call it."

I asked Ernesto if the road to San Vito was passable without tire chains. "Yes," he said, "but I can go; you have now been on the roads for almost 24 hours."

"Let me try," I pleaded.

It was after midnight when we reached the Italian colony. We awakened the radio operator there only to learn that the transmitter had broken and could not be operated. "Go to the church," the operator said, "the priest there has a transmitter."

The priest started his generating plant and at once began transmitting a general distress call. Over and again his voice repeated the message to anyone who might hear. The minutes lengthened, and the silence on the radio receiver grew leaden. "San José, San José, San José . . . ," and there was no reply.

—But the reply must come from the people! the community leaders would exhort. The word *gente,* people, rang with a clarity and a sincerity all knew. In Costa Rican culture there is a particular significance in this word; it means community; it meant at that time in the experience of the emergence of this nucleus of men and women and their children that *we belong to one family; we face a common need!* The community leaders said: It is for the *people* to confront these problems; it is for the *people* to act, not separately but as one.

The settlers who heard these words, the eloquence of the words the new pioneers knew, exchanged meaningful glances; their feet would shift on the ground where all might be standing in a small group outdoors, listening to the speaker. The hands of the men would move along their belts and run along unshaven cheeks and then through their hair. And one would turn to another, the women to the men, and they would nod and say:

This is so.

—Until there grew such a pain and such a hunger and such a despair and such a need . . . , that the people took these things and made them with their hearts and their hopes into a new tool, a tool with which to make a day to dispel the darkness from the night when there was no response—

"I can do no more," the priest said. "No one will answer. I will call again at first light of morning. And I will call for the plane to come at once."

The doctor and I returned to Agua Buena, and I left Cecilia, for I could no longer remain with her; I was unprepared to see her die.

On the following day from Loma Linda we saw the plane make its circling approach to land at the airfield in Agua Buena. I sent our foreman, Adolfo, afoot to the airfield to bring word. At length he returned and his old face—Adolfo was old from much living—spoke with a great sense of loss.

"Cecilia was taken in the plane to San José," he said. "The doctor went with her. An ambulance was waiting. Cecilia died in the ambulance on the way to the hospital."

There was no quarter then—we had brought our wives to this wilderness, asked them to share its hazards and bear children, and we men could not quench the ache which bore witness to our frailty.

Not long ago, I visited Ernesto at the family home in Agua Buena. It is built on a hill there, overlooking the community. Zoraida was in San José with the Araya children, all grown now. Ernesto rose and greeted me as I entered the living room. He walked with a slight limp, because he was just recovering from knee surgery. We spoke of many things, as we always do now when we see each other. But at length our thoughts were drawn to those times in the past, a very different and distant world from the present. At one point in our talk, Ernesto said, "Come, I want to show you something." He led me to the bedroom he shares with his wife and drew back the curtains on one window. He stood to one side, and I looked out on the story that unfolded from that vantage.

Reaching below the hill was Agua Buena. The old airfield is gone now. On its site a coffee growers' cooperative has built several buildings, and a coffee processing factory stands nearby. The road in Agua Buena is paved with asphalt—a highway we call it, connecting this village with San Vito and all other parts of Costa Rica. There is a health center and an ambulance and a school and a church and electrical power and stores and homes and telephones, and, at the old Italian colony in San Vito, a hospital. There is a future made into reality. I was aware as I looked at all this that day from the hilltop that almost everything I saw had been touched by people like Ernesto and Zoraida. My companion at the window said nothing; we were each lost in our separate thoughts, which, in truth, would have been much the same thoughts. We seldom speak of Cecilia; but my memories, and I believe Ernesto's, went to her then. There is no way, I thought, that such a price can ever be reconciled. The loss of life can never be equated with what we learn and attempt to correct, but the loss is made more bearable by making life a continuing pledge to live.

The time of the pioneer of those earlier years has passed. Gone too is the challenge of that frontier. But no age, no time, is without its challenge. The pioneer of that earlier time seized in his or her imagination a vision which was never complete, only a beginning. It remains to build on what was started, to recognize and reassess the exigencies that gave way to those earlier years. We must seek to understand, for we have acted upon scant knowledge. The new pioneer is the student, the researcher, the person who would learn. He or she must deal with the burden which has been brought forward, for we have loved—yet despoiled; labored—yet destroyed; cherished—yet all but lost a world which we must now seek to recreate and restore. This is the frontier which abides today in Coto Brus.

Each of the flights I have described was a means of breaking the grip of isolation upon the settlers. The isolation was a circumstance imposed by the inaccessibility of the lands being settled. It is true that, given enough time and energy, settlers were able to move themselves and provisions over the "King's Highway" during many parts of the year. And, generally, flights between Agua Buena and the outside world were reliable, on a three-times-a-week schedule. The banana plantations in the lowlands usually could be reached; a long wait there in the plantations themselves enabled passengers to board a train operated by the United Fruit Company and eventually reach the port of Golfito; on the following day one might fly from the airport there to San José or catch a ride on a cargo boat to the Pacific port of Puntarenas and then go by train or road to San José. Such means of breaking away from isolation were the normal routes of entry and departure from the frontier. But life for settlers is often defined in terms of its emergencies. It is not satisfactory to be safe most of the time in the full certainty that at other times life itself will be risked. And since it is natural in human effort to identify an external adversary when we must confront the nature of our trepidation, the frontier and, specifically, the rain forest became an adversary.

No father or mother wishes to encounter the sickness and possible death of a child at night by candlelight when the rain around the home is falling like a deluge and all of the trails and roads have become quagmires. Under these circumstances the darkness itself becomes an adversary, as does, by extension, the darkness of this abysmal and unfeeling land which encloses and defies the very entry of the sun. If one must live where it rains and rains and will ever rain, then the roads must not be within the shadow of the forest, with its continual and never ceasing dripping which lingers even when the rain has gone. If the children must walk miles to reach a single classroom, then they must not do so by walking through this forest—for has it not been shown that the forest is alien to security?

People's relationship with their environment then also becomes defined by their assessment of their relative security, whether this be in a crime-ridden city or on the fringe of unexplored land. In the first case, the quality of security is interpreted mostly by human relationships, people with people; in the second it is recognized as people's relationship with a natural environment, an environment which does not express itself in human language, and, hence, an environment which responds to our measures to curb its imputed adversity often only well after our punitive actions have been applied. Most of our acts in the face of conditions we seek to change will have repercussions beyond our expectations; certainly this is so when we attempt to refashion a world and make it into an environment fit for human life.

"Three Flights for Survival" is a segment of history, and, as such, the events related may have limited application in the professional fields of those persons not specifically concerned with the background of the settlement of a particular area in Costa Rica. However, students in certain disciplines might peruse this material to better inform themselves of the antecedents of their investigations into land use. If we put ourselves in the position of these students, scientists at one or another level in their academic careers, we may see why their work will be difficult and how it might become more meaningful.

As scientists, these students are trained to find, sort, and organize information in logical systems. At the beginning of such work they must apply principles of objectivity; in other words, they must reduce to a minimum that which is emotional, nonscientific, unsubstantiated by fact, in the interest of presenting and interpreting accurately gathered and organized data. I work with students who follow such methodologies; indeed, we follow such methodologies in our research work on this farm.

But we must recognize that most people do not conduct their lives under such disciplines. This is something that, as a matter of fact, we do recognize. However, when we come to consider the interactions of people with their respective natural environments, we tend to undervalue the influence of subjectivity. Men and women are acted upon by their environment; in turn it is acted upon by them. And people are emotional beings as well as intellectual beings. Hence, the element of feeling, or emotion, is ever present in these interactions; how one feels today about a piece of land and his or her family's future on that piece of land will affect the home it becomes tomorrow.

In this regard, my exposure to scientific inquiry over many years on Finca Loma Linda has left me with a sense of a widening gap between the methodology of inquiry and the perceived realities of life it must address. The element that too frequently is missing is subjectivity. I am aware that I am treading on sacred ground in making this statement. Yet, as often as we return to the procedures of strict logic to interpret life—our own as the human expression of life, or that of other life with which we deal—we leave untapped a source of information which may well be vital in the overall framework of our understanding. We cannot only quantify so many units of a given designation in our studies and inquiries into life processes; we must seek that which can neither be weighed nor counted nor interpreted numerically but that is probably a motivating force in much that we see today in our environment and will continue to see in the future. These are often the silent places in the hearts and minds of men and women. Might they also be the silent places in the life processes we investigate in the world around us? I am not prepared to say, but I think that this, at least, can be a possibility. The relationship of people to their environment is an immediate process; it changes from moment to moment. There is a cause, an effect, a response; but beyond this there is a heritage, an accumulated voice which speaks through time. Let's call up this voice now to support our present inquiry into the causes and effects of land settlement.

The rain forest here has not been destroyed entirely; its legacy in its principles of life relationships speaks over these acres. The acts of men and women who went before us have not died; they are planted in this earth, in the greater heritage of our planet. Before we superimpose our scheme of logic and objectivity upon this present, we should try to discover wherein is rooted its soul.

FOUR

Subsistence and Monoculture

*A*bove the clearing, surrounded by forest, the morning sunbeams would burnish a gaunt, spectral immobility at the tops of trees, branches reaching like arms against the silhouette of day; a fabric of intertwined fingers of shadow and deeper shadow—and the deep-throated solitude of silence. Then, by ones and twos, the voices would meet upon the sky: the cries of toucans, vaunts of vainglorious squalor within the dawn, guans, to babble in a panoply of shadows, voices seeming to be unloosed from the threads of night, and parakeets, taking wing like scattered leaves upon a wind of sound.

Were there too many more tomorrows, this morning would be now—as then, when the entire vista of this horizon opened and we were young; in its youth this heart within the season spoke but with that voice which we understood and knew for its candor: this land is ours, this moment free.

With some memory that seems to speak from this moment, I have walked within this morning, my footsteps a print upon this ground, the light then caught in the verdure of these trees. Here where begins now all the recourse I have to avail myself of a need to learn the secrets of this place, I may this day take some part of its beginning to guide my hand and thought to make a thing of worth.

The challenge in what I believe is the virility that comes from the logs I hew, and with these make a fence, may test my strength. There springs across this earth so fallen now and cast within the bounds of this forest felled by me a breath of all that may come in time; I am enclosed by each stroke of axe or blade.

In time children will grow upon this place—what pride in bringing forth generation! I must cast the weariness off the evening and make my journey consistent.

Now at dawn my sun of trust arises; it too will shine at noon, and then in west be weighted down and I in furrow plowed across these days will make an arm and hand which yield shall not until the sun be parted and in the west the furrow ended.

Settlers do not speak in such terms. Or is it indeed that they listen to them? There are both: the spoken address of the individual to the environment, and the response of the individual to what is perceived as a reply.

The elements of empathy I have touched upon in the foregoing paragraphs are not inapplicable to the plain facts of the use of the land or to the lives of people. In this work, the beginning of a farm, there is a contact with vital forces to which no individual is a stranger.

During these years we, who took our residence here, felt ourselves to be free. Within this freedom all things seemed possible. We would build homes, bridge streams, make roads, clear the land, create expanse within restriction. We would plant and the land would yield.

This sense of freedom is the character of youth, and in youth the world speaks of all that is yet undone and yet may be. Each element in the perspective of this horizon becomes then a means of expressing a release and a sense of action. Yet all such release and expansion bind in a mold, a future cast. We may begin our day in poetry; we conclude in prose and find that the lyric then was always a reference in later fact.

There were and are settlers who would never utter a word whose beauty might echo the song in their heart; yet their hands would make epics and their lives be written in verse. They worked with the seed; they cultivated its growth. They were planted in their days; they grew across time. They were not deaf to the energies of life systems; they were not mute in the recognition of their power. Yet, they expressed themselves in ways which we need to understand.

How, then, did all this begin?

It would have started on the charred, the blackened land. Here where the fire has swept, leaving but a remembrance of the days and nights in wind, now the rains have fallen.

We take these tools in hand. There is a worth in steel—men feel this; probably we have inherited our response to the touch and weight of tools, implements to extend the force in arms or hands, the momentum and impulse in the legs.

These tools are the *machete de suelo,* a broad-bladed machete with a crook at the handle, used for digging and planting in the ground and not for slashing like the conventional machete; the *pala,* a short, U-handled shovel with a very broad blade, also used for planting and for cultivation; the axe; our long-bladed machete for cutting and slashing; and the *garabato.*

It is interesting to note, from our modern perspective, that the framework of technology—to think in terms of power, to work with power applied—is missing in the early years of frontier settlement and to recognize that the only power would be supplied by us. Here are no power saws, no power machines, no power diggers or movers, sometimes even the absence of the power supplied by animal traction.

So the power is ours.

Out of such a requirement—that of having to supply the power oneself—and from ages past beyond memory, men and women have learned two additional attributes of personal power: rhythm and balance.

With our simple tools in hand, we can work for hours under the sun, through intervals of rain, throughout the day as measured from dawn to evening. And we learn to apply our power, our strength, through the media of rhythm and balance.

There is a third factor here, something that is external to us but present with us throughout the day. It is the response to ourselves in our work.

Initially, here on our land there was order; we did not comprehend it but recognized it and destroyed it. Our name for it was forest. Then there was—and is—chaos, the wreckage of the felled and burned forest. Now we work to restore order.

Today you and I will take these tools in hand—first the axe— and cut these branches, charred and blackened as they are, which cross and crisscross here, obstructing passage over the land, and we will pile them here, by this stump. Two things are happening as we do this work: there is a rhythm and a surge in the swing of the axe, originating from the ground and the feet, as I have said; and when we have cut these branches and we take them in hand to be piled, there is the feel of the rough bark on our hands, and in it there is a response to us.

Response—how?

The response is in the pile, in the cleared sector of land from which these branches were removed. The response is in the tiredness which comes to us from this work, just as the sector of land is free of obstructions and the pile by the stump is taller. A link has been joined here: we have expended energy, power; but this power was never ours, but rather an attribute of this land and of the work associated with it, of this moment; had we not had this moment, this place, the power would have been meaningless, for it would not have been the reciprocal of this relationship in our work.

Now we have *cleared* this sector of land. We will use this word in its various forms repeatedly, *clearing, to clear*. It does not mean during these first years that the land is clear, the earth free of roots and stumps; it means we have initiated the process of so transforming it.

From this sector of cleared land we must extract now a condition in our lives as settlers, and this we shall call subsistence, the means by which we will try to meet as many of our own daily food and goods requirements, and those of our families, as possible. And here there enters a further element of our power, that of creativity. To the rough texture of the bark of the branches on our hands and the smooth flow of the axe handle across our palms, there is added now a sense of purpose; we have the ability through our strength and our determination to produce food, to produce shelter, to produce the wherewithal of well-being.

But the power is not only ours. I have spoken of a sense of freedom. It arises from this sense of purpose. For this is a good thing we do—we believe—to make a shelter, a home, to provide food and well-being on the land. Because we believe this, we recognize that the power is not only ours but is also that of the energies and the life which flow around us. Indeed, there is no separation in this power; it is one and the same, and we are a segment of it or it is a segment of us.

We recognize these energies in the rain. Whereas it is not necessary that we analyze the effects of gravity on the rainwater when it reaches the ground or the relationship of this water to angle of slope (although certainly it is useful to recognize such relationships), we will see in the rain an expression of life forces. Without this rain the soil becomes dry, afflicted with drought. That which grows upon the soil seeks the moisture and is without it. There is a time of need, and the land looks upon the sky as would a human countenance in supplication. We know this, as do all who see these circumstances. But we know too that there is more than the fulfillment of a need in this rain.

In the rain too there are the same release and freedom we acknowledge; here energy is replenished by receipt of energy. The first, the rain, falls and is received by the land; its energy is transformed and renewed. The earth reaches toward the sky with its strivings of verdure and its multitude of small words spoken on silent breaths, and the energy is released and returned to the air.

It is not necessary that we analyze this, although it is useful, because, as part of this system, we know it. It is not an extraneous process we are viewing; we have taken this energy in hand in its myriad expressions, have worked with it and transformed it, and to it our energy has passed and from it its energy has returned to us. This is why women and men who work within the natural environment feel an affinity and a relevancy in their daily contact with life and its associated forces. There is no distinction between that and me, between this and what I do; for, whereas we are, of course, different, I detect and you discern that there is much that binds us.

This may also be said of the sun, its light and its energy. For we know that it burns with an intensity upon us so that our strength is sapped and our arms grow weary. Yet we are aware too that in this also is our strength. For we are not a pampered entity; we, like all else here today, must prove the worth of our commitment and live. Life is an expression of our work this day; and these, the rain and the sun, are our counterparts in expressing trust. We believe the rain will replenish, the sun will engender growth. We believe that there will be a time of lack and a time of surfeit and that across the seasons we and these sources of energy we identify will prevail and sustain.

With these sources of energy we build. We are about to turn the earth. We know that we are not the first people on this land; to be first is possibly meaningless in the context of what we shall attempt. Others were here before us, indigenous peoples—perhaps too we were with them, for there is something that speaks to us in the heart of this land, indeed, our planet—but it does not matter that they were here then or we now in terms of time, but rather that we share with them now this new tenure and its heritage. For we are about to turn this earth and it has not been turned in ages; we have the means of making a beginning, our beginning merely that which is added on those others which have gone before us. We will use the *machete de suelo* and the *pala*, tools which have no counterpart in our experience in other lands but which are needed here.

We cut and lift the earth with these tools, the *machete de suelo* and the *pala*, using both hands on both tools, as required. The *machete de suelo*, as it was used in this early work on the frontier, is a heavy-bladed knife, and with it the earth is turned and pulverized and windrowed. Much the same work is done with the *pala*, although this is a heavier tool. With each tool we work in a stooped position, bending near the ground.

Muscles can accommodate themselves to this work position; in fact, the balance and flow of rhythm so essential to long-term productivity in physical labor are present in this work as we bend and apply strength to these tools.

The sun and the rain are here in the earth. As yet there is little vegetation emerging from this ground; there is shock in this transition—the transition from the primary forest to what will follow—and recovery and response have yet to take place on this ground we have laid open. But here the sun and the rain have written their pages, and we see this in the roots. The wind too is present here, its memories recorded in the tissues of the roots, because in each fiber the root built strength imparted by the wind to brace the tree. These are the pages of past events recorded in this ground.

This clearing is only a small portion of what the farm will become. Yet there is no other land like this; there is no other here or elsewhere. On this hill which rises to the east of us, that high point characterized by such massive trees in the primary forest, where the wind strikes in the northeast season with its starlit darkness and from which the coast of Panama is seen, its line of ocean in haze, there has been a cleavage in the land, the effects of earlier hurricanes in the Caribbean causing lines of faults in the ground to become saturated with volumes of rainwater. All of this and more is written on the earth if we can recognize it. And each segment of land, be it here or wherever we may happen upon it, has its accounts to tell of past events.

Thus, if we walk but twenty paces from here to a point by the forest edge, we will have altered our orientation not simply by having changed place, but by having changed history, because each location is the product of a different combination of forces. Where the ground swells or elsewhere is depleted there is not the same tenor in the earth. Now we must learn the meaning of its nature.

Our soil will one day be called by the name *Andisol,* meaning that its origin was owing to volcanic activity. There is, of course, the volcano, Barú, not distant from us here in Panama. It is inactive now; how it must have painted its name upon the sky when its ash snowed over this land! As we make this start on the land, we wonder: can there be any relationship between us this moment and all this that we perceive in the past?

There is no question but that there can and must be.

This is what we, as settlers, will learn: we stand at a point in time; beyond us the past recedes without definition, its collapse beyond measure. There is no reason to assume that there will be no future. There are persons who contend that we, as a human race, will exterminate our opportunity to know it, but none deny that a future will exist, regardless of its implication to us.

Possibly, no experience is more relevant to this sense of past and future than our work today. As settlers we intervene in processes of which we become aware while at the same time recognizing that they had proceeded without us irrespective of what our wish might have been to be participant.

Through an awareness of this circumstance, that of the human presence in this environment having been neither essential in the past nor necessarily contemplated in the future, we convert our present, which really is all we have, to a knowledge that much is of significance in this environment beyond what is our concept of self.

This then becomes a determinant factor in our relationship with the environment—the factor of the ceaseless forces, energies, processes, systems, forever evolving around us. It is certainly true that not all of the settlers were sensitive to these energies, these processes. Many persons might dispense with a conscious awareness of them. But life systems, their relationships to substrates, do not halt and cease to exist because they are ignored. Men and women could and did come to the new land, the frontier. In the degree that the rain forest represented an obstacle to their progress—however this might be defined—people would raze and eliminate the forest. Yet that forest, its ambient environment, was, of course, not destroyed in terms of its fundamental principles of life and their continuity.

Were the settlers to be indifferent to these principles, they would

A PLACE IN THE RAIN FOREST

prolong their task of learning. To the degree that the settlers separated themselves from a concern with the life-systems principles surrounding them, and always operative, they would drive a wedge between themselves and what they needed to know. The fruit of indifference, or arrogance, would be converted into a harvest of thorns. It would be by a process of a gradual awareness of an expanded identity—indeed, an identity associated with more than what we recognize as us—that we who settled the frontier would come to find our place within it.

I am not speaking in metaphysical terms. There would be no place in this book for such content. But it is my purpose to show, through my personal experiences and those of the settlers whose experiences I know, that we are acted upon by the forces of life surrounding us; that we are acted upon by the energies with which we deal; that in turn we act and seek to prevail with them; and that in the course of these interactions we find that our perception of self, each individual, is changed. Thus the frontier, by a strange and uncertain alchemy, has been converted in both place and instance to become us; the settlement of this land has become its influence on people. We were to start in youth and with a certain sham image of glory. We would be brought to our knees only to rise thence with the dregs of disillusion bitter on the wind and to renew and persist in learning.

At this, the dawn of settlement of Coto Brus, all things might be given to us in our time of youth.

But in reality they were not and are not so given.

Was this then the real essence of the frontier, to learn what could not be done? I don't think so, and I don't think any of my neighbors here in Coto Brus would acknowledge this as having been the outcome of their work as settlers. They are today, as they were at the time of first settlement, people who believe in making success. Yet the experience of settling the South Frontier was that of repeated and endless failure, of finding oneself proved wrong.

Let's examine how these two opposite conditions could live together in the same house. We, as first on the land, would have to accept that we could not look over our shoulders and point the finger of blame at some earlier time for what would go wrong under our stewardship. In most farming areas of the world, farmers may, if they wish, look back at earlier generations and infer that those earlier users of the farm had mismanaged it. We could not do this, although the generation which follows us today certainly can. We would have to answer solely for what might come.

The initiation of the use of a previously unpopulated region entails the realization of two separate but related facts: no one's mistakes here can be used as a crutch for current blunders, and conversely, there is no one to consult on what works and what may not work in the way of plantings and farming systems. That there is no accumulation of prior information about the use of this land is one reason that settlers can be so overpoweringly optimistic about what they will do and how they will make everything work. We recognize, of course, that no one has proved anything yet on this land, and so we give a free rein to our expectations of our own abilities. These first years in settlement will see a lot of trial and error in applications of farming systems.

Let's follow some of our first steps in the pursuit of our objectives on a sector of cleared land.

Few today would agree that simply attaining a subsistence from the farm would be an attractive objective, but where no food whatsoever is produced and the land is yet unplanted, obtaining some food from the future farm is quite an accomplishment. It is also an overriding need, for only limited food supplies are as yet available in the few general stores.

Returning to the blackened earth after the burn in our clearing, we are a little surprised to discover that there isn't much organic matter on the surface of the soil. This we note as we begin to turn the soil with the *machete de suelo* and the *pala*. Certainly, the fire burned the surface leaf litter in most places; but there are some patches the fire didn't touch, and these, too, seem to be lacking in the surface mulch and litter that our impression of the standing rain forest presupposed. What is happening is that we are seeing now what we did not see well at the time of exploration of our forested land: that the surface litter on the forest floor is not as thick and heavy as the stature of the forest would lead us to expect. Of course, in the rain forest there is always a litter—leaves, animal remains, insect tissues, excrements from various forest life—covering the ground, but it is not as thick as many unfamiliar with the tropics believe should be the case.

Here, for the newcomer—and all are new to this land—is a good point to stop and do some thinking. What we are seeing in this rather thin layer of mold and litter is a clear signal of the very accelerated pace of life processes in this tropic environment. It might be compared to life-support conditions in greenhouses where temperature and moisture combine to force rapid growth. No sooner has some living thing become established in this environment than it is seized upon by other living things as a source of sustenance, and while living, or after death, it continues to feed other life. This takes place without respite, without the intervening cold and freezes of other parts of the world; hence, that which drops and succumbs on the forest floor seldom lingers there but becomes incorporated in the tissues and energies of new, living matter. A world ramifies from this simple observation, which might fill volumes of further observations to be written on principles and applications in tropical farming; but, for the moment, we are more concerned with growing some food than with learning why it can't be done in the scores of ways which will occur to us and eventually be proved wrong.

Another surprising characteristic of this leaf litter left at some patches where the fire didn't touch is that its smell doesn't seem to convey the right fragrance of mold and decomposition we associate with a good garden loam. This litter has a rank, wild smell; in other words, it smells like the rain forest and not like a garden soil. This, too, might cause us to do some thinking. The resins, the chemical components in this litter, the arrangement of the different elements which, we know, are necessary to sustain plant life, are not necessarily right in composition or proportional relationships here in this forest litter to support the planting we have in mind. This is not yet an agricultural soil, and the fact that it sustained the rain forest does not mean that it will grow good vegetables.

Here, too, it is easy to jump over clear signals. As settlers, we feel ourselves to be the dynamic moving force; we are changing a world. This is not the time to hesitate and ask a number of extremely complicated questions, such as: If the rain forest thrives, won't most other things grown in this soil thrive too?

The immediate (we do not know about the longer term) answer is that they will not—not at this early stage in the conversion of virgin land. What is important are the reasons that so many crops will not grow well. And if we could understand the difference between the earth and the forest it supports, we might learn one of the pivotal principles of the forest legacy. The principle is this: the fertility of the rain forest is suspended and preserved in its living tissue and not principally held as in repository in the earth. As persons unfamiliar with this environment, we assume that this ground is the source of life and a principal source of all of the magnificent structure of the living forest. A closer approximation to the truth is that life is a source and a sustainer of life, and we have destroyed an entire order of life systems. Simply, we assumed that it all would return here to this ground and replenish itself and be prepared to spring anew at our bidding into any one of a number of fresh living systems. But in felling the forest, we extinguished untold life and life-support mechanisms, and in reality they are no longer in existence. Have they disappeared forever? No; fortunately, we don't have the ability to exterminate *life*, but we can so alter life relationships that we will be compelled to deal with the results of our machinations for decades, and perhaps longer.

How does life sustain and support life? In the rain forest this is accomplished by the continual circulation of what we refer to as *fertility* when we use this term in regard to farming. Fertility circulates in living plants, large animals, insects, and other life forms. It also passes through that matter we refer to as being dead, which, nonetheless, supports and is incorporated into so much that is living. What we must see here is that fertility is not an arrested status, captive and awaiting that moment when it will be tapped and then flourish in hundreds of expressions of, let us say, plantings. Rather, it is the expression of life, the dynamics of living processes.

A PLACE IN THE RAIN FOREST

Here among logs and stumps and heavy branches we will plant bananas and plantains, chayotes, some cassava, corn, and a pumpkinlike vegetable called *ayote*. The soil is dark, steaming now in the early morning sunlight, and the thought comes to mind that some of this seed may be the first ever of its kind to be planted on this land. It has not been easy to get the scions of the bananas and plantains, and the chayotes too—the fruit itself is planted—must be held as precious. Earlier settlers, especially some who have come from Panama, have started this seed, and they have given us our start. Because of its scarcity and importance this seed requires careful handling. The corn is field corn, not sweet corn, and the *ayote* seeds will be planted with the corn. The cassava wood (or stems) was a lucky find; another settler gave us a few sticks. All in all, our small store of seed is a little treasure to be carefully managed.

Our clearing, as we have noted, is free of weeds; as a matter of fact, this is a striking characteristic of the new farm. After the burn very little is growing here. There are, of course, no weed seeds here; there have been no weeds, as such, growing on this land. Some saplings from the primary forest are sprouting and showing vigorous regrowth; however, if we have made our *zocola* (the forest understory clearing) well, by cutting all these saplings at ground level, they will not be with us now to send out shoots.

Here then is a gardener's utopia, a weed-free garden. Consider that if there are no weeds growing here, and the forest is no longer growing, all the plant food, the fertility, in this land must be ready now for our seeds, ready to endow our young plantings with the richness treasured in the soil.

The tool we will use mostly for this planting is the *pala*, the broadbladed, short-handled shovel. It belongs to that select category of hand tools which are truly well made. It has a welded closed back where the blade is attached to the handle and a sturdy U-grip at the end of the handle and can be bought with blades ranging from 12 to 24 inches wide. The work for this shovel is not to dig trenches or to fill loads; it is used for weeding, like the *machete de suelo,* but mostly for hilling. The blade is of thin, high-temper steel, and the edge is kept knife sharp.

I describe these tools in detail because they were universally used in Costa Rica and elsewhere in Central America at this time, and with them farms were made. Today they are not frequently seen in their earlier uses and have been largely supplanted by chemical weed killers. Let's follow their use, because there are many significant differences between the farming systems they came to represent and those in practice today.

To use the *pala* we work, as I have mentioned, in a bending position. We drive the broad, flat blade horizontally into the ground and find that our muscles accommodate themselves with practice to this work attitude. With the first stroke we turn the soil and begin to make a windrow or hill that runs in as straight a row as we can make between the logs and stumps. We have advanced no more than a meter or two when we reach for the axe or machete to cut roots. Indeed, at every other stroke of the *pala* we bang into a root. This collision, like a fumbled axe stroke, takes away a reserve of balance and drains far more energy than it should. In some roots the *pala* gets hung up and we have to pull it free. The rhythmic stroke-and-turn in hilling, so important in this work, is continually being blunted. Multiply this by hours and the inevitable result is fatigue — and some frustration.

What does it mean? This is our first encounter with a definition of the word *clearing,* with which we will live now for the next two decades. It will come to dominate our thinking, our planning, and our work in far-reaching ways during the next years. What we are actually dealing with here is the obstruction of the fallen rain forest. It is an obstruction which will sap energy and reduce limited cash reserves and blunt our ingenuity time and again, defeating our best innovations. It is very prosaic; surely some creative thinking, even some technology, can overcome this fallen obstacle dominating the land. But in the ensuing course of events, none of these do work.

What does work, and only in limited dimension as measured by the surface area of our land, is labor itself, lots of it.

As we turn the soil with the *pala,* cutting roots with the axe and machete as we go along, weaving in and out among the stumps, we see a new and interesting condition in this ground, this soil which is to become the basis of the farm: there are two textures in the soil. Where there are no obstructions, the *pala* cuts into the earth in two stages; the first seems to go through a tough crust in the soil surface, two or three inches thick, then the *pala* moves easily into the lower depths below this surface. It takes more energy to break through the surface crust than it does to drive the blade to lower depths. Let's look at the surface crust and see why it is harder to cut.

It is clear that there has been a surface mat of roots covering much of the forest floor. This mat is not very deep and, generally, it is not composed of heavy roots. The *pala* has the correct weight and balance for cutting as the blade is driven through the soil (although it will not cut heavy roots with any efficiency), and we are finding now that it is able to cut through this surface root mat. Sometimes the mat is so thickly intertwined with roots that very little soil adheres to them. And, again, there is the rank, raw smell in a handful of these roots, for, in reality, there is very little decomposition here. As we shovel with the *pala,* segments of the root mat come up in single pieces, covering a large portion of the two-foot-wide blade. After chopping up these segments with the blade and returning to this land over months as our work goes forward, we will find that many of these rootlets are slow to decay, suggesting that their chemical composition would not be good for making compost.

As I have said, stone and rock are almost never found in the surface soil of Coto Brus. If we work now with the *pala* to somewhat lower depths, below the root mat, we will find that the blade cuts quite cleanly into the lower soil. There seems to be little clay here, and the soil often does not stick to the shovel blade as is so often the case with other soils.

The texture of this soil, its physical properties, seems ideal. It is open, porous; it is not hard to see how rain, huge quantities of rain, will readily pass to lower depths. The rainfall here confirms this, for any other than a well-drained, porous soil could not possibly accommodate the volume of water reaching this ground.

Successful farming, regardless of where it is carried out, is based, with regard to land fertility and crop productivity, upon an important, yet simple, principle. It is that the fertility from a larger area must be harvested, transported, and applied to a smaller area, the farm itself, or a segment of the farm. In today's technology this is accomplished by "harvesting" the energy in petroleum and mineral deposits and capturing the elements in the atmosphere, converting them into commercial fertilizers, and concentrating them on planted lands. The source of plant food, the nutrients, may appear in varying forms—manufactured fertilizers, municipal wastes, manures, composts—but the principle is the same: a larger area of land surface—or a longer period of time in terms of accumulated resources—must yield its stores to a smaller area or a briefer time.

All of these things may seem remote from our labor today in the clearing. The sun has grown hot; the humidity, which is ever with us in the wet season, has brought the sweat through our clothes. Labor becomes toil; work becomes prose. Still, this is only a beginning, and these adverse circumstances will yield. But now we are going to accumulate the resources of a larger area of land and concentrate them in a smaller area. This has been done for generations by Costa Rican farmers, and it is one of the bases of success in traditional farming systems.

With the *pala* we cut off a surface slice of soil, mostly the root mat, and, in a single blade stroke, cut, lift, and turn. We deposit the lifted and turned soil in a windrow. We have taken it from both sides of the windrow; we have reached out at some distance from the windrow and brought the earth from a larger area and concentrated it here, in this raised and elongated mound in which we will plant. Generations of experience have taught us not to dig deeply, but, rather, to slice and transport the soil from around our planting site and to take this transported soil only from the surface. For this reason, our windrows are not closely spaced, there is quite a lot of distance between them, and we have scooped out a hollow trough running between them. In these windrows we will plant the cassava. For the bananas, the plantains, and the chayote, we will make hills instead of windrows, but the principle of mounding the earth is the same. The corn and *ayote* seed we may drill directly into the ground, using a pointed stick to open a small planting hole. But later, when the corn has come up, we will return to this planting with the *pala,* probably a twelve-inch blade, and mound or windrow the soil around the plants.

Now if someone not versed in tropical farming were to visit our clearing, he or she would not be much impressed by our day's work. Here among all the logs and debris are a lot of scattered, scruffed places made with a curious shovel, obviously back-breaking drudgery, primitive methods practiced by people who had no recourse to something better. Yet the ingredients of traditional farming methods of the past, the components of successful tropical farming today, the principles that will orient improved tropical farming techniques for tomorrow—all are in the steps and circumstances I have described in our work of the morning here in the clearing. And all are part of the legacy of the rain forest.

Let's review what we have been doing and discovering.

The scant layer of surface mulch in the unburned patches of land here in the clearing has called our attention to the function of a cover, a living mantle, on the ground. Because there is no practical way to accumulate and hoard wealth—fertility—here in the tropics as a stored resource in the soil, no sooner does organic matter reach the ground than it is activated as a component of living processes, becoming part of life systems. If we wish these life systems to be a basis of our farming system—crops, livestock, or a combination of both—we must keep in view the function of ground cover and mulch in fertility cycling. The rain forest is gone; its life systems terminated. Nevertheless, to some extent we can simulate what the rain forest represented.

The root mat tells us that life is teeming in the few surface centimeters of soil. Here temperature, aeration, light, and myriad other factors combine with moisture to create conditions which we do not and may not ever fully understand but which we must try to reproduce now under an open sky and direct sunlight. The porosity of the soil, its ability to transmit great volumes of rainwater, speaks of a soil which may be highly leached of its plant nutrients. We will not be surprised if soil depths immediately below this surface layer hold few available plant foods.

With these thoughts in mind, let's return to our morning's work in the clearing. It is true that there will be few weeds growing here during coming months. But nature has not ceased to function because we have cut the forest. A successional forest, a diversity of fast-growing annual plant species, and, eventually, many perennials will begin to populate this clearing. As these plants take hold in the ground we are cultivating with the *pala,* we will come often to this planting—continuing over successive years—to use the *pala* as a weeding tool. Slicing under the weeds or successional vegetation growing around and on the windrows and hills, we'll lift this vegetation, cutting it out with some of its roots along with some surface soil, and deposit it, foliage down and roots and soil up, around our planting.

This system is somewhat similar to what is done with a hoe or other tools in other parts of the world. I am not trying to show that we are doing something unique in so turning the soil. But what we are doing is fundamental to maintaining land productivity in this environment, because we are harvesting the living mantle of vegetation covering the earth and using it to restore the plant nutrients it has incorporated in its tissues and will now release through decomposition.

The crops we have planted today and those we will plant during successive days in the clearing all belong to this part of the world and are at home in this tropical environment. In about a year the bananas and plantains will produce their first stems of fruit. For several years they will continue to send up new scions from the mother plants, each scion producing a stem of fruit, and there will be scions to increase the planting. The cassava will take six or eight months to produce tubers, the corn and *ayote* about six months, and the chayote will bear at about the same time. All will provide more seed for new planting. Now, with corn, we can raise chickens and there will be eggs. The corn and cassava and *ayote* will also supply feed for pigs; these and the chickens will be the first livestock on the farm. With our pasture grass, planted at the beginning of the wet season following the burn, we can look ahead to a cow and, in the more distant future, possibly, a yoke of oxen, and later a bull.

Meat at this point in the settlement will come from the forest. The guans will be the first to feel the impact of civilization. Completely unaware of their danger, they will gabble conspicuously in the trees, where they can be shot easily. (On Finca Loma Linda we did no hunting. We also tried to stop hunting by others on our property. However, settlers in the South Frontier generally did hunt.)

All of our plantings in the clearing will succeed. At the end of the wet season, in October or November, we will plant beans, and with them will come the source of vegetable protein for our family. Other tubers, similar to the cassava, will be planted; there will be several kinds of plantains. Sugarcane will be planted early, and, for the settlers able to acquire yokes of oxen — and at the beginning only a few can — a *trapiche*, a raw sugar mill powered by the oxen, will be built. Here will be one of the first products to be sold by the settlers: brown, raw sugar, poured and hardened in molds of a conical form. Sugar in this form was known as *dulce*.

Rice cannot be grown here as there are no varieties suitable for this elevation. We may try potatoes, but their planting will come later. Fruits are nonexistent at this point in the settlement, but one of the first to be planted will be the guava tree, which in time will yield well. Pineapples can and will be planted; here again, their planting will come after the more essential staples. Settlers in the tropics do not face harsh, preemptive winters. Malnutrition was a constant and long-term problem for the settlers of the South Frontier, but actual starvation never was.

As I have said, the crops first planted were those that were at home in this environment. And they grew well on the "rich, virgin land." I say this within quotation marks, because it was in this way that we saw and spoke of our land. And while we worked within the category of compatible crops (those compatible with this soil and this climate), this *was* rich, productive earth. There was a direct legacy from the rain forest here; even where the land was burned—in fact, more often where the land was burned—the response to these early plantings was good.

Now let's look at what we are building. In our clearing there are bananas and plantains, there are chickens and pigs; in the *rancho* corn and *ayote* (it keeps like pumpkins) are in storage; there are the chayote and cassava; we may have planted some cabbage. The outrage some persons will contend we are causing upon the environment through the destruction of the rain forest does not seem to be with us. Perhaps it has not caught up to us. In reality, on our little farm here in the logs and stumps, things seem to be going quite well.

If we move the time frame ahead several decades to the present here in Coto Brus, we can make some useful comparisons. For several years now we have been carrying out here on Finca Loma Linda a number of experiments looking at crop responses relative to different management systems. In many of these experiments our primary focus has been on the soil, particularly on the dynamics of one element, phosphorus, in the soil.

As farmers and as research investigators we are drawn to study and manipulate management practices involving the soil because it responds to treatments of cause and effect in ways we can see in our farming systems. There is much that we can do to alter and rearrange conditions in the soil. Farmers and scientists like to work with the soil. But here in Coto Brus, as in some other parts of the tropical world, the major constraint in successful crop production is not the infertility of the soil but rather plant diseases and in Coto Brus—but not necessarily in other places—to a lesser degree, insect pests. Were we able to deal more successfully with plant diseases in Coto Brus today, an important part of our farming troubles would vanish.

Returning now to our clearing, we are working in pretty much a disease-free environment. Crop diseases are not established in this environment because crops have not long been grown here. Generally, the same observation can be made of insect pests. They are not established because the host plants are not here in a monoculture. This relative freedom from diseases and pests will last for several years. During this time, with the exception of a very few instances of skillful management, soil fertility in the virgin land will be depleted. It will be depleted not so much by crop extraction from the new land, for subsistence farming extracts very little, and as yet there is no cash-crop farming of any considerable scale; rather, it will be depleted by the leaching rains and the absence of an adequate circulatory system of life upon the earth. The methods of planting with the *pala*, whereas illustrative of fundamental and important principles, are not in themselves enough to counteract the degradation of the land after the disappearance of the rain forest. Indeed, they fall very much short of meeting such an objective. So while we are enjoying a season of disease- and pest-free planting and seeing the first produce from our land, we are actually losing not so much the fertility but the system of its very existence. Where does this lead? It leads, of course, to the same results characterizing agriculture anywhere in the world: we will become increasingly dependent upon "imported," manufactured fertilizers to maintain soil productivity and a host of spray programs to combat diseases and pests.

Is there any way that such a dependency, with its degrees of increasing environmental problems, might have been, or might be, avoided or at least reduced? As long as the market continues to reward the farmer who gets his produce to the consumer at the lowest possible price and in the most attractive condition (and I am talking about cosmetics), probably not. It is possible today and probably has been in the recent past to produce food with less dependency on such props to fertility and pest control, but it is not economically profitable to do so.

What we are concerned with at this point in our review of the settlement of new land, however, is that the practice of shifting agriculture and the seeking of new lands—with its consequent destruction of more forest—is less a condition of depleted soil fertility and more a condition of a buildup of limiting disease and pest incidence. Farmers and scientists are often remarkably innovative in contending with soil fertility problems; they are less so in dealing with diseases and pests.

I have mentioned the compatibility or adaptability of certain crops (this is also true of some breeds of livestock) relative to our new farm. But there are many things we will try here which will not be adapted or compatible. In fact, they will be far greater in number—and eventually in economic importance—than those which prove to work. When we do begin to deal with these crops and these breeds of livestock which are not compatible with the emerging environment, we will be encountering our first juncture of two worlds. Our world in this clearing is not a world of universal acceptance of that which we will bring here. In the aftermath of its disappearance, the rain forest becomes a complex of extremely specialized life systems; we recognize this now as we attempt to introduce new plantings in this environment. It seems that our plantings are out of adjustment with the demanding requirements of the life orders prevailing here, yet we cannot define how or why. By comparison with the specialized systems which had characterized the rain forest, our objectives in agriculture tend to be generalized.

But the rain forest and our new land are only part of the picture. Another part is so apparently small and seemingly unimportant that we tend to disregard it. This is the genetic life requirements within the seed itself or in the new breed of livestock. When this seed from another world, the temperate world let us say, reaches us, it comes with its own expectations, its own demands. It is not simply a seed that, planted where there is earth and light and water, will grow here as well as anywhere else. It will not do this; and, what is worse, it may grow only in an indefinite approximation of adapting itself to this new environment, involving us in untold frustrations to assist it in fitting in, in the assumption that its failings are our failings in management. We are dealing in the first place with a variety that is not suitable to the environment.

The environment emerging here in the frontier is a complex of altered life systems which, were we given all the resources of monetary support and scientific talent available, would not yield to us what we have reason to suppose we must learn. At best, our efforts to unravel these riddles are limited. The world that comes to us in crop varieties, cultivars, strains, and the inherited traits of livestock is also complex. But we must add to these complexities our own nature, as individuals, as people. We have, as settlers, a tendency to disregard, ultimately to our detriment, many strong, natural forces which impinge on our lives. We tend to act and alter, allowing such action to deny us an opportunity to learn. In dealing with nature, we will choose the course of imposition rather than one of accommodation. And we will be led repeatedly into believing that we are controlling circumstances by which, in reality, our lives are being shaped and turned in ways we often do not recognize.

The interactions I am referring to are common in principle to life and human life at all times and in all places. Often natural forces are concealed by facades separating causes from effects by many intervening stages of modified transition in such a way that we may not recognize the causes as natural. But there is an unusual opportunity for studying such relationships among different dynamic elements— of which we ourselves are one—at the opening of our frontier and this settlement. Here we have immediate relationships with natural forces, and, as individuals, we have remarkable freedom to act without many of the restraints of social convention. Phrases that have been used in the past to describe such freedom are "rugged individualism," and "the pioneering spirit."

Each of us will come to the settlement of this land with some preconceived and characteristic attitudes. These, our individual traits and our collective endowments as members of a society, are no less forces in our encounter now with nature than the strong character of nature itself. We have these indigenous traits in the environment that we are attempting to alter; we have the introduced traits in the seed and livestock we bring to the frontier; and we have our own inherent manner of acting and understanding. If we were to search for a common denominator which might relate these ingredients in some manner, we would, of course, find many. Life, itself, or life interrelationships, would be in the forefront. As we begin our planting on this land, the stage upon which we act broadens to unforeseeable dimensions and we become aware that we neither stand alone in our venture in environmental intervention nor do we stand unassailed.

There is a satisfaction in producing one's own food and the food for the family. As settlers, we want to feel self-sufficient in this and many other respects. The planting we have made here in the clearing brings us a sense of accomplishment. But this is but a first step in acquiring a livelihood. There also must be planted some means of earning a cash income.

In Coto Brus there were not many choices at the time of settlement. Given the nature of the climate, the land, its condition of inaccessibility and isolation, the production of coffee would become a mainstay in cash income expectations.

If a farmer were to visit one of the farm supply stores or agricultural cooperatives in Coto Brus today, he or she would learn something about the reasons for the establishment of a monoculture in a given region of land by looking at the formulas on the sacks of fertilizer used in growing coffee. Several formulas are available; all are very low in phosphorus. The visitor to the farm supply store, if acquainted with tropical agriculture, would recognize two important features of information. The first would be that coffee can succeed with low inputs of phosphorus. The second would be that it is planted in this region, Coto Brus, partly because of its low demands on soil phosphorus. Now this second conclusion would be dependent on further information our visitor would need to have acquired: that tropical soils in many parts of the world are critically deficient in available phosphorus. By "available phosphorus" I mean that chemical form of the element which a plant's roots can pick up and use for the growth of the plant.

A further look around the warehouse of the farm supply store would reveal to the visitor other aspects of farming here which would tell him a good deal about life and the economy in this district. This additional information would come from the printed formulas on the sacks of fertilizer comprising much smaller piles in the warehouse. On these sacks would be formulas such as 10–30–10 and 12–24–12; both formulas are high in phosphorus. With this insight, the visitor might conclude, without having asked a single question, that other crops grown here require heavy application of phosphorus. He or she might then come to a further conclusion: that even

A PLACE IN THE RAIN FOREST

though heavy applications would be made, these other crops in Coto Brus probably would not be too successful. Let's examine how one might arrive at these conclusions and why, if made as I've described, by a casual visit to the store, they would be correct.

The element, or plant food, phosphorus is one of the three major plant foods contained in most sacks of commercial fertilizer. (Nitrogen and potassium are the other two.) Phosphorus is associated with root growth, seed development, and many other processes in plant metabolism. It is considered essential because without it plant growth cannot succeed. We may assume, however, that some plants, some plant species, through evolution and over long periods of time, have developed the ability to grow well where there are low levels of available soil phosphorus. Why do we make such an assumption? There are large areas of the earth's land surface where phosphorus availability is low, yet many of these areas do support plant populations of different species, among them coffee. Coffee is also adapted to areas of high rainfall, moderate temperatures, days of scant sunlight because of cloud cover—in other words, to areas in many parts of the tropics. Other crops, such as alfalfa, carrots, and potatoes are not adapted to soils of low available phosphorus.

Why is it that I have prefaced the word *phosphorus* so often with the word *available*? It is because phosphorus is often present in soils in plant root zones in such a chemical form that the plant roots cannot take it up and use it for the nutrition of the plant. When this condition of unavailability exists, we refer to the phosphorus as being *fixed*. By this we mean that it is chemically bound in such a manner that it is not available to plants. So, if we return to our farm supply store and look again at the sacks of fertilizer with high phosphorus formulas, 10−30−10, 12−24−12, we may suppose that this is the way to supply phosphorus to plants in an environment which otherwise would not be conducive to plant growth in the soil the way it is—that is, by applying fertilizers high in phosphorus. Here we would be wrong, however; it is not just the phosphorus already present in the soil that is fixed, the phosphorus we apply as an additive to the soil also can become fixed. This means that when we put phosphorus on the soil in Coto Brus it very rapidly becomes unavailable to the plants—so fast that 85% of it can be fixed before the plants have a chance to assimilate it. The condition I am describing is not peculiar to Coto Brus. It is found throughout the tropics in high-rainfall, high–soil-acidity conditions. One further consideration is that farmers who must see eighty-five cents of each dollar's worth of phosphorus fixed and become unavailable to their fertilized crops cannot compete successfully on the commercial market.

These considerations are generally unknown to the settlers in their early work on new land. They know that coffee grows well here and that many other crops do not. Later they will learn why the other crops do not grow, if they can; now that crop which does grow well and for which there is a market must be planted.

During the early years of settlement of the South Frontier two varieties of coffee were planted; neither of them is being planted extensively today. These varieties, the *arabigo típico* and the *híbrido tico,* were both slow to yield. Generally, planters expected to wait five years from the time of the seed planting to the first significant economic harvest. Thereafter, however, the coffee might bear its single harvest a year for forty or fifty years. Both of these varieties of coffee were planted mostly under shade trees, preferably leguminous trees to supply the shade and also some nitrogen in the soil through their root systems. The coffee trees were big by today's standards (many dwarf varieties are now preferred), reaching two to three meters in height. Then, as now, only the ripe, red berries were picked during the harvest, with successive pickings as the berries turned from green to red, thus indicating maturity. And all picking was, and continues to be, done by hand.

Let's return to our clearing and plant our coffee. Across this undulating land we will again apply a vision. Work on a farm such as ours, probably, is never initiated without also becoming subject to a vision of its completion. As farmers—as people—we interpret this vision in terms of ourselves: how will this planting affect us, our family, those who work with us in the future? From this planting we will work toward well-being; there will be a return from our labor, and others will participate in its benefits.

This planting today will sow the seeds of beauty across the land.

In time the remnants of the fallen rain forest will recede and merge with a period whose utterances will lie within the past, a blanket of murmurs abiding on this earth. That stature which had been achieved by this statement of the past, the spoken forest and its expression in serenity, will find no exact counterpart today or tomorrow in our work with this planting. But the coffee under its shade trees will renew through us the pact made by life and respond to the chords of remembrance in this ground. In each stump and log resting here is this symbol of our pledge to reinstate something we have touched—and which in turn is touched in us—so that not a seed be planted which shall not confirm a promise to this forest and its progeny.

The link we would knot between that day and now is not a bastard pretence of our reach; for have we not seen that this same earth, this vital air, this sky will yield alike to both, that forest, this hour in coffee, if but our hand is dropped in grace? With this vision we kneel to plant.

We will work again with the *pala*. Using this tool, we will shovel the earth, again making shallow, superficial slices, and with the earth so collected, we make raised beds about a meter wide and as long as needed for this first step in the work, the planting of a seedbed. Our seed, similar to the coffee beans used for roasting, except that it will be covered by a thin shell, called a parchment, will have been brought to the South Frontier from San José by one of the flights of the light planes to Agua Buena.

The seedbed will be made at the end of the dry season, during March. The reasons for choosing this planting time would seem to be in order to give the coffee seedlings enough time in the ground during the ensuing wet season before the arrival of the next dry months, beginning in December or January. This is true, but as research has begun to show, the time of planting is important, possibly critically so for some seeds, because from the seed's viewpoint, the way it interprets its environment at time of planting is not a matter of indifference. For instance, we are seeing with some cultivars of beans planted in research projects that their sensitivity with respect to time of planting may fall within a requisite short period in the year and, planted out of season, they will not perform well. This consideration brings us back to how the seed sees its world, its genetic requirements. It is easy now, at the outset of our farming experience in the new land, to suppose that these are unimportant or less relevant because of so many overriding and far more apparent conditions on the frontier.

I have known coffee nurseries to perform well when planted at different times during the year, but whether they perform equally well, I am not prepared to say. It is also possible that more sensitivity in time of planting will be found in the older varieties, the *arabigo típico* and the *híbrido tico,* than in some of the newer varieties. What is important here is that traditional methods in coffee growing were followed in Costa Rica up to about the mid-1960s, when many new methods were being introduced. The seed used for the earlier plantings had been selected and planted for generations with some uniformity with respect to the way it was handled. We have reason to believe that such uniformity in prior management may influence the way seeds respond to any changes in the management system later.

On the raised beds shoveled up with the *pala* we will scatter the coffee seed and then cover it very lightly with loose soil. This covering again is a matter of special importance; the tendency to cover too heavily leads to lower germination and weak seedlings with more possibility of damping-off, a fungus disease affecting seedlings.

Rains will not have begun in March, and watering by hand, with sprinkler cans, will have to be done while the dry season lasts. To preserve the moisture in the seedbed and keep the coffee seed from exposure to too much light (some of the seed is actually partly uncovered) banana or plantain leaves are laid over the seedbed, again lightly so that there is some entry of light and aeration.

In six weeks the coffee seed will germinate, and within the next two weeks the hypocotyl, a stem, will push what appears to be the seed itself—actually the cotyledons still wrapped in parchment— out of the ground. At about two months the cotyledons will throw off the parchment and open in what appear to be two small leaves.

Before this takes place, we must make a raised frame of saplings, thin, straight sticks, over the seedbed and remove the banana or plantain leaves from the ground surface so that as the coffee seedlings push out of the ground they will have room to grow under the shade of a canopy of new banana leaves placed now on the sticks. And before the cotyledons open, we will prepare the nursery to which these seedlings will be transplanted from the seedbed. The nursery too is made with raised beds, shoveled with the *pala,* and over these beds we also make a frame, about 30 centimeters above the bed. Here we place more banana leaves to protect the seedlings from the direct sunlight and the direct action of the rain. It is important that the seedlings be transplanted while the cotyledons have yet not opened because the seedlings are stronger, better able to withstand transplanting in this stage.

Let's review the steps in planting the coffee nursery in relation to some of the things we have learned from the rain forest.

We have provided a microclimate under the canopy of shade for the nursery. Within this microclimate, we have created conditions of temperature and moisture similar to those found on the floor of the rain forest. The coffee seed was not planted deeply in the soil; it was covered as though, had it fallen on the ground in the forest, it would have been partly covered by leaves and found its place within interstices in the decaying mold on the ground. Our older varieties of coffee, those we are working with now in the clearing, will not be happy if we expose them to the direct sunlight, especially now during their infancy, again reminding us that this is a plant that originated in the forest of Africa.

The methods of planting a coffee nursery I've described did not originate with study of how coffee might be adapted to conditions in the South Frontier where there was yet much rain forest. They came with the Costa Rican settlers to the Frontier as the traditional methods practiced for decades in the Meseta Central, the central plateau of Costa Rica, where the rain forest had long ago disappeared. It is unlikely that even in the Meseta Central coffee culture had been modeled after rain forest conditions, but it is interesting to see how its management closely follows some of the principles we have observed in the forest.

There will be few diseases to contend with in these early coffee nurseries in the Frontier; damping-off may appear, but if planting has been done well, it will not be serious in terms of number of seedlings lost, and there will be no insect problems. No fertilizers will be added to this nursery, there being no manufactured fertilizers available to the settlers. What we have done in collecting the earth with the *pala* is, in fact, a system of fertilization.

Planted as it is at the end of the dry season, our coffee nursery will be well established by the beginning of the following dry season in January, and it will be able to withstand the dry months without watering. During the latter part of this following dry season, we will be raising and reducing the shade over the nursery in order to prepare the young trees for transplanting to their permanent location in the field. A little more than a year after the planting of the seed, at the beginning of the wet season, the nursery is ready to be transplanted. The little trees are 40 to 50 centimeters tall and have developed four or five pairs of lateral branches. The *arabigo típico* variety will have bronze-colored new leaves, the *híbrido tico* light green new leaves.

We transplant the young coffee trees to the field as the rains begin to fall, refreshing the air and the earth. From the standpoint of how the coffee grows and how it will yield it makes no difference whether the trees are planted in rows or whether these are straight. Coffee, at this time in Costa Rica, is not cultivated as a row crop. During these first years in our clearing, when there are so many obstructions from the forest on the land, laying rows out on a contour across slopes would have little effect in controlling possible soil erosion. Looking farther ahead, however, to the time when the logs, stumps, and branches will have decayed, contour rows will become more important. Most first-time coffee planters will not think this far ahead.

At this point in our work on the new farm we will become aware of some aspects of our future with this long-lived, perennial crop. Clearly, we will not be working with machinery during the subsequent years of its cultivation. All work here in this clearing, and what follows on this beginning, will be by hand. Even in other parts of

Costa Rica where coffee is the dominant crop and where the clearing of the land is a century or more in the past, mechanized cultivation of coffee is not practiced. The time will come here on our land when there will be weeds to control, and it is evident that we will be dealing with them with the machete and *pala*. Working as we are today, preparing for the transplanting of the coffee in the clearing, we may well pause and speculate about where this future will lead. We are planting a crop that requires hand labor in every phase of its culture. In many respects we may never emerge from our present condition of bondage into a time when we will compete on the market with other producers and implement efficient, machine-oriented technologies. Such thoughts are sobering.

On the other hand, our future in working with this crop, we perceive, will entail a personal relationship that will almost certainly have to be intimate. Daily our hands will be applied to this land, this planting, quite literally. We know already that coffee responds to good horticultural practice, that, indeed, it is a plant which will yield rewards when given skillful care in its pruning, its adjustment to its environment, its management over the years. Here again is a marriage, and there is a reward on the horizon for our work today. This living earth, this particular species and form of life, will now become part of our life; our life will be infused and invested in it. To the extent that we may discover within ourselves the secrets it may teach us, will we not be better cultivators of the land, more gifted planters? We will have the privilege of working closely and directly with life; each day in this field will bring us an awareness of a nature of interrelationships in which we ourselves are a component, a part which belongs to something more. In the days of our future there will be sunlight and rain, the air which blows clean and fresh, the earth which is here to take in hand and revere and restore; all forms of living, dying, and release will be ours to know and respect; surely we will come to gain an insight.

Many of the men and women who acquired land at this time on the South Frontier shared the views of the future I have described. Were it possible to implement them consistently, we would have a better environment here today. This has not always been possible, however, and we will see later why these objectives needed to be modified.

There are two general systems in transplanting a coffee nursery. One is to cut the trees out of the nursery, using a *machete de suelo* to shape a ball of earth attached to the roots, which is later wrapped in sugarcane leaves for transfer to the field. The other is to carefully loosen the soil around the tree's roots, separate the soil from the roots, and transplant the trees in what is termed "bare root." Early coffee culture favored the former method.

It is not at all easy to move hundreds, or thousands, of coffee trees in this condition, with the soil attached to the roots, across the debris in the clearing. This is especially so because the soil in Coto Brus is generally light and does not adhere well to a root ball. Any bump against the roots along the way across the clearing as the trees are being carried to the planting sites will almost certainly make the soil crumble and fall off, carrying away a lot of the smaller roots with it. If you have waited a year to see your coffee nursery ready to transplant only to find that, when the tree is being carried to the field, most of its roots are torn away by the disintegrating earth ball, this is not a happy moment. More accurately, *it is something we are not going to let happen.* What does this mean in terms of our work and our life here today? It means that again we will find ourselves in that category of labor sometimes referred to as "drudgery," having little or nothing to do with modern technology but relying heavily on physical effort, in this instance the effort of carrying, individually or in small batches on a stretcher, seemingly endless numbers of coffee trees. And we will blame this condition on the uncleared—obstructed—condition of our land. Such work is not necessarily a misfortune; it can bring a particular sense of satisfaction and accomplishment at the end of the day, in both body and soul, and can seem to be at peace and in agreement with much else that has been part of the day. It is not, however, efficient as productive work.

As we transplant our coffee nursery into holes we have dug across the clearing, we leave the earth from each hole at the edge for refilling. The spacing we use between trees is much wider than such spacing will be some years later when new coffee varieties are introduced. But now our spacing cannot be precise because the fallen forest does not allow for such precision. We carry each tree over the logs to its hole, carefully set it in the hole, remove the sugarcane leaf wrapping, and firm in the earth around the roots. The earth here is moist; there are many roots—roots from the forest—that we must cut, sometimes with the axe, at other times with only the shovel. There is a cloud cover above us obscuring the brightness of the sun, and moisture impregnates the air; such conditions are good for transplanting.

I've used the word *monoculture* in this chapter, and its meaning should be put in context with this stage in our work. The coffee monoculture which has been developed over time in Coto Brus is not a contiguous planting of adjacent pieces of land all forming one solid block of a single crop. Coffee is grown over most of the country, but almost all of it is raised by small farmers, farmers whose landholdings are small. Among these coffee plantings, distributed across many farms, there are pastures and areas of successional forest, and occasionally a patch of primary forest still standing. Coffee production did not begin in Coto Brus as a small landholding enterprise; many of the initial plantings were on large estates. Nevertheless, partly for the reasons I've referred to in its requirement of hand labor, the production of coffee became increasingly a small landholding operation.

Coffee did constitute, at the outset of the settlement—and it continues to do so today—a monoculture in an economic sense. That is, the livelihood of a large percentage of the farmers came to depend on the successful production of this single crop. And as this crop faced vicissitudes of different kinds—low international market value, production problems in the forms of diseases and depleted land fertility, and the consequences of poor land management—all of the farmers and the residents of this region became affected in a similar way. If there were any possibility of prosperity, all would prosper; if hard times were in store, all would suffer.

Many efforts were made to overcome the grip of this monoculture during such hard times, a catch word being *diversification;* but these efforts were not successful. This should give us some pause for thought. A great deal of resourcefulness was brought to bear on the problem of monoculture, yet it did not yield to such initiatives.

There are many reasons why the monoculture would not, and does not, relinquish its hold upon the lives of the people of the South Frontier, and we will look at some of them later in this book. But for the present, as we stand at this threshold of our new life on the farm, shovel in hand, the earth falling through our fingers as we plant, we have the faith of this labor and this day. It is unlikely that we will be troubled by the dark prospects as they loom over the future; we have touched the earth and through it the sky and the air and the rain. Life flows through us and returns. We will succeed.

FIVE

The Singletree and the Collar

*T*he hand labor I've described for planting coffee, and its continuity over ensuing years, impressed me with its limitations. If we could not farm on Finca Loma Linda as a segment of the modern world in terms of some of the more efficient modern production methods, then we might at least be able to move for the present beyond this heavy reliance on *pala* and machete, tools with which I was not as skillful as my Costa Rican counterparts. But there was more than the use of tools in my thinking. Our plan as a family for Finca Loma Linda was to make a small diversified farm. We purchased 130 acres. Today about a third of this area remains in primary rain forest; it was always our intention that it should. The balance of the land I wanted to use for more than just coffee production.

My farming experience has been acquired here in Costa Rica. But my mother and father had a background of farming in Connecticut and California; my wife spent part of her childhood on farms in

Chiriquí, Panama. Out of such experience a blueprint for Loma Linda emerged from our earliest work on the land.

Substituting for the word *subsistence* the term *self-sufficiency,* the plan envisioned a farm on which much of the food requirements for the family and some food embellishments would be produced. Finca Loma Linda would be both a livestock and a crop production farm. These two general systems would complement each other. We would have milk and butter and cheese and cream; eggs, meat, goats, possibly sheep and hogs. In the field we would plant a number of grains and forages: corn, sorghum, peanuts, beans—the whole range of vegetables, both for home consumption and for sale.

Early in the farm development work we would plant fruit trees, citrus, loquats, avocados, guavas, and nuts, and to these would be added berries and pineapples. We would keep bees for honey. Our plan also included fish raising in a farm pond. Coffee would be the first planted farm income crop, but in addition to this, these other farming projects would be carried out, and we expected some eventual income from most of them. In effect, we implemented almost all of these projects. We did not raise the sheep or the pigs, and we never put in the farm pond, but all of the other projects, plus some additional ones, were at one time or another part of the farm program.

Loma Linda would also have some home industry. Some of the produce from the farm would be converted into more saleable products through simple kitchen processing. The making of cheese was especially attractive to us.

None of these activities, including the coffee production, would be large-scale. A main objective was to integrate many different farm projects, bringing all together under a system which would be dependent on careful management of the productivity and fertility of the land. From the earliest work, our farm development plan envisioned contour planting and the segmenting of small areas of land so that each might be dealt with individually, studied and treated as a separate section rather than just as another piece of generalized terrain. Not only would the actual planting be laid out on contours, but roads and fences would be also, thus reducing erosion of the soil where traffic of farm equipment or livestock would occur. There was no particular policy regarding the use of chemical spray materials until many years after their use became generalized. Then I began to restrict them so much so that, today, they are practically never used.

The earth on Finca Loma Linda had not been exposed to misuse. It would be up to me to see that my management of this land would not bring with it a residue of contaminants.

Looking at the land with these thoughts in mind, it became necessary to survey and map the overall farm development. Gradients were measured, roads, building sites, land-use allotments laid out. I don't mean to convey that a lot of capital and time were available for planning and surveys; my family and I worked early and late doing this work because we believed that this was the way to make a farm. We were not wealthy.

Today, with computers, it is possible to do this kind of work in far greater detail and more comprehensively than was possible then. There is a potential for improved land management in this field of data analysis by which so many features of an environment can be analyzed digitally, compared, and some correlations made. Such a system is particularly applicable here, where the influences of the rain forest play an important role. But well before this electronic technology became available, my father and I had begun collecting data and information from our earliest work in recordkeeping. These records became a basis for much future planning.

To succeed with this program for a diversified farm, the land would have to be cleared, the felled forest removed from the clearings. Interestingly, no one knew just how long it would take for logs and roots and stumps to decay. The settlers actually did not have this information at the outset. But it was clear that this natural decomposition of the fallen forest would not be completed soon. All of the land where the forest had been felled could not be cleared—by whatever means we might choose to hasten this work—at one time. Certainly, the land planted to coffee would not have to be cleared immediately, perhaps not at all. The coffee would grow there without the clearing, but its maintenance, weeding, and pruning would be more costly. Pastures, too, might be left partly uncleared. The livestock could find their way through the logs and stumps, with some paths and openings being cut for their entry. But the efficiency of such grazing would be very low. Fruit trees might be planted, like the coffee, within the fallen forest. But the actual planting of row crops and tillage of the land would need to be carried out where the obstruction of logs, stumps, and roots had been removed. Such work would be slow and costly; only small sections could be handled this way. Without some progress in this direction, there could not be a diversified program; the farm would have to operate with simple and what to all appearances would seem to be backward methods of subsistence.

The principle of tillage had not been tested on this land. Certainly work with the *pala* was not the same thing as tillage. It was clear that the *pala* was an extremely useful tool when handled skillfully, but it was also apparent that its use must probably be a consequence of necessity rather than good, generalized farming practice. A plow, a disk harrow, a cultivator would go far to displace the *pala*. With such farm equipment the land could be made to produce with some efficiency of scale. It was unlikely that large machinery would ever find a place on Finca Loma Linda. Even though the land had been carefully selected for its more uniform gradients in topography— this had been one of the requirements of purchase—many gradients and slopes were too steep for conventional farm tractors. Such machinery would not have a place in the future of this farm, in all probability; in some respects it might be just as well if it did not. However, the soil would have to be limed (lime would have to be incorporated in the plant root zone). The soil would have to be turned, exposed to aeration, made uniform.

I would be looking for good seedbed condition. The method of throwing up the earth with the *pala,* making in effect a raised seedbed, impressed me with its tedium and awkwardness; farming at this level is dependent on one's ability with a shovel in hand. There would have to be better methods, even now while we were starting in this tangle of obstructions in the clearing. So went my thinking.

Many things our family had learned elsewhere in farming came to bear now in our decisions. In our most intimate thinking, we who undertake an enterprise in farming harbor the feeling that an agricultural soil must be turned, tillage being fundamental to farming as we have experienced it. It has been a principle of farming almost everywhere. It is not difficult to persuade oneself that, where it rains as it does here, the "good" in the soil—its nutrients—is being washed from the soil surface into its lower depths, where, eventually, it will be lost through leaching to the plant roots of the crops we will plant. As farmers it would be up to us to carry out periodic tillage, deep plowing, and other efforts designed to bring these nutrients back to the soil surface, thus keeping them in a kind of circulation. In fact, deep plowing might well be the secret of success in long-term soil productivity.

Doing this, tilling and plowing, would also bring about a condition of soil uniformity, the incorporation of surface mulch into lower soil depths, where, through its decomposition, it would be included in the soil structure, in time releasing its nutrients within the soil itself. The planting of cover crops, probably leguminous crops, would be implemented, these periodically being turned under with tillage. Eventually a condition of uniform texture, approaching a condition of seedbed structure and possibly uniform fertility, might be attained.

We must keep in mind as we explore some of these extensions of planning—plans which became work, work which molded the land and life on it and changed the future—that we, as people, are subject to a desire for security in formulating plans; we need to feel that we do know what we are doing and have a pretty clear idea of where we are going. One way of doing this on a frontier, where there is no background yet of proved work, is to espouse concepts which have proved practicable in other places at other times. If they worked then, why should they not work for us now?

There are many reasons why they should not, but such reasons are elucidated only through the exposure represented by experience.

Concurrent with these plans on how to be successful farmers on this new land, each family of settlers—and most settlers are families—will build plans for the heart of the farm life, the family itself.

When planning the farm's herd of dairy cows, our thoughts will integrate the work among the children and the father and the mother. As parents we may hope that our children will enjoy working with calves, will come to look upon the young offspring, the litter of pigs, a foal, as part of farm life. Sons will work with fathers, brothers, and uncles in the field; mothers and daughters will work in the homes. If this seems archaic—a division of work between men and women— it requires no apology; it is simply the way Coto Brus was settled. It is the way many Costa Rican families live and work together today. My family and I worked together in this way.

But the operative word here, in terms of building the farm and making it a viable economic enterprise, is work, work which is shared by a family. When we plan our farming systems by the way they meet the expectations for ourselves and our families with respect to our work, we are being realistic about the forces that will make the farm operate.

Such work is seen in the planning stage, as I have noted earlier, in terms of a vision of its accomplishments. We plan a pasture, we see its extension over the hills as a green carpet, the debris of the felled forest no longer an obstruction, a herd of dairy cows freckling the grass. There is a barn, its wooden structure a solid measure against the rain, the wind; within the barn the lantern lights at evening, the shapes and sounds of the cows and calves at milking; the fodder in the mangers, the moths in clusters in the light; the darkness falling at day's end. The milk, the froth in the bucket, the work in quieting union as the day joins evening, the residing labor beyond the darkness in the land—we see these things; we see the sons and the daughters looking from the stature of childhood at these calves, each a youngster, their promise and ours in sons and daughters. And we plan.

All must come to rise from this earth, this environment, the fertility to nurture the grass; the pasture to carry the cows; the offspring in the barn; the children by the light of lamps with faces grown sleepy; the day, our plan, this work. This family must know the smell of sweat, the burnish on brushed and groomed coats, the warmth of the stable and the smell of the livestock and its life, the sharing and the reward.

All plans are, in reality, kinds of visions; on Finca Loma Linda thinking such as I have outlined here led to a decision around which many other parts of our farm life were built. We needed the power, the power beyond that of the shovel, the *pala*, the machete, the hand. We needed to move the logs, drag the branches; we needed to integrate the management of the farm with a means of creating power, expansion, fertility, continuance. This decision was to work with draft horses in the clearing, tillage, and planting of the land and in the transport to and from the farm of supplies and farm produce. Our vision of the accomplishment of this plan projected a time when the well-trained teams would bend into the collars, the trace chains tighten and tense, the concentration of muscles and bodies leaning into the loads, the smooth flow of the forest debris being dragged across the land, and, in the glow of the lantern by evening, the teams stabled and at rest in the barn.

I had worked with draft horses here in Costa Rica. My mother and father had used them to farm in Connecticut. One further principle should be mentioned in support of this plan, a well-known part of traditional farming experience: livestock, through their manure, return nutrients to the ground. The use of draft animals is thought to be a good way to help maintain the fertility of a farm.

I was aware when I decided to work with draft horses that the decision represented a considerable gamble. In Costa Rica oxen were the traditional draft animals, pulling carts, doing logging work, employed on a much smaller scale in plowing. It was for this latter work where the oxen seemed to me to be particularly unsuited, because the way oxen are driven in Costa Rica is actually to lead them, the oxen teamster walking ahead of the oxen and commanding them with a goad. In order to plow, two people must work with the oxen, perhaps a boy leading with the goad, the father using the plow. We have worked with oxen on Finca Loma Linda; I have a lot of love and respect for them. But they are slower than horses in draft work. The decision to work with draft horses was a departure from known practice in Costa Rica; I would be attempting something people were not acquainted with, introducing a new element in farming. My family and I had a background of working with saddle and draft horses, but no one in the family had worked in logging or land clearing with teams.

Most of the saddle stock in the South Frontier and elsewhere in Costa Rica and Panama where I had traveled was too light for heavy draft work. Horses such as these saddle animals would not be successful in the hard hauling of land clearing, moving logs, pulling stumps, breaking out roots. However, in making inquiries of the Ministry of Agriculture, I learned that the Costa Rican government had, a few years prior to this time (1955), imported several purebred Percheron draft horses with the intention of using them as breeding and demonstration stock to teach Costa Rican farmers the merits of farming with horses. The Percheron horses had been brought into Costa Rica from the United States. My wife and I left the Frontier in one of the flights of the light planes from Agua Buena to San José and went from there to the province of Guanacaste, where some of the Percherons were on pasture. We bought three mares and a stallion in Guanacaste and later in San José acquired two more mares at pasture on a dairy farm.

To bring the horses to Finca Loma Linda we would have to lead them over the Camino Real. It might also have been possible to ship them from San José by rail to the Pacific port of Puntarenas, then by boat to the United Fruit Company port at Golfito, then by rail again to the rail terminal at Corredores, then by truck to the edge of the South Frontier, and finally over trail to the farm, but this option was never a realistic consideration. Shipping fever would have been a likely outcome of such a plan. Two years later we did bring a pickup truck (a truck my mother and father had driven to Costa Rica from California) to Loma Linda by the route I've just described, by rail and sea; fine for vehicles, this route was not a practical means of moving livestock. My experience on the Camino Real, the King's Highway, convinced me that we could bring the horses overland. Many thought the plan a wild scheme, but they also had to acknowledge that there was no other route.

Moving these heavy draft horses over the trail during the wet season would be impossible. I had come to use mules on our trail packing on the Camino Real because they usually were stronger and more sure footed than horses. Even for light saddle stock the trail posed risks. To move the draft horses, weighing a little under a ton each, over the trail from San Isidro to the Frontier could only be thought of as a dry season possibility. River fords would not be an obstacle during this season, the lack of water itself and the absence of pasture along sections of the trail posing a different kind of challenge; however, this was a challenge that we could meet.

We bought these horses in the midpart of the wet season of 1955. With a farm employee, Juan Vargas, I led four of the Percherons to a ranch at Buenos Aires, a settlement in the El General Valley. A friend there, Fred Hardin, agreed to hold these four head on his ranch until the beginning of the following dry season. I had left one mare and a filly in a paddock near San José. The mare had a suppurating sore on the rear of her back left fetlock, and the Ministry of Agriculture, through its veterinary department, was treating her.

Toward the end of the wet season that year there was a hard rainstorm over southeastern Costa Rica. These storms, called *temporal,* are usually caused by clouds blown inland from hurricanes off the Caribbean coast. The rains were severe through the South Frontier and the El General Valley as well as along the Caribbean. At one point in the storm, Fred had to move all his livestock and our Percherons off his farm, which became flooded by rivers, onto the upland *sabanas* of natural grass at Buenos Aires, and the stock had to be held there for several weeks.

Of even more importance than this exposure of the livestock to the days of rain on the poorly grassed *sabanas* was the likelihood of landslides and heavy erosion having been caused by the storm along the trail. Mass slippages of land are common over this terrain during these storms. The King's Highway would not be the same trail we had known on earlier journeys.

Dad joined me on the farm, having just arrived there from California with my mother, who would stay on the farm with my wife. Dad and I flew to San José from Agua Buena early in the dry season of 1956 to arrange to have the mare, Jean, and the filly, Ginger, trucked to San Isidro. Two days later we reached Buenos Aires and Fred's ranch with the Percherons, having led them afoot. The weather had become dry; the northeast trade winds had been blowing and the grass on the *sabanas* at Buenos Aires had turned brown and was shriveling.

Our livestock there was in poor condition. Fred, a former cowpuncher from Texas who raised mules and cattle at Buenos Aires and with whom I had worked before my family and I bought Finca Loma Linda, confirmed what I had known: the Percherons had been exposed to the sunless sky during days of almost ceaseless rain; now the sky had cleared and the sun shone with a fierce, unrelieved intensity. The Talamanca Range rose very steeply above Buenos Aires, the forested serrations in masses of terrain austere, mostly unpopulated. To the southeast the range ran as a backbone in the direction of the South Frontier, distant under this open sky, the wind here in Buenos Aires gusting and picking up dust on the parching *sabanas,* grown poor and scant in sustenance.

That afternoon I rode one of Fred's mares to the settlement at Buenos Aires, a short ride from his farm. His pastures had been depleted by the flooding from a river and a smaller stream; it would be some time before they would recover and carry his own livestock. There was no place on them for our horses. During those years at such outposts as Buenos Aires and Agua Buena in Costa Rica, the government maintained a shortwave radio service for sending what were referred to as "radiograms." I went to the radio office in Buenos Aires and sent a message to my wife. The message would be picked up in Cañas Gordas, near Loma Linda. In the message I asked her to send Juan Vargas with our strongest saddle animal to meet Dad and me with the Percherons at some point on the Camino Real.

The Percherons would have to be moved within two or three days, enough time to give Jean and Ginger a rest after their trip by truck to San Isidro and then over the trail to Buenos Aires. Each day on the *sabanas* here only further weakened the heavy animals. Dad and I conferred and came to this conclusion: the prospect of getting the six Percherons safely to Finca Loma Linda now was not good. We knew there had been landslides over the area to the west of the South Frontier. We had seen some evidence of this on our flight out of Agua Buena to San José to pick up Jean and Ginger. The message to Loma Linda to bring us Juan and the extra saddle animal was now an acknowledgment of what we expected to face on the trail.

Walking over the *sabanas* alone that afternoon, I looked to the east. The area around Buenos Aires was open. There in the distance toward the frontier was the lowland forest and, well beyond it, the more distant highland. That would be our objective, the hazy line of higher land, indefinite now under the dust and sporadic puffs of wind—the highland where the rains were yet falling, the air cool, yet moist, and, beyond it, Loma Linda. The smell of dryness was on the air here in Buenos Aires, the dry air and traces of smoke from the burning land. One upon another now the next days would come.

Dad and I had walked from San Isidro to Fred's ranch, but here we arranged to buy one of Fred's mules and borrow a saddle horse to move the Percherons on to Potrero Grande, where we expected to meet Juan. Fred offered to come with us as far as Potrero Grande; he knew, of course, what moving the Percherons over the terrain immediately to the east of Buenos Aires would mean. On a morning early in the latter part of January, we started, the three of us riding saddle animals, driving and leading the Percherons. The sky that day was cloudless, the land already parched and dry.

By midday the heat had become a palpable barrier in the air; we moved slowly with the heavy stock, feeling the heat waves as invisible, tactile curtains as we went through them, the horses working their way over a trail deeply eroded and showing projections of rock and stone. The air had grown calm; there was no wind by this hour. In several places in the distance columns of smoke arose above the landscape where settlers were burning recent clearings.

The hours had passed and we had met almost no one on the trail. We were moving through forested and *sabana* country, some pastures and successional growth off from the trail, a *rancho* here and there to be seen, but actually few inhabitants. For some time we had been descending, and the trail reached now the edge of a river canyon where it broke steeply in switchbacks, down its banks. The horses were strung out; Dad rode ahead leading two mares, Fred was at the center of the line behind two Percherons and a filly which we were driving without lead ropes, and I was at the rear of the line, leading the stallion on a rope behind my horse. There was the rhythmic clop of the stallion's hoofs striking stones on the trail and a high-pitched, constant, rising and falling whine of cicadas. As the mares came to the bottom of the canyon bank, they began to lengthen their line, skirting a sand flat at the edge of the river.

The heat there was suffocating, the sand flat gray and seemingly vibrant with the radiating reflection along the river. Suddenly, one of the mares, Rocksy, broke from the line and ran with a stumbling tired gait out onto the sand toward the river. A shout from Fred caused Dad to turn and then head back from the front of the line. I dropped the lead rope on the stallion and put my horse to a gallop. Fred and Dad had already turned their horses back from the sand and were on their feet with Rocksy when I reached them. They were sinking to their shins in the sand oozing in the shallow water which came to the surface wherever they stepped. I left my horse with Fred's and Dad's and waded out, feeling the sand and water sucking, retaining, yet cool.

Rocksy had gone down on her side and was partly submerged in the sand. She probably weighed about eighteen hundred pounds. There was no likelihood of her drowning—this was not quicksand, and it was solid with gravel and rock about eighteen inches down— but there was a good chance that we might not get her back on her feet. She struggled violently, sinking deeper, then lay motionless.

While one of us held her head above the seeping water and the sand, the others went to some saplings along the trail and with machetes, which we had carried on our saddles, cut branches and brought them back, dragging them across the sand, floundering and pulling each leg and boot out from its suction. We shoved these under her, propping her head and neck. Each time she struggled she tended to sink deeper, settle more solidly. We tried to keep her quiet. The minutes lengthened; the heat and the whine of the cicadas became one, and slowly we raised Rocksy a little above the sand in her forequarters—only to have her sink again when she flailed with her legs in spasms of panic and then lay motionless. Then we would start again to fill in under her with the branches.

We attempted to put ropes on her and pull her with the saddle horses, but initially she was too heavy to raise. At length we did get enough branches under her to pull her partly up at the forequarters; with a gigantic pawing she came to her feet.

The toll had not been easy on Dad or Fred or me. We were drenched with sweat as well as with the water and sand and we were more worried now about the horses. The Percherons were not bred for this climate or for trail work, and the heat here in the river canyon was far too much for such heavy, weakened animals.

We bunched the horses in the shade of some saplings by a stream that fed into the river, let them drink, drank with them, and took some lunch from our saddlebags. There was not much talk among us; we all knew the trail ahead, and the prospect of getting these heavy animals out of the canyon weighed heavily on us during the minutes by the river.

We started up the bank with the Percherons, and for Dad and me this was a first test of whether we would get these animals to the South Frontier. Fred knew the trail only as far as Potrero Grande; beyond Potrero Grande, however, there would be much steeper, longer climbs than this we were making now. The phrase "riding over the Camino Real" was misleading. Over much of the trail a rider would go afoot, climbing or descending and leading the horse. None of us attempted to ride up the banks out of the canyon. We took the saddle horses up afoot and then began taking the Percherons up one by one.

It was heartbreaking to see the heavy animals struggling on these banks. They tried frantically to keep their footing, fell, went down on their knees, and lunged up only to lose footing and fall again. Each of us took one of the animals on a short lead rope, holding it, stopping it, forcing it to hold and stand until it regained its wind and balance. Then a few steps more, and again we held the animal. As the horses that had gone ahead dislodged the dirt along the bank, this became less stable and more difficult for the horses that came behind. Just as we were reaching the top of the canyon wall, I heard Dad shout: "Juan is here!"

We made camp that night above the river; we had been far longer in reaching this point on the trail than we had expected. Juan told a dismal story of the conditions ahead on the trail. He had traveled day and night to reach us, moving at night by flashlight.

The following day brought us to Potrero Grande with a lame stallion. The stallion, Dick (the names were on the pedigrees, for this was purebred stock), had banged his huge hoofs so much on the trail that he had bruised the sensitive linings under the hoof and an infection had started. Fred said goodbye to us in Potrero Grande and started back to his ranch. With his light saddle stock he would reach Buenos Aires in a single, long day. Dad and Juan and I began doctoring Dick's bruised hoofs. Actually, both forefeet had been damaged. More than half of a horse's weight is carried on the forelegs.

With my pocket knife I pared away part of Dick's hoof, looking for the seat of the infection, trying to release the pus and pressure. The big animal was patient. But there were times when he would put all his weight on us as we held his foot; then we would have to release it and it would go down like a pile driver.

Grass was in short supply in Potrero Grande, and we were having problems finding pasture for the other horses. What grass there was was drying or had dried. We were able to buy some sugarcane from a settler, and we hauled this each day from a field at some distance to our stock, which we had paddocked under some shade trees. Dick's condition became worse, and eventually he could not stand. Some antibiotics were available in Potrero Grande; there was an airstrip there serviced by the same single-engine planes which flew into Agua Buena, and we had been able to get some penicillin injections for Dick. But they were doing little apparent good. After several days of working with Dick and waiting in Potrero Grande we realized that we would have to leave him and go on. The other Percherons were becoming weaker from the heat and limited forage.

There was another of the Percherons that might not get to Finca Loma Linda. This was a soot-brown filly named Dumpling. She had not been strong when we bought her in Guanacaste, and the hard weeks on the *sabanas* at Buenos Aires during the end of the wet season had not improved her condition.

Juan had taken a particular liking to Dumpling. I think he knew she needed special help. He came to me one morning when we were getting ready to leave Potrero Grande with a plan he must have been thinking about for several days. He would take Dumpling on alone, leaving Dad and me to take on the four Percheron mares, all of which were stronger. Having just come over the trail, he didn't want one of the saddle horses. His plan was to take Dumpling on afoot, leading her, traveling mostly in the early morning and late afternoon to avoid the heat while in the lowland. He would beg some sugarcane from the few settlers along the trail. Gratefully, I agreed to Juan's plan; it was not likely that we would be able to reach the Frontier with Dumpling without risking the remaining energy of the other mares.

Juan left that afternoon, carrying some provisions in a pack, leading Dumpling. We did not see him again on the trail. The following morning Dad and I took the four Percheron mares across the Coto River ford. Getting them to the ford and across took all of the morning and part of the early afternoon. We decided to put up that night with a settler on the other side of the river who offered to let our horses graze for the night in his pasture. We had left Dick in the care of a settler in Potrero Grande, leaving some money for sugarcane and some hauled grass. As soon as we got the other horses to Loma Linda, I would ride back to Potrero Grande and try to bring Dick on alone.

Jean, the mare who had been left with her filly, Ginger, in San José under veterinary care for the sore on her fetlock, had been cured of this problem when Dad and I picked her up at the government paddock near San José, but on the trail the sore had reopened. That night while the Percherons were in the pasture, some stray horses got in with them and ran Jean into a barbed-wire fence. On the following morning before dawn, when Dad and I went into the pasture with flashlights to rope and saddle the horses, we found Jean with a cut shoulder. We had been doctoring her fetlock with a black liquid product used for screwworms and cattle grubs, called Smear 62. Off and on through the day we had to stop and put this on the fetlock and now too on the cut shoulder as the white fly eggs that would hatch and become worm larvae appeared on the wounds.

We made an early start, and at some point on the trail we must have passed Juan, who would have left the trail with Dumpling to wait out the heat by a stream in the shade or stay with a settler at a *rancho* to rest and feed the filly. Our goal now was to reach Finca Loma Linda as quickly as possible. At the farm good pasture waited. We would be in the highland; it would be cool. We could doctor Jean's sore and cut and feed and care for the other horses. And I would go back for Dick.

That day Dad and I planned to take the Percherons and saddle stock over the most difficult part of the trail. This was La Cuesta de la Pita, about four hours' ride beyond the Coto River. At La Cuesta de la Pita the trail rose from the lowland up a long, steep escarpment to the highland. We felt that if we could get the Percherons beyond this point we would have put behind us the major hazards of the King's Highway. We reached the foot of La Cuesta de la Pita a little before noon.

We dropped the lead ropes on the horses, left the saddle stock tied to trees, and began to explore the conditions on the trail. At this point the Camino Real entered the primary rain forest and would not emerge from the forest until just a little before reaching the Italian colony. Behind us toward Potrero Grande and Buenos Aires, there had been some open country, particularly *sabanas,* some clearings and pasture, sparse settlement, rivers, streams. But the trail would pass for the balance of this day's journey and for the following day through the forest.

We found the trail as Juan had described, badly cut by the earlier rains, with some parts of the banks having slipped away. Juan had come down the escarpment, leading our mule, Babe. Babe had been over this trail several times; she was strong and trail-wise; still, in some parts of the escarpment, Juan had found her sliding and skidding behind him.

Dad and I had spent only a little time at the foot of La Cuesta de la Pita when we concluded that we would have to cut a new route through the forest along some parts of the trail. We did this with our machetes, realizing as we cut these detours that the ground in the forest was not solid on such steep slopes and would loosen and break out under the pounding of the horses' hoofs. More time here would have given us a chance to do this preparatory work better, but we needed to get the horses to the top of La Cuesta de la Pita and on through the forest to a place called Sabanillas, a small patch of pasture grass planted in midforest where we planned to spend the night, so we could turn the horses out to forage in the little, unfenced pasture. We made the trail slash quickly and came back to our horses at the foot of the mountain and decided to take the heaviest mare, Rocksy, up first. I would lead with a rope on her halter and Dad would come behind.

The next hours were torture for us and the horses. They were printed on our senses in a kaleidoscope of shouts, lunging bodies, flaying hoofs, slipping, wild-eyed horses, legs pounding down and throwing out the earth, the dry catches of breathing in short halts and starts, and the grunts and impact of the horses, the heaving, sweat-soaked bodies trembling and fighting for stance.

Again and again we narrowly missed being hit by the horses' legs and smashing hoofs. Our feet slipped out from under us on the loosened clay; we went down as often as the horses; we were as smeared with the red clay of the banks as they. Out of these minutes grew a fixed impression: these animals could not take much more of this; we would have to reach the Italian colony; we must get them to Loma Linda. The afternoon on La Cuesta de la Pita seemed to have been arrested in this paroxysm of struggle.

The last Percheron to climb La Cuesta de la Pita was Dixie, a three-year-old, broad-chested mare, the colt of Rocksy. Dixie was jet black, a fine Percheron type. She had tremendous strength and vitality, even then on the trail. She fought to keep her footing on the bank with a power that was stunning. Repeatedly I dodged on the trail ahead of her as she lunged and drove her hoofs into the earth.

We took the saddle stock up last, and here at last was a respite. The trail-wise animals picked their way, occasionally lunging, but never panic stricken. Our drinking-water container, on one of the saddles, was damaged on the way up La Cuesta de la Pita, and we found ourselves without water now as we moved on to Sabanillas. We had stopped at a stream to let the horses drink before starting up La Cuesta de la Pita, but our own supply of water was now gone. There would be no water between here and the Italian colony. Just before nightfall we reached Sabanillas. There would be some dew on the grass during the night to refresh the horses. After picketing the saddle stock and checking the Percherons for stones that might be lodged in the soles of their hoofs, Dad and I broke out some dry rations from the saddlebags. Later we found a little water in upturned palm fronds lying at different places on the forest floor. There were mosquito larvae in the fronds, but it didn't matter to us.

On the following day we had to leave Dixie in the forest. She was the strongest of the four mares, but she had become so dispirited that she refused to lead or follow. Led, she would go to the right of a tree that the saddle animal had passed on the left, bringing us to a halt until we rode back and circled around the tree. This happened repeatedly and our saddle stock was getting worn out. When we tried to drive her without a lead rope, she bolted off the trail into the forest and stood there, indifferent to being left behind. We were about four hours' ride from the Italian colony when we decided to leave her tied to a tree in the forest and return for her the following day.

That afternoon, at about three o'clock, there was a shower of rain. We were about one hour's ride from the colony, passing through a fairly level stretch of forest, breaking out now into some of the first clearings around the colony; ahead there was a downgrade, and across this grade the trail had cut deeply with the passing of livestock and erosion from the rains. The trail had become a knife-edge V here, enclosed by high banks on either side. Such cuts made by the trail were not unusual, and riders and horses became accustomed to them. Seldom did anyone ride through such a V cut, because there was not room between the clay walls on either side for legs in stirrups. This was just one more place where you dismounted and led your horse through. This happened to be a particularly deep V cut, however, and after the rain the footing on the narrow bottom had become slippery. This close to the colony, Dad and I were thinking that we were coming to the end of the ordeal, and we started the horses through the V pretty much as a matter of course.

Dad went through with the saddle stock first, using them as a guide for the Percherons to see and follow. I followed at the rear, leading Rocksy behind me. There was a turn at one point in the cut, and for a moment we lost sight of the horses ahead. At the same time Rocksy, with her big hooves, lost her balance in the tight footing, panicked, started to fall, and reared.

I both heard and felt this happening, as I was looking ahead at the time. I heard her grunt and slip; then the lead rope in my hand pulled up, lifting and burning through my hand, and I turned to see Rocksy rising above me, her great, white belly over me, her forelegs pawing at the bank sides above us, her eyes wild as she rose on her rear legs higher and higher.

I threw myself and partly fell back, seeing her huge body above me, seeing that she would fall on top of me, pinning me certainly under her in the crevasse at the bottom of the trail. She did fall— but just short of my body.

After a lot of flailing with her legs, she came down with a sickening crash. In a moment Dad appeared around the bend in the cut, his face ashen. He expected, probably, to find more than a hurt horse.

We both thought that Rocksy had broken her back by the way she had fallen. She was lying motionless, stunned, her eyes wide, staring, seeming almost opaque. "My God!" I thought, getting to my feet. I climbed over Rocksy; she was twisted in the crevasse, her legs bent above her, her back down, streaks of red clay crossing her gray coat. She was breathing in short, labored breaths. In a moment she began to struggle, beating her legs, raising her head and neck and beating them against the banks. The same thought came to both Dad and me: she hadn't broken her back!

We half crawled, half ran out of the cut to the horses and brought back our machetes from the saddle sheaths. The machetes were short with broad, stiff blades. With these we began digging at the sides of the banks, loosening the soil and letting it fall on Rocksy. As we dug, we widened the banks in the narrow bottom.

When we had a mound of clay so loosened, I lifted as much of Rocksy's head and neck as I could, and Dad shoved the clay under her. Then, using two hands on the machete blades, we dug some more. Gradually, we widened the space around Rocksy, lifting her forequarters, straightening her twisted body. From time to time she struggled, throwing herself against us—there was no room to avoid her—and we had to lie on her forelegs to keep her from hitting us, and we tried to keep her quiet. The afternoon early dusk began to fall, with clouds closing above us with the threat of more rain. We dug, scraped, lifted, filled. Trickles of clay-reddened sweat ran off us, making rivulets along our chests and arms. I began to see that my hands and arms were shaking and that Dad's face was becoming pale. We seldom spoke; there was only the heavy, rhythmic breathing from the mare at our side, the heat from her body, the smell of her sweat and of the moist, rain-wet dirt.

Dig, scrape, lift! Would she never help us? The weight of her body seemed to be growing heavier; my arms would not lift. My God! Could there be no way to end this?

I looked at Dad. The pale blue in his eyes was overcast; his face was a mask of streaks of clay and sweat and exhaustion. He shook his head wordlessly and turned, half rising, reaching for support at the sides of the cut; then, partly crawling, he went to the point beyond the cut where the horses were standing. I followed. We dropped on the damp ground beside the horses. *Rocksy should have been able to come up*, I kept thinking; she wouldn't help us! There she was, wedged in the cut at the bottom of the V. Why wouldn't she come up?

We lay on the ground for several minutes. Then there was a tremendous beating and thumping from the trail around the turn in the V. We rose, thinking to go back, when an apparition materialized at the mouth of the cut. It was Rocksy, on her feet, smeared all over with the red clay, unsteady, but walking with short, spasmodic jerks, coming toward us.

We reached the colony that evening, paddocked the horses in a fenced pasture near the center of the settlement, and went back for Dixie the following day on foot. The next day we reached Finca Loma Linda with the four Percheron mares and our saddle stock. Four days later Juan arrived at the farm alone. He had left Dumpling at the colony, in a pasture there. She had been too weak to come any farther. I received a shortwave radio message that Dick had died in Potrero Grande. Juan returned to the colony for Dumpling several days later and brought her to the farm. I had promised him a colt from this filly, but she died after many days of doctoring and care on the farm.

From the Percheron stock we bred and raised many strong draft animals on the farm. We did not again ride over the King's Highway. Today it is part of the Pan-American Highway, connecting San Vito, the old Italian colony, with all parts of Costa Rica.

Experiences such as these were not unusual in the settlement of the South Frontier. It is true that no other settlers attempted to work with draft horses as a central part of a farming system, and ours were among the few Percheron horses in all of Costa Rica. In addition, most settlers in the South Frontier had not spent as much time on the Camino Real as we. But the nature of these experiences was not uncommon to the early years of the settlement of this land.

What is this nature?

At the outset of their experiences in a new and unpopulated land, men and women and their children face more directly and more intimately the natural forces around them than these same people will at a later time in life or than do most people in developed societies where such forces usually are not directly felt. Rain; sunlight; heat in terms of the absence of moisture and consequent shortage of food; distance in terms of the personal, physical effort required to overcome it; gradients as encountered when one's own energy must supply the motive power to surmount them—these and many more are forces we come to know directly.

Today, for instance, buses and passengers drive up or down the escarpment at La Cuesta de la Pita without requiring any personal energy of the passengers or drivers beyond that of being passengers or drivers. All do provide the energy to make the highway, the fuel, the vehicles, as part of a complex and widely dispersed society in which the benefits of one technology or another ramify and become available to many, who in turn through taxes or consumer spending support the technology and industry; all this is indirectly part of being a passenger or a driver on such a highway. But this dispersed and separated involvement in meeting the requirements of overcoming the force of gravity, the displacement of oneself over distance, is less direct than walking or climbing over the trail. Today we experience many things indirectly; we are divorced from their most immediate nature as we might know it if those components of society and civilization which we have interposed between them and ourselves for our comfort and well-being were removed. We do not remove them and we do interpose them for good reason—no one wishes to walk or climb endlessly up La Cuesta de la Pita.

The point is this: when we do so walk or climb, our lives receive the imprint of these experiences. We then act and think accordingly. As settlers, the first here, the way we think and act will, in its turn, carry an imprint to this environment more deeply, more extensively, than had we ourselves or someone in our place spent a similar number of years on this land at a later time, after its settlement.

A time of settlement then becomes a critical time in fixing the direction of systems in an environment. The natural forces acting upon the lives of the settlers and the lives of the settlers reacting to them become a process which has no counterpart in later years. If we wish to understand the roots which produced our present, because their superimposed structure is the fabric of what we have now, we must not see the gradient on the hills on La Cuesta de la Pita from the viewpoint of a passenger on a bus. Nonetheless, this same passenger will inquire: Why is it important to know these roots? All of the present has a past; why is it necessary to understand how people reacted to given conditions at some time—which is gone now—when in the present there is so much that must engage and challenge our continuance?

The answer to such a question is this: We are still on the frontier; the elements of natural systems, their forces, are no less with us now than before; our lives are not less affected by these forces, these systems; their impact is with us as it was with others; when we are talking about a continuance of life, we are dealing with ourselves, regardless of time. None of the essential components of the frontier has disappeared, nor has the relevancy of the acts of those who lived before us, regardless of when they lived—!; each aspect of application of relationship may have been modified, but our lives are still being influenced as we ourselves are exercising influence. This is the central problem of environmental issues today: how to convey to ourselves that we are not independent of these elemental forces of nature, of this present and its past, and of the relevancy to the future of what we do. We are not independent in time; we have separated ourselves from such elements, but we have not removed their impact from our lives or the impact brought about by us from theirs. The effects of their nature have been dispersed, both in place and time, and may be less directly felt; they may not even touch us directly, but only our children or later generations; nevertheless, they *will* make themselves known.

Let's return to our home on the frontier, our clearing in the rain forest, and see if we can identify and understand some of these forces which we must meet. We will do this in a way that is appropriate to settlers, not by studying these forces but by living, working, and struggling with them. The bounty of such an experience may be that we will never be able to articulate what we have learned but that what we have learned will be written upon the pages of the experience we know as life.

This same rain which, in other character and other season has caused the slippages and displacements of parts of the King's Highway, is now falling tonight around us, its patter on the metal roof a constant reminder of our security here within our home. Our children will lie in bed as on this night, listening to the rain—we have felt it on the trail, we have felt it here in the work in our days—and we know with something that responds within us that this rain is a provender of life, is at times an opponent, at others an ally, but, more fundamentally, always something which, through our residence on this frontier, is becoming intimately a part of us.

Outside, in the grass in the pasture just freshly planted, our horses graze in the rain. But this is not a cold rain; there is energy in it, energy in the grass it provides, energy in the grass being eaten by the horses, and this energy is supplying warmth. Still, we must make a stable so that our horses will not always need to stand in the rain.

The stable will be built of timber cut from this clearing, the posts once having been trees, the rails cut of smaller trees. We will finish the stable with metal roofing.

By evening, by the light of the kerosene lantern in this stable, we will groom and care for these horses. We will trim their manes and tails, brush their coats, care for their hooves. In time, we will learn the skills of a blacksmith and shoe them. Here in the stable there will be a forge and a small smithy. The glow of the charcoal fire in the forge, the hand-operated blower, will create from the iron in the shoes a print that will trace its pattern over the undulating surface of this land.

These Percherons are among the very few now in Costa Rica. With the loss of the stallion, the ability to raise purebreds was also lost, but we will raise a strong, heavy crossbreed of draft animals from these mares. By the light of the lantern at evening in the stable we will make these plans as the brush strokes on the coats of the horses speak in the dusk of our day of work.

During the days, in the mornings before the rains in the wet season and throughout the day in the dry season, we will work with the teams in the clearing of the land. There is a light team, the two mules, and a team of Percherons to be made up of Rocksy and Jean or Dixie. The filly, Ginger, is too young yet to work. Only Rocksy and Jean have worked in harness; the other horses and mules must be trained. The clearing of the land will require steady, well-trained draft stock.

The harnesses and collars must be oiled; here in the tropics mold deteriorates leather. We will use a logging chain in the land clearing, a set of singletrees and a doubletree as eveners to distribute the weight between the companions in the team, chains for traces, strong hames against the collars. We know the clinking of the chains, the squeak of leather, the clack of the metal eveners as they are drawn by the team out into the field in the early morning.

A thin carpet of mist covers the land, higher stumps and branches showing above it. All around the clearing to the west, the forest enclosing that side is bathed in the fresh light of day. To the east the shadows of the preceding night cling to the foot of the trees in the forest at that edge. The toucans are perched on the highest trees and throw their beaks up at every cry.

There is the probity of metal in the chains, the freshness in the earth, inertia, weight, power in the log. We have been here working with the axe, bucking these logs, removing branches, cutting them into lengths the teams can move. Now, as we snub the chain around the log and link it to the clevis on the doubletree, the honesty of the smell of the horses, the leather in the harness, the smell of old iron on the eveners where it is caught in the sunlight, steam arising as moisture from the earth—the scope and the freedom—are all part of this morning.

There is a ripple in the reins as we shake them, the leather dark, worn smooth with the work of other times, and then the command: "Take it up!" The team, gray and in symmetry, moves into the collars, the traces tightening. There is a moment of hesitation; the team veers off to the left, bending, legs planted and bodies arched, momentum hesitant, inertia on a point of escape, forward, tightness draws across the lines of the hames and into the collars—and the log breaks free. The motion is flowing now, the reins crossed and doubled through our fingers, a tug to the left, to the left, the left, resolutely and taut, to the left and around, the long drawn-out line of chain, the massive legs veering, and the command: "Rocksy!" The response comes on the rings on the bits, and the team swings to avoid a stump, side-stepping to keep the traces tight so that they do not cut across their legs.

The hours wear on; where there were logs and branches on the land, now a small space of clearing opens and grows. Skid marks trace a figure across the ground where logs have made shallow trenches, deep hoof marks in the earth. The sweat flows, the sun having grown hot, the collars, the harness showing the impregnation of wet from the horses, a light froth around the shoulders. The sore on Jean's fetlock is now gone, the cut on her shoulder having left only a scar. The team of Percherons, their gray coats darkening with sweat, bend into their work. A log snags on a root, catches, pivots; there is slack in the traces; the log begins to roll; and around, around, the team sidesteps, taking small deliberate steps in a diagonal to bring up the slack in the traces, take up the tension on the chain, and repurchase the snub on the log; and the regained log skids and makes a dark streak across the ground.

We are moving the logs to a low point on the slope, dragging the weight of the logs down, coming back with the unburdened team. In time we dig around the stumps, cut their roots with the axe, then try them against the team. They are hard to pull. The horses start into their collars, feel the solidity of the load, ease and bend into the collars again—and the load does not move; legs begin to dance in nervousness, the mares pulling unevenly now, worried by the anchored stump; then comes the command: "Back! back!" and the team comes to a standstill. Off goes the chain, the singletrees and doubletree loose on the ground, the team standing, and again we search for the hidden roots with the shovel and axe.

In time a space on the land is clear, and we can see the exposed face of the earth. Here it is crisscrossed by the many trenches made by the skidded logs, there by the holes, refilled after pulling the stumps. Everywhere roots have been yanked from the ground, leaving crevices where they broke free in a zigzag as the team pulled them out with the chain. Now this land is released from its bondage to the forest. The earth is free and loose; the earth crumbles easily; the earth smells vaguely of mold and yet virile too; this earth retains the power, the character of an earlier time.

But what is this power? Is it not power that we have been applying to the land, to this clearing, to each day's work? We have brought these horses to our clearing because they represent power, tractive power. With their power we combine ours, the strength in hand and arm, the motive power of the leg; with this, our combined strength, we have confronted what we recognize as a residual power in this land.

The definition of this element in the land as that of "power" is really the reciprocal relationship we noted earlier, for we cannot live and succeed here without discovering in ourselves a kind of strength. And because the task of living here requires of us this expenditure of strength, we construe that our opponent in this work of establishing life—our way of living here—is also strong (we expect and sense that it must be far stronger than we) and therefore an expression of power.

This is true if we correlate such an expression of power with energy. For here we have the energy of photosynthesis, a million processes in the structure of tissues, and the functions of life systems in the forest we remove, in the earth we expose. Here we have energy in the displacement of air; we feel its action in the evaporation of the perspiration on our skin. We have energy in heat as it extracts from us and this team the maximum of our labor. We have energy which comes not only from substance and sustenance but also from the reflection of our gaze across the hours of this place in the knowledge that we are winning from each stroke of sinew or blade a sense of value and worth in ourself.

We recognized this same kind of power when we encountered the soil displacement along sections of and on the gradients of the Camino Real. The extension of the expression of this power over distance, the hours of travel through heat or rain or dryness, the infiltration of the water in the sand became for us expressions of a power, requiring of us a strength to counteract its influence on us.

What we are interpreting here is our place in a scheme of life and energy systems; we exist with these. We therefore respond to them, finding that they have a means, through our response, of communicating with us. We have only to meet them to discover that we must make a response to them; our strength is required to meet theirs. We do not exist independently; surely we must be as one.

If we return now to our clearing and our work with the teams, we will find that we have uprooted and dismantled many established orders, all of which represented one or another form of integrated and dependent relationships, all of which required an application of energy to be thrown awry. There has been resistance to this process of disintegration; these structures did not willingly abandon their tenure. In what measure can we prevail in binding our tenure and our order?

We might conclude that this will become a test of relative tenacity, ours against something we must overcome here. In this test we have a better understanding of our resources (although this is far from complete) than we do of the resources of what we confront. In the absence of any clearer insight, we refer to these perceived external resources by their magnitude: rain, heat, distance, weight, darkness, mass—all these and others impress us by a degree of scale which might diminish us; but it does not, for we deny their ability to be separate from ours.

Now we turn the surface of this ground, using a team of horses and a disk harrow instead of the *pala* and *machete de suelo,* and again we will be impressed by two forms of one character: our work and that of our horses, and the resistance to this work of what we undo. On this day the earth is to be turned under mechanized tillage; this must mark a fresh point of beginning.

Ours is a riding disk harrow with independent adjustment of each of its two gangs of disks, long handles ahead of us where we sit on a springy, sulky seat allowing us to "set" the angle of the disks for either deeper or shallower cuts. Looking out over the rumps of the gray Percheron team, we sight a line across the clearing, shake out the reins over the horses' backs, and cluck to them. The sulky harrow sinks into the earth below us as it moves forward. There is the swished, mellow sound of the steel disks cutting through the surface soil into the fine roots below; and, as we look down, a marvelous thing is happening: this virgin ground is turning, and a rich, dark furrow follows behind each disk, the black loam curled and turned up. Ages unfold behind us; so have men and women turned the earth since time in memory, planting, bringing into growth. The harrow rocks from side to side as the disks roll over unseen roots yet to be grubbed out. The pace of the team is steady; each pass with the harrow makes a half lap, one-half the width of the preceding cut; the tilled earth widens; an entire transformation is coming over this segment of our farm. Somewhere in humanity's past, we feel, is retained a counterpart of this moment when men and women so tilled the land, the certainty that the moment did exist, that this is valid work.

The harrowed soil is loose, exposed now to the air; the energy of oxygen enters it and sunlight falls where before it had not reached; a new life will emerge here. We turn the team at the end of the row. This is what these animals have been bred for, the steady pace across the furrowed terrain. Was it not this that we saw that day when the whole of terrain and sky spoke across the distance of the Camino Real?

At the end of this morning's work in the clearing, we drive the team back to the stable; each muscle we feel has been thrown in a new way, it seems, today by riding this harrow, but there will be other days—many—and our muscles will harden to the work. We curry down the team, massaging the shoulders where the collars have seated, releasing the moisture from the coat; these animals have earned their rest. One of the first crops we will plant must be forage for the horses. Oats would be a choice, but oats will not grow here—not yet, but maybe in time. We feed the horses now, later giving them water, and return to the clearing to walk over it and study the day's work. How loose, how soft, how yielding the soil has become!

In the evening it rains. The sound of the rain comes, as so often here, from the distance, approaching over the forest with hurrying footsteps. The first drops strike the roof of our house, making an impact—these are big drops! In a moment comes the beating of a thousand massive drops, striking, disintegrating, shattering into droplets. Here in our home the kerosene lamps cast light against this night. There is light, in the wood-burning stove heat; glows of warmth escape at the edges of the firebox door, bulwarks against the night and darkness and rain. Within the house is the closeness of a family, rest and withdrawal from the work of the day. But beyond this warmth, the glow, the light, this second-story level elevated above the ground, is the clearing, the freshly turned land, the horses at stable. For an hour and a half the rain continues to drive; in all somewhat less than three inches will have fallen. Then a heavy mist settles over the farm, wrapping its stillness around the house. The home is an even tighter sanctuary against these elements, the aftermath of rain. But we must live on this land. The source of our livelihood is not here at home; it is outside where we have tilled and turned with our team and machine.

Taking a flashlight and raincoat, for the rain continues to fall ever so lightly, we will go into this night to see this thing—for something has happened: there has been a tremendous release of energy over the farm. First, we check the horses in the stable; here all is well. But in the field where we harrowed in the morning, the beam of the flashlight through the droplets of mist and light rain shows a stunning change. Gone is the soft texture of the loose and aerated earth.

The surface of the soil is washed, flattened. Water is puddled in hollows; in many places it has broken down little slopes, washing the soil away, leaving gutted trenches. Where we step, our rubber boots sink into the soil and when we withdraw the boots there is the sucking sound of saturation. Had we planted seed, it would have been washed out of the soil, washed away in the soil, been buried under the soil, carried by the rainwater. In a matter of hours we have lost control over this little world. Had control ever been ours—or was all this pretension but delusion? Worse: *I* have committed the unforgivable sin of the farmer; *I* have allowed the soil to be carried and washed away by erosion. In the name of all that is sacred—and this earth must be so held—what force has been let loose this night?

It is again that force which is easily seen. Combined with the work of our morning, our input and that of our horses, and the energy in the rain, we have brought about a condition worthy of despair to this segment of our farm. By the light of day the conditions here look no better than they did by flashlight.

Yet once more we are identifying factors which influence our life as settlers and farmers by their magnitude; we become aware of them only when they have almost overwhelmed us. In truth, they are operating around us, constantly, within us—many moving forces. We are aware of some of them, but of most we are unaware; none of them do we really understand.

We might make the following comparison: As human beings we are aware that we breathe; we inhale and we exhale. We know how to do this, and we certainly have control over our breathing. Yet most of us do not know the mechanism of nerve and muscle at the root of this vital process nor could we say that we actually do control our breathing in this more fundamental sense. We rely on processes completely unknown to us to support this life function. We hold ourselves to be in control of our breathing, but consciously we forget about it almost entirely.

Around us in the clearing this morning, as we look at what seems near devastation where we have tilled, life and energy processes are constantly at work, and by one definition of work, energy is being expended, recovered, transformed. This energy is not only in the form of life processes. It is also the energy of physics, the molecular

A PLACE IN THE RAIN FOREST

energy of bonded atoms, the energy of liquids passing through the walls of membranes, the mechanics of soil structure, the energy of moisture evaporating in the air—many expressions of energy which may or may not be directly associated with a particular vital process. As farmers, we are almost totally in the dark about them, yet none may exercise more influence in altering these processes than we. It is possible that we will pass our entire lives on this farm becoming aware only of the "great" forces which surround and affect us and never of the "little" ones, which are operative constantly. Yet, as we look at this soil today, having been so washed and altered by the rain, we are seeing no less the effects of an altered condition of molecular relationship—because of our tillage—than of that of the apparent surface conditions produced by tillage and rain. It is far from certain that either is greater than the other; it is quite probable that both are part of a single complex in which, when any part is altered, all others are affected.

To what extent is it necessary to learn more about all of these "little" processes, those which we do not readily perceive or feel? Such a question will be answered differently by each person. If we feel comfortable about the way we are managing, and being managed, in our environment, we may consider that things are going pretty well. If we do not, we may conclude that we need to learn more. On the basis of what has taken place in Coto Brus, my own viewpoint is that we need to learn more. But how much of these "little," fine considerations can we learn? I have no idea; the more we learn on Finca Loma Linda, through research and scientific study, the broader becomes the horizon of what we perceive that we must understand.

But this matter of learning is not so much a matter of completeness as a matter of *process.* It is the process of learning that will enable us to better live with ourselves and our environment. We certainly will never finish learning. But as long as we continue to proceed to learn, we will have the sensitivity to understand that we do not know everything and therefore must act carefully.

These are the forces and the power I refer to. In reality, they become transformed in us and resolved in us as attitudes. Our attitude relative to what we do or do not do is fashioned by the forces we daily meet in life and by our responses to them. We may stand today by this clearing where we have made the tillage and see the mischief we have produced. But we will not abandon this work; we will make a farm. We have a right to live on this earth as do other forms of life. We will learn what has gone wrong and then try to correct it. For the moment, let's hang the collar here on a peg in the stable and leave the doubletree and singletrees by the harness and see what we must do tomorrow.

SIX

The
Nature of
Our Adversity

*S*een from the air, as from a low-flying plane, the primary rain forest has a tufted, irregular texture, the trees—some overtopping others, some pockets of lower vegetation—having an uneven tapestry of many hues of green, occasionally the gray or white of a tree trunk or a barren branch. Seldom does one see the land below the canopy of trees. In the region which became Coto Brus, the Talamanca mountain range, clothed too in forest over most of its slopes, formed a barrier of a purple or dark blue, seen from a distance, against this more immediate green of the nearer forest. Although uniformity is not a concept usually associated with the rain forest, this region, as seen from a plane, might indeed have seemed quite uniform because it was intact and one segment of canopy looked much like another.

The land below the plane would be at this time of uninterrupted forest largely unexplored. Rivers would make themselves known by crevices in the features of the forest; the canopy there would be indented and follow the snakelike course of the river. Steep gradients could easily be discerned, even though completely clothed by the forest.

The forest canopy—if, indeed, it should be referred to as one, as it always is a multistoried complex—was also an unexplored realm. Here were strata of life and life-supporting conditions, one above the other, each perceived through different intensities of light, each subject to a different microclimate in terms of relative height above the ground. Many species of life roamed freely among the several strata within the forest canopy; others, we may assume, might have been quite specialized in their requirements of habitat, remaining within the specific conditions of some given level. Clouds came to this region of forest, and, borne on wind currents and subject to the heat-transfer dynamics of land and air, came to represent within weather conditions certain norms, subject, of course, to some deviation, but generally behaving in consistent patterns.

This was a lonely land, if only because we are led to use such a description when we meet conditions in nature that cause us to feel that there must have existed in a past, now remote to us both, a time when we were more closely linked with all this that we perceive.

Based on the senses which are ours—those of sight, sound, smell, touch—we know that this region of forest embodied an element of eternal struggle in which all life was committed. Yet in this struggle, vitality was detected more often than fear as a dominant expression of being. Over the whole region, the entire tapestry of forest, there seemed to be an all-pervasive insurgency of courage.

Now all of this has come to change; the uniformity of diversity, if the forest might be so characterized, has given way to an interceding simplicity—or so it appears. Again, as seen from the air, the forest no longer is intact; it remains in ever more circumscribed stricture. Pastures, coffee, farm lands appear. They seem to be less complex than the forest they replace; they stand out as the same kind of thing, thereby gaining an assumed character of simplicity.

Over the region can be seen homes, roads, villages. Where it had appeared there were rivers, it now can be seen that these are only streams. And the streams do not look as picturesque as our imagination had envisioned them. What was seen of the rain forest was the

A PLACE IN THE RAIN FOREST

countenance of a mystery; what is seen now of the land which has emerged from it is the mystery of what has disappeared.

In each of these new segments of pasture and coffee and roads and farms there is the tedium of the known, and this challenges the mind, whereas the unknown challenged the imagination.

Because this region, which has come to have a name and a geographic and political identity, can be seen from the air, certain features are attributed to it. This region can also be seen now from its land surface, and here also attribution of character is made. Beneath the earth's surface of this region, however, the perceptions which are ours have little effect; little in terms of character features are ascribed to what is concealed from us within the earth. Time also here is an element which is elusive. At one point in time volcanic ash fell over this region, but such a time is past. This is a place of many characters; possibly these have no beginning; perhaps their sequence will not end.

These characters are of a fluid condition; they take on many guises, are present in many semblances. Of the many semblances which might be recognized by us in this compass of geography, a place now having acquired an identity and a name, none will impress us more than that which acquires a human face, a human form.

It is night. For several days and nights it has been raining—a *temporal*. Along what appears to be a ribbon of water extending over the ground, moonlight glints, for some light passes through the cover of clouds. Shadows, inert and lightless, intercede at the sides of this liquid reflection, standing vertically, masses of vegetation vaguely sodden in their shapelessness, appearing as darker segments in the heavy saturation of the air.

All is silent, if rainfall can be so described; or all is the monotony of the spatter of drops falling on a million wet surfaces, always this soundless sound, in which nothing that speaks to the soul can be discerned, save this overriding dreariness of indefinition. This rain has soaked into the very memory of a drier time, so that even the sunshine in recollection is cast in a pale of uncertainty.

At some distance along the ribbon—indeed, beyond its farthest discernable reach—a light appears, peculiarly white and unsteady, faint, burning strangely in the rain. In a moment there are one and then two more lights, all burning with about the same intensity. And now there comes a sound above the rain. It is the sound of men's voices and, too, a peculiar metallic, clacking sound, irregular, sharp, stuttering occasionally, but coming with frequency.

The lights approach, and, as they do so, the ribbon becomes more visible in the faint illumination approaching with the men. The ribbon can now be seen to be an extended quagmire, a surface of mud. And the men approaching are walking in this mud and carrying on their foreheads carbide lamps, such as those used by miners. Each lamp projects a small, white flame behind which there is a silver reflector. The flame is accompanied by a hiss and a strong smell of the gas from a carbide generator. The men move slowly, one arm extended behind them, grasping the yoke of an oxcart, the other arm, held at an angle, projecting a long ox goad. Two oxen, with massive horns, come directly behind each man, and behind each yoke of oxen, a cart, heavily loaded. There are four carts and four men but among them only the three lamps. The carts are lined out along the length of ribbon.

As the first cart reaches a point in the ribbon where the surface seems to be only water, the man walking ahead of the oxen and guiding them sinks to his thighs in the watery mud and the oxen move cautiously into its depth. The night is split then by a series of shouts: "*Buey!, buey!*" The man in front flails the goad round the oxen, threatening more than actually goading, and from behind, other men touch the rumps of the oxen with goads. The great beasts sink to their bellies, lose their footing, go down on their knees, come up, seesawing. But the cart has become a dead weight in the quagmire, its axle dragging well below the watery surface, and the oxen, breathing heavily, their eyes wide, come to a stop. With difficulty the men move around them, mired almost as much as the oxen.

From a cart which has not yet entered the deep part of the quagmire, the oxen are unhitched from the cart tongue and brought forward through the mud to the mired cart. The second yoke of oxen is brought ahead of the yoke which is mired, and the two yokes are hitched in tandem to the cart.

Again the insistent sounds of men's shouts break through the darkness: "*Buey!, buey!*—." The cart budges; the oxen bend to their knees; they sway and stumble; the men hurry around them, pulling on the yoke, their voices breaking in exhaustion; and in a moment the cart sinks deeper and comes to a stop.

Wearily, the men throw their goads to the side of the quagmire and ply their hands to the ropes binding mud-covered, burlap sacks on the cart. The sacks are soaked in the rain. There is a sweet, vaguely fruity smell coming from each sack. Grasping a sack, two men lift it to the shoulders of a third. This man staggers through the mud, barely keeping footing, to the edge of the quagmire, bent almost double under the 150-pound weight of the sack. Then, tottering along the edge of the quagmire, with a square of plastic like a cape tied over his shoulders, he climbs up an incline in the terrain to a more solid place on the road. Each man in turn comes out of the quagmire in this way, carrying a sack.

When the cart is partly unloaded, the men return to the oxen, and again the cries ring into the night—"*Buey!*"—and the great, patient oxen move the cart along. Each cart makes a clacking sound as the narrow, wooden, steel-rimmed wheels ride loosely on their iron hubs and worn axle bearings.

At length all four carts are brought through the quagmire, and the sacks, having been portered by the men, are reloaded where the road begins to ascend a hill. Two hundred meters beyond this point is another quagmire, on the hill itself, and here again the oxen and the carts become mired. Earlier in the afternoon, these same men with the same oxen and carts made it through this quagmire, but now in the darkness the oxen founder, and the sacks have to be off-loaded again. The men are barefoot, or wearing broken or torn boots, their skinny legs looking hardly able to support them under the load of the sacks, their pants tied at the waist with cord; they are muddy from head to foot.

At length the men and the carts reach a small shed, built at the edge of a rock-surfaced road. From the shed the light of a kerosene lamp glows, and inside is an official measuring box, the *media fanega*, for measuring ripe coffee berries. The men empty the coffee berries from each sack into this measure, from which the berries are then dumped on an inclined floor which feeds to a chute at its foot. A four-wheel-drive agricultural tractor drawing an open-bed wagon receives the coffee berries below the chute, waiting there until the wagon is fully loaded.

Each man delivers the sacks of coffee from his own farm, receiving a white paper receipt written out by the man who measures the coffee, writing either by lamp or candle light. The man delivering the coffee takes it in a muddy hand and puts it under his waterproof hat or in a pouch under the belt. Then all the men climb into their empty carts and, driving the oxen from behind with the goads, return along the road, back through the quagmires.

The coffee berries picked that day on the respective farms must be delivered this night; they cannot be held until the following day because coffee berries ferment within hours after picking, and by law fermented coffee cannot be sold in Costa Rica.

The third trip of the day with the oxen and carts still has to be made to bring the last of the day's coffee to the receiving shed. Huddled under their plastic capes now, the men return to their farms. A breeze comes up; it grows cold. The unshaven faces are weary. They look closely ahead at the water on the surface of the road as moonlight breaks through the clouds. Mostly the oxen pick and find their way. Occasionally, a cart will stop and a man will get down and lead the oxen through a hard place. The carbide lamps continue to hiss and throw a flickering light. Through the rain, ever the rain, at length the men reach their farms, load the last sacks of coffee, and start back to the receiving shed. And with each trip over the road by the carts, from the first in the afternoon to the last somewhat before midnight, and in subsequent days, the quagmires become deeper because the steel-rim wheels of the carts cut more deeply with successive loads into the earth under the mud.

As each man returns to his farm after the third trip with the carts, he stables and cuts sugarcane for the oxen. Then, mostly unwashed, he sits by the hearth in the rude, dirt-floor house, watching the slow glow and fading of the embers of the firewood, drinking steaming coffee from a glass, thinking, thinking into the hours of darkness. At last he climbs into bed beside his woman, perhaps a baby in a box beside the bed. All in the house will smell of the wood smoke from the hearth, and as the minutes lengthen before sleep, there is the sound of rain.

Throughout the Frontier on this night there is the darkness, the rain, the clouds moving slowly, behind them the light of the moon. A million instances of life are afoot and about their separate pursuits, each tiny segment of this complex a universe unto itself. There is a rhythm and a sound which comes over this land which cannot be seen or heard or felt. Yet it emanates from the darkness, is part of the night. It is the perception of each creature of its existence, its relevancy in this instant to its environment. It is not a separate perception, as from one or another of the senses; it is a conglomerate of these, and something more: an awareness, the synthesis of perceptions coalesced. This common awareness (it shares a common moment in time and a common environment) becomes a common sentience in this darkness. At the end of its extent, a root tip grows, a single cell is added to an earlier cell . . . in the dark, damp wet of the earth. A spider above the ground takes a step and secures a thread so fine as almost to be unseen and hangs like a jewel in its web in the moonlight. A mouse hunches and becomes small, a furry ball, then darts within the leaves to a hole in the ground. And ever the reluctant, fragile drops of rain.

In this place in time gone by, there was never this which is about to become — or perhaps only the seed of this which now will root and flourish upon the face of a living tissue, a structure of life. This new thing, its being, is a fungus, and it lives upon the tissue of a leaf. In the night it excels in the wet and the rain, bathed in the cold light of the moon. This fungus alights, secures, penetrates, establishes, procreates, disseminates, knows the brilliance of its tenure in the wet and the shadow, multiplies and is fecund. It spreads its kind across the face of the earth — upon the surfaces of leaves. Had there not been coffee here, this fungus would have languished; in the presence of coffee it is king. And there remains within it a separate mechanism ready to trigger a modification in its makeup should a threat arise to its existence.

This life, these integrated units in multiple life systems, are active, sentient, responsive, and ubiquitous tonight under the drops of the rain. They comprise a vast, unmeasurable scheme, a scheme in which the men and their carts and their oxen and their coffee are but a component—one among those others which, in their total, are countless.

Now, as the woman in the home of this man who worked the night before with the other men and their carts awakens on the morning of the following day, still it is raining. In the darkness of the dirt-floor home there is damp and solitude. The baby stirs and wants to cry but for the moment is silent. It is three o'clock in the morning and the moon has set. In the hearth the ashes are cold. The man grunts and turns as the woman leaves their bed, pulling on a second dress over the one in which she slept, padding in bare feet across the pressed earth of the floor. The woman pokes in the hearth by the light of a candle. The man will not get up until there are tortillas and hot coffee. The baby begins to cry.

The woman gathers some kindling and arranges it in the hearth. The kindling is damp; all in the house is damp in the darkness and the presence of the rain. The woman touches the tip of the candle to the kindling, and for some time it refuses to ignite. Then a tiny flame emerges and goes out. But it has left an ember, a single, faint glimmer in the dusky film of dampness. Gently the woman blows and the ember brightens. She takes a breath, and the ember starts to go out. Again she blows and the ember widens, becoming fiercely white and trembling. Then it fades as the woman draws in another breath. Gradually, the woman coaxes the fire to life. She coughs, she has inhaled the smoke. Languidly at first, the fire smokes and trembles. At length there is the crackle of the tinder; larger sticks of wood begin to burn.

In the light cast now by the fire, the home is seen to be but a single room. It is made of rough-sawed boards as exterior siding. These were green when they were nailed to the walls, having shrunk as they seasoned, presenting wide cracks where earlier they had joined. The roof of this home is of metal; there is no ceiling, and heavy drops of condensed moisture can be seen clinging to the undersurface of the corrugated roofing, the drops discolored, having taken on a charcoal tint from the smoke and rusted metal. The rafters supporting the roof, one-by-four scantling crossed and braced, are blackened from the smoke from the hearth and carry accumulations of soot and cobwebs.

There are no glass windows in this house. Shutters close out the night now, opening out, when they are open, on two walls. On a third wall is the door.

The floor is of packed earth, hollowed and troughed in places where it has been swept heavily with a home-made broom, the fibers the branches of a weed. In one corner of the room a hen blinks at the firelight, mistrusting this activity now. She arranges herself more protectively, spreading and fluffing her wings over a clutch of eggs in a nest made of a box. A dog, emaciated and looking apologetic, watches with doleful eyes as the woman begins the day; from time to time it shakes long ears and nuzzles close to the ground, nostrils twitching to catch the first scent of the cooking food.

On a wall next to a window is a wooden slat frame, the *fregadero*, for dish washing. This frame projects beyond the outside dimension of the house, about two feet. It is sided and roofed with slats to keep possums or skunks from crawling into the house through this route, and on the *fregadero* are two aluminum pans, blackened from the fire; a cast-iron *casuela* (an open cooking pan); some enameled plates and cups; and a few spoons and a fork.

The woman goes to the hearth, where the fire is burning brightly now, and uncovers a large, aluminum kettle. In it is a grey liquid looking a little like mud. She stirs this with a wooden spoon and kernels of corn come to the surface. The corn is submerged in a mixture of wood ashes and water, the ashes helping to separate the corn kernels from the skins, which come loose when the corn is soaked over night.

The baby cries more now—it is a one-year-old boy—and the woman goes to the box and lifts him, wrapped in a blanket, talking to her son, smiling into a diminutive, sleepy face. There is a strong smell of urine in the blanket and in the box used as a crib.

Holding the baby in one arm, she gives him her breast, stirring the corn in the ashes with the other hand.

The woman is young, no more than eighteen. She has a strong, robust frame. All of her upper front teeth are gone, decayed, and this gives her a strangely foolish look. But the impression is only momentary. For seen as she is now, holding her son, there is beauty in her face, by firelight, a warmth and depth in her dark eyes.

Although she is only eighteen, already her body shows the burden of work, work in which the body is subject to many things. She is barefoot now as she will be throughout the day, wearing this same dress too that she put on yesterday; at present she has but two such dresses.

Having given the baby her breast, the woman puts him back in the box, covering him well with the blanket (it is still cold and damp in the house), hoping that he will sleep now. She goes to a post, a wooden post that her husband has planted in the floor by one wall. On this post, at about waist height, is a hand-turned corn grinder. After washing the corn several times from a bucket of water brought the evening before from the well, she begins to press the corn into the mill, turning with one hand a crank and feeding the wet corn in with the other. There is a pulpy sound as the *masa*, the ground corn, comes through the mill. It is slow work; it is hard work, and perspiration comes to the woman's face. She turns with a full bending sweep of her body, generations of such work seeming to precede her.

When the ground, moist corn meal has been collected in a dish, the woman takes it to a planed board, filmed over from earlier work with corn meal, and deftly begins to pat the meal into tortillas, seasoning these with pinches of wet salt taken from an enameled cup where the salt has accumulated the moisture in the air. Putting a little pig lard in the shallow *casuela*, the woman flips tortillas onto the greased surface, and the smell of food begins to fill the air. The dog raises its head and looks lovingly at the woman. Water has been boiling at the fire in a pan, and the woman now pours the boiling water through a little sack, like a man's sock, at the tip of which there is ground coffee suspended over a cup. The aroma of coffee combines with that of the tortillas.

Outside it is still dark, but already the guans have begun to babble in the forest at some distance. The man has stirred, looking sleepily from the bed. He yawns and gets to his feet, wearing long shorts and an open shirt. He goes to the *fregadero* and splashes water on his face from the bucket, then, slipping on his boots at the dirt threshold, steps out onto a little dirt-floored porch where a rooster and a few chickens are bunched against one wall. Taking an old towel from a peg by the door, the man throws this over his shoulders and walks out into the light rain. Seen with the firelight coming through the open door behind him and the vague lightening of dawn in the east, his frame is light; his dark, unshaven face is the color of the hair on his chest. Standing by a stump, he urinates, gazes for a moment at the lowering clouds, then walks quickly into the house. The smell of coffee and tortillas is strong.

The man goes to the box and picks up the sleeping baby. The woman looks at him scoldingly for a moment, the trace of a light in her smile. Once this morning she has gone to the door of the house, stepping over the prostrate dog, opened it, and looked out. A bat, hanging under the eaves, had taken flight. The chickens and rooster had stirred and fluffed and settled again by the wall. The woman stood in the doorway, the light of the fire behind her, her figure in its white, shapeless dress silhouetted against the dark. She had sighed heavily.

Always, she had thought, it is the rain.

In the home of a foreign settler—"foreign" in this context meaning a nationality other than the Costa Ricans—a group of land owners are having a meeting. The home is by the side of the road connecting the Italian colony with Agua Buena. The home, by all comparison in the South Frontier, is elegant. In the Frontier there are only a very few homes like this, these few having been built by "foreigners." This home stands somewhat in from the road and is surrounded by the beginning of a lawn, although at no great distance from this site there is evidence of recent land clearing in the fallen forest, stumps and logs.

The house can be seen from the road, which now is a series of quagmires. It is painted white, built up on posts above the ground (a style of building popular in the Frontier among those who can afford it), and is spacious. Within the home there are a number of antiques, a grandfather clock brought here from London, some oriental rugs and vases, several oil paintings, and a cast-iron Franklin fireplace brought here from Florida. In the fireplace a fire is burning. It is early afternoon; outside the well-framed and curtained windows, the rain falls; for hours, days, it has been so; this is the same *temporal* mentioned at the beginning of this chapter. Seven men are meeting in this house today. They have come here from different parts of the Frontier, from the colony, from Agua Buena, from Cañas Gordas. The owner of the home, a bachelor, is American. He has offered his house for this meeting.

Along the slopes of the Talamanca Mountains on this day, the same day on which the woman and the man with their baby face another day of work in picking coffee and delivering it to the receiving shed, the rain continues falling. It falls in a vast and undisturbed stillness here, for no settlers are yet living in this wilderness. The summits of the mountains, rising to nine and ten thousand feet, cannot be seen because the low clouds have obscured them. This tract of mountain slopes is clothed in shadow, a pervading shadow of diminished light and ceaseless rain. The rain and the clouds combine to produce a wet, close-adhering twilight which clings to the ground. Within this twilight, the drops find their way from leaf to leaf, falling and trickling along the wet surfaces, gathering at apexes and falling again, reaching the litter covering the forest floor. All here is a dark patina of browns, burnt and raw siennas, and gray.

Trickles of water flow through the fallen leaves and root mat comprising the forest litter, gaining in slight, diminutive volume, growing bolder with the descent in slope and aid of gravity. A group of these trickles bursts upon an instant of juncture, combines and flows as one. The water flows clean in the cacophony of splintered raindrops, all falling and splaying from leaf to leaf.

Now the nascent water finds its way to a spring, welling darkly from the leaf-moldered ground. Up from the depths of earth, seamed with roots and searching filaments, comes this lucid, dark water, smelling of earth and decay, and into it flows the little streamlet, formed from the drops which collected and flowed from the leaves. Now the stream welling from this spring flows ever down, searching for its union in water. And so flow a million drops and a hundred springs, into the Río Negro, into the Río Cotón, into the Río Coto Brus, and into the Río Cedro.

Days earlier, over the Caribbean, this same water had lifted from the surface of the ocean and formed in clouds. These clouds were driven to the shore and, by mechanisms unknown to us in the weather, interacted with clouds brought in from the Pacific, and the water thus borne into the atmosphere was released and fell as rain. As this rain, converted now into rivers, finds its way through the darkened forest, it occasionally breaks over the precipices of stone, and its thunder in waterfalls is lost in the solitude and desolation.

For the men gathered in the home in Las Cruces, the rain has meant hours of struggle for some in jeeps and four-wheel-drive trucks with tire chains and winch cables to get over the road and reach this destination.

"My land is being invaded by squatters," one of the men at the meeting says.

Others nod. "My land, too," they respond.

And through the deep seams in the forest flow the surge and the thunder of the rain-swollen rivers.

Each of the incidents I've described in this chapter was part of the collective life of the frontier. The road leading to the coffee receiving station was the road passing in front of Finca Loma Linda. Our oxen and cart were part of the effort to bring the coffee to market. The home of the man and the woman and their baby was that of my neighbors; the meeting at Las Cruces was one at which I was present. Always in the remote forest along the Talamanca Mountains there were the solitude, the rivers, their story in the night, and the shadow and the rain.

These circumstances were all part of a single fabric inasmuch as they were joined by time and place. We do not know how to characterize this fabric; is it life, are we joined by common experience, some common elements we do or do not know? The answer to such a question, its definition, is the task for the individual. But as individuals we know that these circumstances have been to us a moment in a synthesis of many things.

I used to carry my daughter Juliet on my shoulders through the rain forest in a section of land briefly added to Loma Linda, which we referred to then as the lower section. Julie was two or three years old during this time. The lower section was a sixty-six – hectare tract of primary forest we had purchased because a Costa Rican friend and his family was to acquire it some months later and become our neighbors. As it turned out, this family couldn't buy the land, and it remained ours for a few years.

For a time I thought of including it in the development of Loma Linda. I mapped its important land features and streams, planning to use the Percheron horses in clearing some areas and farming there. But it was always too much for me and my family to do. Finca Loma Linda then comprised, as it does today, fifty-four hectares. Such an area was all we could reasonably expect to develop.

After we found ourselves the owners of the lower section, it became necessary for me to check it frequently, for at this time in the settlement of the Frontier, squatters were taking over forested land.

Who were these "squatters?" What was their relationship to those of us who were landowners? Some years ago I wrote a background report for students and faculty visiting the Organization for Tropical Studies field station at the Wilson Botanical Garden, here in Coto Brus. This report, like "Three Flights for Survival," described some of the things other settlers and I experienced in the early years of the settlement of this land. There follows some excerpts from this second report. The people described here were my employees or neighbors, people I knew, or know, personally.

The People Who Needed the Land

In the midpart of the decade of the 1950s, and as this decade drew to a close, many of the plans for the settlement of up to three hundred families in the Italian colony were beginning to appear unattainable. The agency running the colonization scheme, the Sociedad Italiana de Colonización Agrícola (SICA), attempted to accommodate its management to the unforeseen and decreasingly favorable circumstances of obtaining financing for the program. Construction of homes continued to go on; new colonists arrived at the colony; the airfield there was built, thus making this place in the rain forest less dependent on the airfield at Agua Buena. Great efforts were made to build rock-surfaced roads, and coffee was planted over more extensive land areas every year.

But even while these strides were being made, momentum was flagging, and the vision which had imbued the beginning with such promising prospects began to vanish. While these attempts at permanent colonization were being made by a handful of foreign adventurers, and the first warning signs of the eventual failure of many of the planned objectives of the project were appearing, another immigration was taking place which, taking its momentum from many of the developments made by the Italians, would carry the task of settlement into the future and create from the South Frontier the community of Coto Brus.

This immigration could be seen on many days toward the end of the 1950s. A man and woman would trudge up the rock-surfaced road from Corredores in the lowland at the fringe of the United Fruit Company banana plantations to Agua Buena, for the surface of rock had then been completed as far as Agua Buena. This extension of the rock-surfaced road was of some use to those making this trip by jeep or truck because the extra rock from Campo Tres to Agua Buena lengthened the surfaced road a little between Corredores and the Italian colony and made the distance where there was only a dirt track a little shorter—but not much; and it didn't matter really to the man and woman walking over this road, and, actually, it was easier to walk on the dirt than on the rock, because most likely they were not wearing shoes.

The man and woman carried a baby and a bundle. The bundle, a sack tied with twine, contained their belongings. The wife carried a second baby, for she was pregnant. So they walked up the road and hoped that a truck or jeep would come by and pick them up. Sometimes the drivers of the trucks and jeeps would pick up the people trudging up the rock road with a bundle and a baby. But sometimes there were no trucks or jeeps—or these would be full—and so the man and his wife would spend the whole day walking from Corredores to Agua Buena. During their journey it might, and often did, rain. These people, the man and the pregnant wife, were looking for work.

"Would you have work?" the man asked. They would do almost any work. The wife could work too, for a time before the baby's birth. They had almost nothing, no money, and would need first to find shelter and a means of buying food. So they went to the big landowners, people who did then own large tracts of land which they had not yet developed, and asked for work and a place to live. Now often the place to live was only a hut, because the landowners then were not making much provision for these people who came to look for work. But this hut was shelter, with its dirt floor and its rough siding and metal roof, and the man and his wife with their baby lived in the hut and worked on the land. In their hearts was an earnest wish: that in time they would have their own hut and their own land, and from these—with the help of God— move ahead.

In these years too there were single men who arrived in the Frontier—itinerant laborers they were sometimes called when it was thought necessary to group them and call them by name. These men were spillover, a consequence of the South Frontier's location adjacent to the coastal, lowland United Fruit Company banana plantations, which required the labor of hundreds of men. In the early years it was difficult to recruit labor on the South Frontier, and so any laborers who wandered up to the highland forest from the lowland banana plantations were usually offered work.

When these men first came to the highland, they said—if they said much at all—that it was cold. When they arrived looking for work they would have with them their belongings—a blanket and an extra change of clothes. They owned little else, earned only a little when they worked in the Frontier, and often spent what they earned on solace and an anticipated euphoria from liquor. So they looked forward through the work week to Saturday, which usually was payday, and which they hoped would be big, for then they could spend their money—and begin the next work week with nothing at all.

Often, when they could, they took their money to the brothels and bars in Villa Neily. When they returned to the highland, if they did, they appeared to have enjoyed very little comfort, only having spent their money trying to do so; they came back to work looking dejected.

To accommodate the itinerant laborers in the South Frontier, wooden barracks were provided on the bigger landholdings in the early years when the land was being cleared and planted. In such barracks the men would sleep on bunks in tiers or on canvas cots, hanging their clothes on nails on the walls, which were unpainted. In various niches and crannies of the barracks walls melted candle wax was stuck, blackened and adhering to the wood. Although no one read, and few knew how to (some of these men could sign their names), all liked to have a little light from a candle before going to bed. They did this usually still wearing their clothes, with a soiled and little-washed blanket pulled over, because here it was cold.

Meals were served at the barracks by a woman who cooked and her children, who were mostly young and who had runny noses and bare feet and were mostly unwashed. The woman who cooked, and washed clothes too, was usually pregnant—until she became old, which happened while she was still young. Her shape was not trim, because she was pregnant, but even when she was not pregnant—and this was not very often—she looked like she was pregnant because her body was stretched and tired in those places subjected so often to pregnancy and work. And the little girls, the daughters of the woman who cooked and washed, looked at the mother and tried to understand the men.

But they could not, really, for the men did not quite understand themselves—and a man who does not understand who he is or might become cannot impress children, other than in ways which make children slightly apprehensive of men.

This was the situation because the barracks was not a home, and the mother was not a wife, and the children were not the children of a family, and the men were not men who recognized themselves as being needed by a wife and a home and by children, and hence could not see themselves as really being needed in any important way.

But these conditions began to change in the South Frontier. More horses began to appear at the hitching rails and hitching posts in front of the little stores—*pulperías,* they are called in Costa Rica—which came in the course of early settlement. These horses meant men who had come to buy provisions to carry back to homes. The men would stand around the stores and talk, their pants tied or held up with an old belt, wearing boots and spurs, usually hats. There would be mud on the horses and on the pants of the men in the wet season. The men, gathered in groups of two or three in front of the stores, would say to each other, sometimes squatting, to get a better grip on their thoughts:

"I calculate . . . "—they meant the word as *feel*—"that I'm going to get a good yield from this planting." And they would squint and look at their thoughts in this way through narrow eyes.

Another man, who had been listening and thinking, would look down at the man who had spoken from below, squatting, and say: "Cripes! I have to figure out how to plant more!"

The men would go on talking like this, and in reality their words would not say what they meant—for they were men who had not paid any particular regard to learning a lot of words—but they would know what they thought, and they would communicate this to each other in these words, which if heard by someone else, a stranger, would not mean the same things they meant to the men. All of these men talked in this language they knew—abbreviated, given to short statements and to pauses, so that if you listened to their conversations it seemed that they could really not be saying much or meaning much.

"I calculate," someone would say, "that the *vieja* [the old woman] can help me with the planting. . . . "

When these men had gone back to their landholdings, which were to become farms, and worked on them for another number of days, they came out of the forest and mountains to the store on their horses and hunkered down and thought—with each other. But no one would have guessed that from this there was to grow a communality of understanding in the settlement of a frontier.

Almost all of these men were poor, and their families were poor. But they were not poor in spirit as were the men who went to the cantinas and brothels looking for an identity, to see if they could gain a perspective on how they should be men. The men who came from the forest on their horses knew who they were; they did not have to go in search of this recognition of themselves. They went home from the store, and when they got home they spoke to the *vieja*—who was "old" only because she was dear—and said those few things sometimes spoken by men. But they retained much more; they had thoughts which needed to break open, like seed in the earth, and this had to happen within, and then the men too would see better what was there.

A turning point came in the settlement of the frontier, and it turned upon an identification with home, which is more than an identification with self. This turning point began to appear when the men ceased to think of the women as a means of filling a need and began instead to think of the women as *fulfillment of* the need. "*Tengo que hacer la chosa para que la vieja y los chiquillos . . . ,*" the men said then when they were together. "I have to make a home . . . for the wife and the kids, and it, the home—and the future—have to be better than now . . ." became the pivotal concept upon which this future turned. So the future of the frontier lay in this desire to make a home—for my woman and our kids.

The kids at this time went to school wearing mostly the same clothes washed and put on again each day. Most had very little help from the parents in learning what had to be learned in school, because the parents could not read or write. For this, if not for so much else, the children must go to school. The father would say, when he must sign his name, "I can't write or sign"; then he would make his mark, and the sweat would almost come as he took the pen and made a sign. It looked like a scratch of ink or pencil scribble on the paper, but it spoke more than had the father written a lot of words about why the *chiquillos*—the kids—would go to school. The *vieja* never did learn how to sign her name or make her mark.

But her children, collectively, went on to win scholarships and attend universities all around the world.

The fathers would squat by the *pulperías* and say, "*Y hubo que echarle ácido a la jodida . . . !*" and look mean and angry—and sad. They, or the *vieja*, had had to pour battery acid into an ulcerating sore on the arm or the leg or the cheek of one of the kids to clear up a *papalamoyo*, a parasitic sore that ate into the flesh and wouldn't stop. They didn't know what to do when the parasite just kept eating deeper and wouldn't stop, making this hole in the flesh and later a deep scar on the child. Someone had thought of the battery acid—because you had to think of things to keep going—and sometimes the acid worked, if the person receiving it could stand it. The mother and father had also used the acid on themselves for the *papalamoyo*.

From these days and nights emerged a determination, a feeling, held deep by the men who spoke in truncated words and the *vieja* who couldn't write or sign, that this would get better. And it did.

In time.

But first an inertia needed to be created, for this was like the growth of a giant tree, this immigration and struggle with the frontier. The inertia began to gain strength when rickety buses crept along the narrow rock road clinging to the cliffs rising above Villa Neily and leading to the South Frontier.

Traveling on these buses were whole families—not like the man and his wife who had trudged up this same road afoot carrying their sack and their baby, but families who had sold a farm somewhere in Costa Rica and were now coming to this new land to make a home. They would be cautious, for they had not sold their former home and land for very much money. Here in the new land, all would be dear. Yet these people traveled in the cramped and uncomfortable bus with joy and an eagerness in their faces. Here was this new place, and they might make here a fresh beginning. Had ever a land looked more promising than this?

In this kind of family were a mother and a father. The mother was not so old, but she did not look young. She had not looked young since she had been a girl, a very pretty girl. Now she was a mother and she looked like a mother, like one who knows the feeling of love, given and received, and of pride in her children. And there were many children, the older ones taking care of the littler ones, except the baby, who was carried in the arms of the mother. Often on the long trip the children would want to pee, for they were not much accustomed to having to be on a bus, and the baby's diapers would have to be changed. So the bus would stop and the children would get out. The men would get out too and unbutton their flies and stand behind the bus. When the bus came to a filling station or a little place to eat, the women would get out too and all would go to a privy, the mothers lining up and waiting their turns.

Families traveling in this way always had something to eat. Usually there were things to buy along the way: almost always many kinds of fruit, ice drinks with condensed milk poured over the top, candies and cooked meats and tortillas. The children would eat with merry faces; it was not so often that they could have all these treats. They had been told about this bus trip and had been talking about it for months—and now they were riding on the bus and there were lots of things to eat. And the baby had its bottle with a sweet drink so that it wouldn't cry.

The father looked keenly at the other passengers on the bus. Maybe someone here would be an owner of land in the new region to which the family now journeyed. The father was alert, because the first test in the new land would be to find a place for the family to live and for him and the older boys to work. He would lean forward and look with a friendly face at the man across the aisle on the bus—for the man looked as though he might know about this new place—and say, with an expression of both humility and pride (he was humble because he was coming to a new land, and he was proud because this was his family), "Are you from there?" and the father would look at the stranger with genuine interest, wanting to know. If the man was from there, from the new land, if this was a man who knew of this place, the father would listen with a friendly, studied face to what he would relate.

The stranger would say, "We came"—and he would mean himself and his wife and their children—"three years ago, and the corn— and, listen, you should see the beans—!"

And the father would lean forward and his eyes would be alert and intent, and he would hear this report of the man and his family on the new land. The older boys, the sons of the father, would look a little askance at the man because here was someone who had experience about this new land and would know. Then the father would explain to the man how he and his family were coming to the new land—coming from another place, Guanacaste, where they had sold their little farm. "But they still owe me some payments . . . ," the father would say; and the man who listened would understand and know that land was seldom sold for cash, or bought for cash even, and that always there would be payments. He had sold his little piece of land too—for this man and his family had also come from Guanacaste.

"The lands are tired there," he would say, this man who lived now with his wife and their family in this new place.

The father and the sons—for the sons would now be listening, and the mother too, although only from a distance, for this was the talk of men—would listen and nod, and the father would say (and the sons would look as though they would know), "But listen, this new land has a fame . . . , and the reports about it . . . ," and the father would look wise, but only in the way a man looks who is new and does not wish to look wise but wishes too to show that he has appreciation for this new land, so that others can see that he has appreciation for it and for them too.

And the man sitting in the seat ahead of the father would nod and say: "But listen, you should see the corn . . . and the beans, and the coffee!" and they would all smile and the sons would nod and be knowing. Then a big buxom girl in a simple plain dress—she did not have any particularly fine dress for traveling, but this was her best dress, and she did use it for just special things, like traveling, only the family had never traveled—with her strong country legs and her open, good-natured face would get up from her seat in the bus and go to help the mother with the baby. In the faces of the mother and the girl there would be much similarity, for the mother was what the girl would become. And then all the family would look out the window of the rickety bus, because it was creeping now along the edges of the cliffs on the Fila de Cal, this bus made on a truck chassis and put together by hand, and the girl would say: "Oooo, *papá! Mirá*—look at the great hollow!" And the whole family would look from the windows of the bus, and there would be a big expanse of land falling from and below the edge of the road beyond the bus; and the family would look timidly at this road, the father and mother exchanging glances. The father would look knowing and smile too, but in his eyes there would be a caution and a watchfulness, for he must be attentive and quick to learn in this new land. The bus would bump and groan on, and the little children would eat their candy, their faces in smiles.

All of this became part of the growth of a tree, the tree which grew from the land. And it was part of the earth—for all trees which grow do so as part of the earth, and they are of the sun and the air and of the rain—and such a tree as this grew now from this place where a few had sowed a beginning and others had come or were to come. Then each who came, or those who would, in time became part of this settlement.

Thus, when the family reached the South Frontier, they looked keenly and swiftly and deeply for any opportunity at all—for they were not wealthy, and they would make their start now . . . , for they must work, find in this new place some work . . . , because the small reserve of money brought here must not be diminished. And the father said, speaking to a landowner:

"You wouldn't have work?"

He smiled, and he showed by his smile that he needed work and that he would work here and put something of himself into this place for hire—"because we are poor," the father said without shame—and he would say, "And I have sons too," and hold up his hand to show not that these sons were of a particular stature but that they were of another stature too because they were his sons; and if the landowner were wise, if he knew by then the language of this father, the language spoken from the roots from which this father and his people came, he would know that the father held up his hand, palm forward vertically, and facing the landowner, to show not just the stature of the sons, but the stature of the father in the sons and the sons in the father. They were a family, and this was important, and it must be known.

And the landowner would say, if the father were fortunate, "Yes, I might have work for you and your sons. What can you do?"

And the father would explain that he and his sons could do all that people who grew on the land could do—work with their hands and think the thoughts that from such work would come and take these thoughts and make them with their hands into something planted. The landowner would nod, if he were wise, and say, "You can live in a tenant house here on my land. We are clearing land to plant pasture and coffee. . . . "

Then the father would shake the hand of the landowner—this was always done—and he would go back to the family and take the news that work and a place to live had been found. "And there is a house," he would say to his wife.

This house was not much of a house—the landowner had no income really; he was hoping to make an income from his investment on the land and his planting of coffee, and so he had put up a house that was really a pretty wretched house, but it was a place to take shelter. The mother knew this, and the whole family lived in this house.

There was no room in the house for such a big family—and the mother was expecting another child—yet they all lived together. There was an intimacy in this togetherness that was imposed and shared. Because it was imposed by circumstance—circumstance that all could see and know, the circumstance of being poor—it was an intimacy that grew strong. The family was engaged in a struggle to grow beyond this house and beyond this work.

Who were the squatters? Many were people who shared the attitudes and motivations I've described in the preceding pages. But like others of us, these people acted in response to many motivations. It is not the purpose of this book to analyze the characters and lives of the settlers of Coto Brus. Rather, it is to show how certain dominant feelings and attitudes, held collectively by a group of people, altered an existing environment and produced new arrangements of relations between the people and the land. Certainly the motivations of home, of acquiring land for a home and a farm, of family and the unity of family were strong motive forces in the settlement of this region. They continue to be strong motive forces in the community of Coto Brus. But the people of this community today, as was the case with those who were among the first settlers here, do not act and did not act solely with noble intentions. They are, and were, able to act selfishly and deceitfully, were prepared to recognize their self-interest and how to gain it. The people I described on the bus trip were my companions that day, for I was also a passenger on the bus. Later all in this family, at one time or another, became my employees; many of them today are my neighbors. All have acquired their own land, farms, homes. They are astute and hardworking; they represent no less today than they did thirty years ago the values I have described. But the tenure of land, its acquisition and subsequent management, represents many things other than these values.

Let's pursue this matter of land acquisition and ownership, for it has many implications in culture, economics, and environmental sciences.

The outcome of the meeting of landowners that rainy afternoon in Las Cruces in the well-furnished home of the American settler was, in one sense, a decision on the part of some of the owners to fell the remaining sections of primary forest on their land. Some of this land was titled and should not have been subject to threatened invasion by squatters. Nonetheless, threats of such invasion and even actual invasion did occur, land titles notwithstanding. Once land was occupied by squatters, it was difficult to get them off. Prevention, above all, was the preferred course to meet this problem. The common denominator for land tenure during those years was the indication that work was being done on the land. Again, "the land is for those who work it."

On Finca Loma Linda I did not have serious confrontations with squatters, although I lived with threats of such for decades. The main reason we did not have major problems with land tenure on Loma Linda is that we worked directly in all that was done on our land. We did not, and I still do not, delegate work to others, my employees, as an overseer. There is no work that has been done on this farm that I have not done with my workers in the field. Thus, the single, overriding divisor for land tenure—that of personal involvement in the work to make and operate the farm—was established.

However, among the men whom I joined that afternoon in Las Cruces were some who did not follow this policy of personal labor on their farms. These landowners saw themselves as separate and above the laborers they employed. Also present that day were owners who owned far more land than they could personally become involved with; no matter how energetic they might have wished to be in the operation of their lands, they could not possibly meet the requirements of personally dealing with all of it. In such instances expedients were adopted to maintain ownership.

The simplest—in effect it was indispensable—was to cut down any primary forest yet standing on the land. All recognized, as I have said, that it is work to cut down the forest. And so laborers were hired and remaining tracts of forest were razed. One farm which had at that time some extensive reserves of primary forest was, within a year of the date of that meeting in Las Cruces, almost completely cleared of any remaining forest. In this particular instance, the land so cleared was titled.

For a time such measures would hold the threat of squatter invasion at bay, but the time often was brief. In many places in Coto Brus squatters were moving onto land which had been cleared—i.e., the primary forest had been cut. So the next step the landowners took was to burn the land in the dry season. Here again, work was being demonstrated, conspicuously—and its conspicuousness was important. It might be added that less visible work, such as surveying, mapping gradients and streams, consideration of topographical and soil conditions, and the balanced progression of moving from one phase to another in the land-development plan, was not conspicuous and so was not looked upon as "working the land." It was part of conventional thinking at the time that burning was a step toward developing productive farmland from primary forest. But none of the landowners then knew how to successfully farm these large tracts of land. So some pasture grass seed would be scattered on the burned land, but mostly weeds and successional growth would come up there without adequate maintenance of the grass, and it was thought expeditious to burn the land again during the following dry season. After all, cluttered land with a lot of successional growth and the remaining logs and stumps from the forest could not be efficiently farmed, so burning was called for to bring the land to a state in which it could be farmed.

Such arguments were advanced to sustain the policies of razing the forest and subsequently burning the successional forest. But in reality, for many landowners, the motivating force in reaching such judgments was that of demonstrating their work and development of the land so as to keep it.

On Finca Loma Linda I did not have to follow such a policy. We had titled land to begin with; it was not an unreasonably large tract for a family to own; and it never crossed the minds of any in my family that someone else would make this farm for us. The people who would have moved onto Finca Loma Linda and taken possession of it—and there were many—were aware that I was as ready as they to pick up the axe and machete and work from morning to evening on the land. And it would have been awkward to find themselves side by side with me doing this on my land.

This matter of working on the land should be carried somewhat farther, for it is fundamental to considerations involved in the management of the environment in the tropical New World. As I have said, I used to carry my daughter Juliet and later my daughter Elizabeth, and would so have done with my youngest daughter, Rebecca, had circumstances yet required it, on my shoulders when they were tots during my walks through the lower section. It was always fun to explore the rain forest this way together. We would cross streams on logs used as bridges high above the streams themselves. This was our land; my wife and I wanted it to be their land.

Another reason for making these walks through the lower section was to ensure that the land was not being invaded by squatters. Squatters acted under cover of the forest; only in special circumstances did they act in the open. A first step for acquiring tenure in the forest for a squatter family would be to make a *zocola*. This could not readily be seen from a distance, many times not even readily from the air. Then a *rancho* would be built and the family would be moved in with the children. When the mother and children were in residence in the *rancho,* it would be difficult to move these people out, for they would be dependent for their livelihood on the land. Then they would demonstrate their ability to use the land by finishing the clearing of the forest and planting. The initial part of this work could happen in a matter of days.

One afternoon when I was putting the tools away at the end of a workday, one of my employees came to me and said, "I and some of my friends have moved onto the land you call yours on the lower section and we want you to go there with us so that you can see the boundaries we have made and see what is ours."

The lower section was titled, and I had a copy of the title in my office file. I took this copy with me in our pickup truck to the Rural Guard station here in Cañas Gordas, showed it to the lieutenant there, and explained what had happened. The lieutenant and two guards came with me in the truck, and we drove to the home at some distance from the farm where most of the squatters were then staying. By candlelight that evening we had a tense meeting with them.

"This man has valid title to the land; you are acting illegally in attempting to take possession of it," the lieutenant said.

"He is not using the land; it is worthless in forest," they replied.

"That is beside the point; the land is legally his."

"The land is for those who need it, those who work it. He is doing nothing with it."

"It is titled land; you can be arrested for invading it."

There was a moment of testing, of tension in the candlelight. Then one of the squatters said, "Then he must pay us for the improvements we have made. We have made a *zocola;* he must pay us for this work."

"On the contrary; he can charge you for damages on his land; you had no right to do the work."

The matter ended here; there was no further trouble with these men. They recognized that they could be prosecuted under the law if they persisted in their work on my land.

But as an interesting sidenote on Costa Rican culture, let me add that my employee's family, the employee who had been one of the squatters, returned at a later time to work for me. And one of the men who was that evening among the group of squatters visited Finca Loma Linda twenty years later with his wife and their children on an outing for the children, and the man said to me, "You know, this is the only farm now where we can come and bring the kids to see the forest. It is good that you have left some standing."

What I mean in introducing these incidents is this: In a new region that is being settled, ownership, tenure, and management are constantly being tested. There is no such thing as a relaxed tenure of land under these conditions. Just as every creature and incidence of life in the forest and the environment which ensues from it must constantly be prepared to meet a threat to its existence, so too must owners of land in a new region be prepared to demonstrate that they are competent to be owners. I know of no condition that weighed more heavily on those of us who owned land during the early years of its settlement than this. It required a tenure far more strict in the sense of this word than is normally attributed to the term. For no sooner had a landowner left his farm for even a matter of a few months, for whatever reason, than someone was prepared to move onto it and take possession—even of developed sectors.

The tragedy was that demonstration of ownership was made—or forced—in the wrong manner, and the rain forest was sacrificed. Instead of rewarding deliberate and long-term planning, a husbanding of forest resources over a period of decades while understanding and learning about the requirements of the management of the new lands, conditions on the Frontier created pressures on landowners that often led them to follow the easy path to show that they were working and thus to raze the standing forest and to carry out subsequent burning.

A general impression is that squatters are landless people who are deprived of access to a livelihood by large landholders who are not using this land and refuse also to make it available to the people. Instances such as these were seen in the early years of settlement in Coto Brus. Such large landholdings were eventually subdivided and made available in family, farm-size holdings. This redistribution of the land usually occurred when one or another Costa Rican government agency intervened.

Another widely held impression is that financially powerful foreign interests have held large sectors of land and kept these away from the citizens of a given country. This happened much less in Coto Brus than, I understand, has been the case elsewhere. What should be noted, however, is that native landowners, the Costa Ricans, were threatened by efforts to take over their land by other Costa Ricans. Specifically, here in Cañas Gordas and within a few kilometers of Finca Loma Linda, a number of sectors of land held and being farmed by Costa Rican farmers were threatened or invaded in attempts to dispossess the resident owners. These attempts did not follow the norms I outlined earlier, in which landless families moved onto forested land. In the case of two such attempts here in Cañas Gordas, developed, fenced pasture land was the target, and some families attempted to take possession of land which belonged to their neighbors, even while they had some land at the time themselves. These efforts did not succeed, but they underscored attitudes relative to land tenure prevalent at the time.

The scope of this focus on land tenure should be broadened. Recently (between 1990 and 1993) many families in Coto Brus have moved away and left their farms because they were not able to make a living there. They left Coto Brus in search of employment in other parts of Costa Rica, usually in nonagricultural work. Ownership and residency on the land then was not a means of ensuring the support and well-being of the family. The possession of a farm did not, in itself, constitute a basis for this security.

The romance of what is new and unknown does eventually fade. While much on a frontier is yet untried and conditions for livelihood in the unsettled region are unexplored, this element of unknown possibilities poses a promise of reaching many exciting goals. Such were the aspirations of most of us in the beginning. It is only when many years of persistent work have failed to produce the reward envisioned that adjustments between objectives and the efforts to reach them are made. In the presence of our best efforts, much has been attempted; many of the attempts have not gained their purpose. These thoughts figured in the decisions of the families who left their farms to look for employment somewhere else. The home farm had not become a means of meeting the needs of the family; indeed, it would not meet the needs of another family who might move onto it. The whole picture of land's being a basis of the family's well-being began to change. Finally, in some instances, it became an anchor, a limitation preventing the family's achieving better things. The children needed opportunities and education; chained as they might have seen themselves on the farm, they concluded that they could not reach them. Far better to move to the city and chance its uncertainties than to remain with the known limitations of this place.

We might say that we have come full circle. In leaving other parts of Costa Rica or other places in the world, we have come to this unexplored frontier in quest of what may be discovered and found to be superior to the limitations we know. Now, these same limitations have emerged here. We know their ability to bind and restrict us; we have come here, we realize now, to find mostly what we already knew. But the truth of this matter lies somewhere else: it is what we do not know that must concern us, for we know very little indeed.

Returning to our aerial view of the forest region which became Coto Brus, we will see the same tapestry of forest canopy below us as noted earlier, that integral forest region which had not yet been settled. Had we the clear eyesight of a bird, we would distinguish differences among many species of trees from this aerial vantage. We would also see in the canopy itself—the epiphytes, the moss, the arboreal fauna and flora—separate elements in an overall complex of life. This view with such enhanced eyesight would be three-dimensional in a sense beyond that to which we are accustomed. We would not only see into the depth of the space from the top of the forest canopy to the ground; we would also see a multitude of strata in this space, distinguishing, as our eyesight pierced these strata, a natural world denied to human vision.

If we assume not only the bird's better vision, but also its ability to soar and hover in flight, we become aware that there is a further sense of depth and space in our realm. This is the physicality of the atmosphere itself. It is the air which supports us now in this overview of forested terrain. We become aware of currents within this air, of relative moisture in certain sectors of our flight, of changes in temperature from place to place. Relative to our height above the ground, we will feel differences in the composition of the air.

Were we able to use this same exceptional eyesight to see within the ground, we would discern from this high vantage many strata of life in the earth. We might so identify and give particular importance to what we call life, but there would be many other components of this overview of the forested region of Coto Brus which would be active, forming part of an interconnected, dynamic structure. Minerals in the soil would be changing in molecular structure. The passage of water through the soil would be altering the relationships of substances through which it passed. The droplets of moisture in the air would be affected by the energy in the sunlight and would interact with the elements in the air. The darkening of an area, through the passage of a cloud, would slow processes dependent on a relative temperature in the soil.

As our flight over the area of Coto Brus progressed, we would become aware that this part of the earth's geography was composed of more and more things. Coto Brus, then, would not be a moonlit quagmire where men are struggling with oxen and carts, the grinding of corn to make tortillas in the hours before dawn, the concerns about land tenure and who owns what; in other words, it would not be only a cross section of human life but also a three-dimensional complex of many others things. Some of these things would not be what we refer to as life; nonetheless, we would recognize that they are important.

The "masters of the earth," as I referred to them at the beginning of this book, the men and women who work closely with much in our environment and whose daily lives change things there, must become aware of their relationship to this "earth." The nature of our adversity is not that of a few perceptions, relative mostly to our conceived self-identity, which we interpret and think we understand, but only exclusive of what we vaguely assume to be a total complex which we do not know; it is the condition of our ignorance of who we are and what we are doing in what may be termed an ecological context.

While we were a smaller number of persons on this earth, we might have moved more freely from place to place, allowing for time to intervene between our venture at some given point of geography and another. Such an interval of time would have reduced whatever effects our presence upon that given segment of terrain might have caused. And before we might return to the same location, we might have spent time in a number of others.

There are more of us people now. It is no longer possible to move from one place to another as before because many of the available places we might choose are already occupied. We therefore must stay more stationary and accept as more closely related to us those products of our lives which, under less populated circumstances, we might not have had to recognize as our progeny.

In less than fifty years the frontier of Coto Brus has emerged in a world of tighter population, more exigent demands upon the resources of our environment. A half-century has bridged the gap from a time of isolation and adventure to one of a complicated social spectrum of human needs and desires.

But to the extent that we identify this present condition of our life in Coto Brus—and I am using the comparison figuratively—with a set of limited, human, personality characteristics, we will increasingly run amok in our management, and our condition of being managed, in this environment.

This is because we are not simply managing; we are also being managed. The environment around us, its life systems and their substrates, is not a complex of indifferent entities waiting to be influenced by us. There is much in this complex which seeks the fulfillment of its existence, and, in so doing, affects us.

It will be difficult for us to attend a meeting of landowners on a rainy afternoon in a comfortable home in Las Cruces and, while we are pondering our troubles about whether or not we really own our land, be aware too of the thunder of the rivers in the mountains along the slopes of the Talamanca Range. Or, while we are struggling to get the sacks of coffee through the mud, perceive that the mud also is a condition related to the physics of the soil. We may wish to dwell on those things which are peculiarly ours when analyzing the nature of our adversity. However, as we become more tightly enmeshed in the results of our work in this environment, we will not have the same opportunity to simplify our perspectives that we enjoyed earlier.

There is much in this environment that we would like to manage. We would like to see our soils become more reliable storehouses of plant and animal foods without being subject to much that, as farmers, we must do to them today. We would prefer not to be doing many of the things we are doing to the air and water. We might look forward to a time when we would carry out more reforestation. We would prefer not to produce food which we suspect might be contaminated by residues of chemical pesticides.

Certainly, at the beginning of our residence on this land we were able to isolate many of the elements in nature as our adversaries. We needed roads, electric power, schools, hospitals. We have them. We also need to learn that, when our most apparent needs have been satisfied, we share this segment of the planet with much that is just as well established and just as firmly committed to continuance as we. To the extent that we recognize this counterpart of existence as something separate and irrelevant to ourselves, we will make the task of understanding it more difficult. We had better look for the insights in our own nature which will help us understand this other nature, which, too often, we hold to be external.

SEVEN

The Grain of Gold

*I*n Costa Rica the coffee bean is sometimes referred to as *el grano de oro,* the grain of gold. The country has a long tradition of coffee production, with many of the highland areas in the Meseta Central producing some of the finest-quality coffee to be found on the export market. The *grano de oro* classifies as "strictly hard bean," a term in coffee grading denoting highland Arabian coffee for brewing. Although the quality of its coffee does not rank as high as some of the coffee-growing areas in the Meseta Central of Costa Rica, Coto Brus some years ago became the country's highest-yielding area in coffee.

The crop bears a single harvest annually, and in Coto Brus this occurs during the wettest time of the year, during the months of September, October, and November. During the early years of settlement in Coto Brus, under the heavy rains by evening at the coffee processing factory, called a *beneficio,* oxcarts, packhorses, trucks, jeeps, and tractors arrived at the receiving platform laden with ripe berries.

The *beneficio,* a large complex of connected buildings roofed and sided with corrugated metal, several stories high in some places, is divided between the "wet" and "dry" sides. The wet side is built on a sloping gradient in the land so that the coffee berries can be carried by gravity in flumes of water through the processing machinery. The receiving platform is a large concrete slab on the ground, partly under roof, partly exposed to the weather, located at a high point of the gradient in the *beneficio.*

On this night at the *beneficio* the rain is falling steadily and the drops appear as relucent streaks against the electric lights illuminating different points at the receiving platform. Coffee growers, wearing raincoats or plastic capes, are arriving from several places in the region, some many kilometers from the *beneficio.* Those growers coming down from the mountains above the *beneficio* at Agua Buena have arrived with pack trains of horses, each horse carrying three sacks of ripe coffee berries. Men and horses are marked with the mud of the trail and the late afternoon weather, the mud showing above the saddle girths on the horses.

Few oxcarts have come from these mountains, the trails there being impassable now to all save pack and saddle animals and people afoot. Oxen and carts have come in from other areas, not from the higher mountains, but where the roads are less steep. But here, too, the heavy spatters of mud reveal their story on the oxen and carts and drivers.

From some districts around the *beneficio* tractors and four-wheel-drive trucks and jeeps are bringing in coffee from a few receiving stations and some farms located by rock-surfaced roads. The elements unifying the men, the animals, and the vehicles around the *beneficio* now are the starless, close night; the rain; the ripe, fruity-smelling coffee berries; and the slow, tedious, and deeply interrupted roads and trails.

For days now the sound of the big engines running the generating plants at the *beneficio* have throbbed through the hours of daylight and darkness. Shut down only for servicing, the engines run constantly, supplying the electric power for the maze of machinery in the factory.

At the receiving platform the men are tired, but they wait patiently for their turn to deliver coffee. The packhorses are unloaded immediately; sacks of coffee, piled in groups, clutter the platform periphery. The horses, relieved of their loads, stand in the rain, steam rising from their bodies. Jeeps, tractors drawing wagons, and trucks jockey for position among the horses and sacks and men, moving eventually up to large, steel boxes, beside each of which a steel lever stands upright. The coffee berries are poured from the sacks, or directly from the beds of the wagons, shoveled into an unloading chute in the tailgate here, into the metal boxes, the official measure. As the ripe, red berries fill to the top of this measure, the man taking the measure smooths the berries across the top of the box with a steel rule, and when the measure is complete and thus leveled, pulls the lever to release the coffee berries through a trap door at the bottom of the measure into a tank of water below the concrete floor and to one side of the receiving platform.

In the tank (called a siphon) sound, completely developed coffee berries sink to the bottom; immature berries float and are carried off through a flume opening near the top of the tank. The heavier berries leave the siphon through a lower flume.

Coffee is being delivered at two measuring boxes on the platform this night, the factory workers taking the measure and emptying the coffee into the siphon, marking on a pegged, numbered counter the number of measures poured into each box. Each producer's coffee is delivered and accounted for separately.

All around the wet side of the *beneficio,* for days and weeks, there has been the slightly fermented, pleasant smell of ripe coffee berries. It bears no resemblance to the smell of roasted coffee beans, but for coffee growers it is just as much a part of the story of coffee as the fragrance of brewing coffee is for consumers. Seen from this hilltop at the receiving platform tonight, the lights of approaching tractors bob along the road coming to the *beneficio.* Carbide lamps can be seen too, approaching slowly with the clack, clacking sound where men are coming with laden carts and oxen. As the men carry their sacks of coffee up to the measures after off-loading them from the horses on the receiving platform, they pour out the coffee into the metal boxes, then shake out the wet sacks and fold them, for they will go back on the pack saddles, and the men and their horses will be making yet another trip down from the mountains tonight.

Below the platform and the siphons, on levels descending from these, is an intricate complex of flumes, whirring belts, the great turning drums of graders, the coffee pulping machines shuddering constantly and disgorging films of freshly pulped beans, electric motors, lights, catwalks. Shadows and light play across the belts and turning pulleys. Moths and nocturnal insects swoop and flutter around the lightbulbs. There is a sense of efficiency here, of an ongoing process which does not halt, with each machine doing its part; the ever flowing water in the flumes; the ripe, pulpy coffee berries; the beans after pulping, flowing from one channel, from one level to another. Men with flashlights move along the catwalks, checking adjustments on the machines, making corrections. Occasionally there is talk, but mostly there is the clatter and shaking of the machinery and in the background the throb of big diesel engines rumbling into the darkness.

After leaving the pulping machines and going through grading drums, the silvery-white coffee beans, covered by a transparent mucilage, flow along flumes to the fermenting vats. These are large, concrete tanks filling now with coffee and water from the several gates that allow the pulped coffee beans to enter. Depending on ambient temperature, the coffee beans themselves, and the condition of the water, the beans may remain in the fermenting tanks from twenty-four to forty-eight hours. In the tanks, a natural fermentation process causes the mucilage adhering to the beans to soften and dissolve. After remaining in the tanks until this process is complete, the beans are drawn out to a lower level in flumes, where they are washed in clear water in narrow, concrete channels just wide enough to admit long-handled paddles which men walking at the edges of these channels use to force the beans against the current so as to create a washing turbulence.

Fermenting and washing carry into daytime work. Almost all coffee receiving is done at night, leaving the morning and afternoon hours of the following day for other steps in the processing. As the coffee leaves the washing channels, the beans, now completely clean of the mucilage with which they had been coated, are deposited by a discharge flume on a concrete drying patio. In some coffee-growing regions these drying patios may be extensive, covering many hundreds of square meters, because the climate allows for some morning hours of sunlight for natural drying. But in Agua Buena and most of Coto Brus, there is little morning sunlight during the coffee harvest, and the drying patios in the *beneficios* are used mostly for drainage. Here the beans are piled by men working with aluminum scoop shovels; the surface water runs off the piles and is carried out at drains in the patio.

The livelihood of most families in coffee-growing regions, such as Coto Brus, is dependent on what takes place in each stage of processing in the *beneficio*. The operation of a *beneficio* is partly an art, partly a science, and traditionally the men in charge of the overall process, the *jefe de patio* and the *beneficiador*, have worked hard for their positions, moving up to them from boyhood. Any mishap in the processing of the coffee in the *beneficio* can drastically reduce the market quality, and value, of the final product.

At the same time that the fresh berries are being received, pulped, graded, fermented in the wet side of the *beneficio*, fires are burning in furnaces throughout the night in the dry section of the complex. The furnaces, made of firebrick, are stoked with firewood by shirtless men in shorts, sweat gleaming on their bare backs and legs. The steel door of a furnace is thrown open, flames glowing white, and large chunks of firewood are thrown in. The furnaces are fired by forced air from turbines, and the heated air is forced through wide, overhead pipes to the dryers. These dryers are massive, revolving drums, turning on heavy arbors, rotating slowly. Temperature, air current, load, and relative entry moisture of the coffee beans all come into play to decide the length of time the beans will be turned under the hot air circulated within the drums. An error in drying time in these drums can cause an entire batch of beans to be overdried, become brittle and glassy, and, when finally leaving the *beneficio*, be sharply degraded in value.

Throughout the dry side of the *beneficio* at night, strange phantoms in firelight dance around the furnace doors, the rumble of the drying drums wearing into the lengthening hours, the electric lights everywhere illuminating men tending the machines, and a different fragrance impregnates the air, a drier fragrance, that of the drying coffee beans, a mellow aroma.

When the beans emerge from the dryers, they are carried on conveyor belts or worm elevators to holding silos where the coffee may be stored for several weeks, even though not yet completely dry. This allows the *beneficio* to operate at peak load during the height of the harvest; once the harvest begins to decline, some batches of beans held in the silos may be taken back to the dryers for a few hours more to complete the drying time.

As the berry picking ends, usually in December or January, the engines and machinery in the dry side of the *beneficio* will continue to rumble for several more weeks as the final steps in the processing are completed. These are the removal by machinery of the parchment membrane clinging to each seed, or bean, the grading of the beans, and the polishing to remove the "silver skins," a finer, inner membrane. The parchments are stored in warehouses near the furnaces and will be used to fuel the furnaces, burning with intense, short-lived heat.

The export-quality coffee beans are readied for shipment in burlap sacks bearing the trademark of the firm operating this *beneficio*. The coffee is sold to bidders all over the world; quite a bit of Costa Rica's best coffee went during these settlement years to European roasters.

I have had no personal experience in the operation of a *beneficio,* but for a few years I served on the board of directors of the Agua Buena Coffee Growers Cooperative, the owner of the *beneficio*. I was also a coffee grower over a period of twenty-five years, and I delivered coffee from Finca Loma Linda to the *beneficio,* first with packhorses, then with our oxcart, then with a four-wheel-drive pickup truck, and then with a tractor and wagon. I never used the Percheron horses, however, for coffee delivery. The road conditions were always too muddy for the heavy draft animals.

During any year at the time of coffee harvest, the *beneficio* is the center and pulse beat of the whole coffee-producing area. But the nerves ramify from this central point to each farm and outlying district where growers are trying to bring in the harvest. It is a tense time for the growers because many things may happen over a period of but a few days to cause the loss of a substantial portion of the crop. It is a time of opportunity for the pickers; all members of a family, from the children to the older adults, may now earn money.

This book is not about coffee production. However, the lives of the people of Coto Brus are closely connected with the crop. Let's see how the lives of these people and this plant intertwine.

The coffee seedlings we planted earlier in our clearing in the rain forest find themselves in an environment full of many diverse things. From our point of view, this environment, resulting from the clearing of the forest we have just felled and the single burn following this clearing, holds much that appears to be uniform. There is a regular opening of space above this land now; all of the forest has been felled. The sunlight will enter equally at all parts; air circulation should generally be uniform; the land is on an approximately uniform gradient; certainly the rainfall will be the same everywhere. So too will be the temperature, and because the surface of the land looks about the same, we expect the soil fertility to be pretty much uniform. In short, we expect uniformly good growth from this planting of coffee.

We have also planted the same kind of seed. In our nursery all of the seeding was with the *arabigo típico* variety. This, we have been assured, should be a good variety for this climate, this soil. We know that it does very well in other coffee-producing regions of Costa Rica. It is true that the seedlings we have transplanted here in the clearing, at one year of age, did not all look as uniform as we expected—some were taller, some with better foliation; still, here in the field, things should even out.

These are all very human assumptions; they are also quite ingenuous.

We think in terms of uniformity and hope for uniformity because we would like to have uniformly high, sustained yields. This is our objective.

But the sunlight actually does not reach all parts of this clearing uniformly; some coffee seedlings will be in the shade of stumps and logs, others will be at the edge of the standing forest. Because of this, and for many other reasons, the temperature will not be uniform.

Air circulation will not be, either. Rain may fall in the same way over the clearing, but its impact will be felt differently in different locations because of the canopy of obstructions from the fallen forest as well as the nature of the cover of leaf litter or some vegetation on the ground. Most of all, we will learn, the soil conditions will not be uniform; in fact, they are about as dissimilar as can occur on a section of ground under natural circumstances anywhere.

Are all of these things important? For instance, how important is a slight temperature difference in one section of the clearing as compared with another?

The truth of the matter is that we don't know. I am speaking now on the basis of many years of research on Finca Loma Linda. The complexity of the systems we are investigating suggests, however, that these small differences are, in fact, important.

Possibly, one reason we question the importance of these minor variations in the environment of the clearing is that we have mentally classified them as "minor." Certainly, small differences in light and shade, humidity and temperature, a little more or a little less litter on the surface of the ground, don't affect us as we move from place to place in the clearing in our daily work. However, it is the coffee that must grow and develop well here, and all of these conditions may be perceived differently by coffee.

It won't take much time for some of these questions to be compounded. We might hope that it will not take much time for them to be answered. Yet at the outset of our experience on this frontier, questions will multiply and be confused; rarely will they be answered.

As the coffee grows or sometimes fails to grow in this clearing, dissimilarity becomes the one overriding circumstance of uniformity. Nowhere, really, is there any consistent line of growth similarity. The coffee planting here is a world of confusing signals; we suspect that we do not even detect most of them.

In the face of such considerations—and all farmers, particularly those who begin where there is no background of accumulated experience to build on, do face such considerations—the natural response is: *What can I do to intervene? How can I make a change, an improvement?*

e many of the things we may do will require a good deal of time—years in some cases—to prove their worth or lack thereof, we tend at this early stage of our work to equate "change" with improvement. As farmers we must act. Now, at this early stage of our work on this new land, we must assume that our actions will be the right ones.

It is because we feel called upon to do something decisive in this maze of uncertain possibilities enveloping our planting of coffee—on virgin ground—that we tend to work so much with the ground. We can shovel or hill, hoe or weed, dig water runoff diversion ditches, make terraces, undo things done earlier; all of this can easily be seen, and its extent and alteration of the surface of the earth makes us feel that indeed we are taking significant action. Later, we may think about altering the currents of air relative to our planting, take measures to influence intensity of sunlight and temperature, modify the humidity relative to certain sections of the land—all of these things will, in fact, be somewhat within our control, but first we are led to manipulate the surface of the ground.

Let's look ahead many years now to a time when some of the variables I have described in our coffee production will indeed be partly within our control. I am describing systems of planting carried out on this farm and followed generally elsewhere in Coto Brus at the time.

This clearing, with all its obstructions, which saw our beginning, now has become a coffee plantation, a single tract of coffee; the term for it in Costa Rica is *cafetal*. All of the branches and many of the logs and stumps from the forest have now rotted away in the field. There are yet the biggest stumps and logs, but they are much decayed. Our coffee trees stand at about two to three meters in height. They are willowy, bending gracefully, rather than growing rigid and straight. Each coffee tree is composed of two, three, or four vertical stems, and all along these stems are the lateral primary, secondary, and tertiary branches. The leaves are a dark green, except at the growing tips of the *arabigo típico* variety, where they are a light bronze. The mature leaves are full; they are wide, well developed. Each coffee tree here seems to have reached an adjustment with its environment. And this adjustment is positive; the coffee is growing well.

Above the coffee are shade trees. These are *inga* (*Inga edulis*), leguminous trees of a low stature, with many lateral branches and broad leaves that are somewhat pubescent, rough to the touch, and marked in places with silver. These trees are traditionally, along with the *Erythrina* family, the trees most used as shade in coffee production in Costa Rica. There are two worlds in our coffee plantation, our *cafetal*, now. One is the world of the wet season; the other is the world of the dry season. The *inga* trees will carry about the same amount of foliage during both of these seasons. We manage these trees in conjunction with the coffee. Under the *inga*, and carpeting the ground in the *cafetal*, is a thick carpet of leaves, some freshly fallen, others in different stages of decomposition. The depth of this leaf carpet from the shade trees, from its top surface to the ground, is impressive. In places it is as much as eight to ten inches thick. In the dry season this carpet is crackly, the leaves sonorous underfoot. In the wet season it is moist, resilient, yet never sodden.

Taken together, the coffee trees and their shade trees form an environment. In this environment we manipulate many things. We prune the shade trees as well as the coffee. We have determined density of shade as well as density of the coffee tree population on a given tract of land by our planting spacing. Because of this we have considerable control over light and shade, and, as a consequence, control over temperature. Air circulation within the coffee-shade complex is also a matter over which we exercise some control. Through pruning we may open more air space or leave it less open.

In the soil we have created an ideal growing medium. There is no tillage here; weed growth is only light because we have spaced our coffee trees and shade trees in such a manner as to take advantage of the light reaching them from the sky but not to allow so much light to reach the ground as to encourage weed growth. Nowhere is the soil exposed to either the sun or the direct action of the rain; everywhere it is covered with leaves. If we reach into these leaves we discover that there is leafmold at the bottom of the carpet. In the dry season there is moisture, and in the wet season the mold remains aerated. At the interface of the mold and the earth there is a place where the mold begins to become part of the mineral soil. Here there is such a mat of coffee rootlets as to be almost beyond belief. There are hundreds of square meters of what appear to be spiderwebs of fine rootlets, most belonging to the coffee trees. These trees are feeding at the surface of the soil; their roots are everywhere underfoot as we walk through this planting, only a little below the surface of the leaf carpet. Just below this fine web of coffee rootlets are heavier, more fibrous roots, the roots of the *inga* trees. And clinging to the finer ramifications of these roots are large nodules, the nitrogen-supplying nodules of leguminous trees.

Erosion does not affect this *cafetal;* we have been here during the heaviest rains. The water strikes the surface of the leaf carpet, then seems to disappear within it. Under the leafmold, the fine segmenting and fragmenting of the surface of the earth by the roots causes the rainwater to enter the soil and be transmitted to lower depths. No matter how rainless the dry season or how heavily overlaid with rain and cloud the wet season, this soil is always moist in driest times, always resilient during the heaviest rainfall. We might pride ourselves on this environmental adjustment and balance in coffee culture. Not even in the rain forest was there such a carpet of leafmold, such a nice association among a few species of plants.

Under the conditions I describe, the coffee trees bear neither excessive harvests nor deficient ones; production is moderated by the control of light and the nutrient balance in the soil. There is a tendency toward a surprising uniformity in the annual yield of the coffee. At the end of the dry season there are delicate, fragrant white flowers on the coffee branches. In October, November, and December these same branches are festooned with bright, plump red berries.

Why will this Eden not last? If we return to our comparison of the coffee plantation with the rain forest, we will have some clues in answering this question.

For those who have not worked and lived with it for most of their lives, the tropical rain forest may be seen to be in its own way a kind of Eden, a place where much seems to be in balance, perhaps even harmonious balance.

Ecologically, this balance impresses us as possibly the finest, most intricately tuned arrangement of seemingly incomprehensible diversity that we know. This is probably true, but how to define its harmony? What more readily comes to mind with frequent contact with the rain forest is an element of struggle—teeming, resurgent, innovative struggle. It is this that may characterize the tempered adjustments of the rain forest, the peak and intensity of its multitude of life forms reaching for the highest degrees of individual and separate behavior. Finally, when you bring together millions and millions of such individuals, you have the most baffling and involved complex of separately vying entities of life imaginable. All come together in what we refer to as the rain forest; yet we haven't the slightest idea of what this all entails.

What is missing, then, in our *cafetal,* our coffee plantation under the shade trees? It is precisely what we would prefer not to encounter here; it is the same element of diversity in complexity and struggle we meet in the rain forest. For as it emerges upon the face of this environment, our youthful *cafetal* is, in fact, itself very innocent. It is a youngster, an upstart in this environment, simply poised to become the habitat of many other forms of life which have no place in our scenario for success with this crop. In planting the coffee and its shade, we have taken the first small steps in a journey of a thousand miles. We thought we had covered a considerable distance; in reality, we have hardly started on our way.

The *inga* shade trees and the coffee are new species to the environment; neither was part of the rain forest during the centuries it remained undisturbed. The complete removal of the forest in a matter of days created a pause, a short interval, in which many organisms would be compelled to seek new interrelationships. Into this pause we introduced our farming system. At the beginning we found our coffee growing very badly in the new clearing. As is often the case with new ventures in farming, we tended to blame the soil for most of our troubles. But eventually we found that light, temperature, and moisture relationships also were important in our successful establishment of a coffee plantation. Over a period of a few years we put together an arrangement of plant associations within a managed environment which appeared to be a solution to most of the problems we had faced at the beginning of the planting.

Now into this environment many other organisms have moved. Were we to study for a lifetime we would not be able to identify or understand even a small part of them. It is necessary to single out but one to illustrate how fragile and actually rudimentary our managed environment was. This organism is a fungus, and because it attacks our farm crops we refer to it as a disease. Its name in Costa Rican Spanish is *ojo de gallo;* to pathologists it is *Mycena citricolor.* Both the *inga* shade trees and the coffee are hosts to this fungus; it infects and produces circular (like a rooster's eye) lesions on the leaves, multiplying to such an extent that, on coffee, it produces extensive defoliation.

This disease thrives in just such an environment as we have created with the *inga* and the coffee. Now there are a thousand other organisms rushing in to take up residence in this new environment, which, we believe, we have gone far to create. Many of these new organisms will be parasitic on both the shade trees and the coffee.

What is taking place, of course, is what we tend to admire so much in the rain forest—partly because we do not have to make a living by cultivating the rain forest. Diversity is being introduced in this new environment. It is not, apparently, nature's plan that *inga* and coffee should exist here compatibly and relatively at peace. If *inga* and coffee are to survive, they should do so naturally, beset by a multitude of opposing forces, giving rise to whatever inherent or acquired strengths our two crops may generate. In time, if we were not to intervene, there would be a few *inga* trees here, a few coffee trees, a great many sickly and senescent plants of both species which, we assume, would shortly die out, leaving perhaps a few hardy individuals to battle for a place in the future.

We do, of course, intervene, and our intervention takes the form of all that technology, science, and personal resourcefulness can supply. As one kind of life within this environment, we are using those attributes peculiar to ourselves to fight our own battle and win our place here. We may feel that we are using unfair means in employing some of the measures we follow and that we have, because of our superior intelligence, an advantage over most else in this environment; but this is an assumption, and it has not yet been proved.

Because we are intelligent we have the ability to evaluate the measures we are following to maintain our place in this environment, and by such evaluation we often are led to reflect that our procedures might become better than they actually are. It may be that we will not prevail over an indefinite period in this environment, but if we are to be defeated it would be preferable that it not be by our own hands.

The point is this: In order to maintain the supremacy of our privileged group of plant or animal species within our managed environments, we are attempting to hold diversity at bay. It is possible, however, that there are other viable approaches to our objectives and that a wide diversity of life relationships may eventually be found to suit our needs.

Today in Coto Brus and elsewhere in coffee-producing regions, coffee is being grown differently than I have described. New, high-yielding varieties are being planted more densely; shade is little used; the coffee trees tend to become exhausted and need to be replanted over the years; producers rely on fertilization and spray programs. In other words, coffee production is much like the production of other major crops in different parts of the world. In *cafetales* coffee growers like to see coffee taking up space on the ground and as little of anything else as possible. This is very contrary to what we believe we understand about the rain forest. Are we right? Was the rain forest right? Possibly in time we will have some reason to think we know.

But all we are accomplishing here is a transition. We are not quite certain of where this transition originated and, certainly, we do not know where it will lead. In the process of moving from one point to another in terms of life interrelationships, one time stage to another, we make adjustments and surmises, and we presume we know what we are doing and where we are going. But there are further elements of this relevancy to our environment that we see in ourselves. Let's pursue a little further the story of coffee in Coto Brus.

In the morning before dawn the candles are lit in the shack at the edge of a stream where the family has slept. It is cold and damp in this shelter and, even though there are rough, unplaned boards on the floor, there is no sense of warmth, of this place's being a home. It is not a home; it is merely a coffee pickers' shack on a producer's coffee farm. The family here—many children, some but infants; the father and mother—are staying now in the shack, but they have come here to Coto Brus from another part of Costa Rica. They will be here for several weeks during the harvest; all in the family can work picking coffee and earn extra money. When the harvest is over they will return to their own farm, which is in an area of Costa Rica, the lowlands, where coffee is not planted. In contrast to the families described in earlier parts of this book, this family has come to Coto Brus looking for neither land nor a home.

In the shack this morning the mother and oldest daughters are first up to light the candles, make the fire in the hearth, and prepare the tortillas and the coffee. The men will be getting up a little later.

There is not much room here; all the members of the family are sleeping on cots, the children doubled or tripled in their beds. In the single room there is the strong, sweet smell of the syrup of coffee berries. This adheres to the wet clothes hanging on nails on the walls.

The clothes are wet because even when it is not raining the *cafetal* itself is wet most of the time. These days during the harvest are often sunless, and within the *cafetal*, under its shade, sometimes for days here in the close foliage, sunlight does not enter. The wet clothes hanging on nails and seen now by candlelight will be worn again today as they were yesterday and will be again tomorrow.

The men are the first to leave the shack, a little after dawn; the women will remain for two or three hours more, preparing the lunch to be carried to the field, getting the whole family ready; the whole family will be in the *cafetal* today.

The picking will be good; the family has been calculating the expected earnings from this day's work. As is usually the case in Coto Brus, the *cafetal* is on a steep hillside. The rows run diagonally across this slope and, seen even from a distance, the dark green coffee trees in the rows are burdened with clusters of red berries. There are three brothers and the father who have come from the shack; they meet now in the *cafetal* with other pickers and with the foreman. All pickers are assigned rows by the foreman.

Using baskets woven from vines cut in the few remaining segments of rain forest, the pickers move into the coffee, the baskets tied at their waists. Sometimes two pickers will work on a single row, but mostly each row is picked by a single person. There is talking, joking, some singing; for a few minutes sunlight appears in the sky. Soon the little stinging ants, the *cuiscalas,* which live in the clusters of the coffee berries, find their way into the clothing and onto the bodies of the pickers and sting, leaving a burning, mildly painful sensation that lasts for up to an hour. Fingers fly among the clusters of berries. Only the red or partly red berries (these are the berries that are mature) should be picked. But all coffee pickers will rake off whole clusters of green and red berries if they are not caught by the foreman, stripping the branches of their mature and immature berries and leaves to fill their baskets quickly. From time to time leaves are thrown out of the baskets, the green berries mixed in well with the red. The weight on the belts, against the back, becomes heavier.

By midmorning the women and children have joined the men, with the smallest children, one a baby, two just toddlers, parked on a couple of burlap sacks and a sheet of plastic spread on the ground, where they soon begin to cry because of the wet and the ants. Two of the older girls are pregnant and cannot tie their baskets at their waists. They put the baskets on the ground under the coffee trees, throwing the berries as they are picked into them. Weak sunlight now breaks through the clouds, and the wet clothes begin to dry. Still there is the pervading, not unpleasant smell of ripe coffee berries.

At about 10:30 the family takes a break for lunch. The baby and the little ones have been nursing from bottles of dark raw sugar, or *dulce,* water. From time to time the bottles stray from the burlap sacks or plastic and find their way to the ground, where the rubber nipples become covered with leaves and dirt. Now the mother and the pregnant sisters care for the little ones, cleaning the bottles and nipples, rearranging the sacks, trying to coax the children to sleep. There are about twenty-five coffee pickers this day in the *cafetal;* most have stopped to eat lunch. The family from the shack have rice and beans and plantains and tortillas, all wrapped in banana leaves. They all drink the *dulce* water. The meal is eaten from chipped enameled plates with spoons (forks or knives being considered superfluous). All sit on sacks spread on the wet ground.

Someone this morning has found a poisonous snake on one of the coffee trees; the matter created a moment of excitement. The foreman killed the snake, but, worse than the snake, really, are the caterpillars. The snake was unusual; the caterpillars are always everywhere. Like most Costa Rican countrywomen, the women in the family staying in the shack loathe the caterpillars, the "worms," as they call them. The very thought of having one on the skin is almost terrifying. Partly for this reason, today in the *cafetal* the women and older girls are wearing a peculiar garb. They have come to work wearing pants and shirts over which they have put on dresses. As yet in this culture, women do not wear pants; however, bare legs in the *cafetal* are subject to all kinds of assault from insects and stinging weeds, so the pants must be worn, but the women still come to work in dresses.

It is hard work. The waist and back become numb and cramped from the cumbersome weight of the baskets as they are filled with the coffee berries—and the reaching, ever the reaching for the higher branches, and the wet coffee foliage in the face.

In Costa Rica each seed, each coffee bean, is picked by hand. The berries containing the seeds—there are two in each berry—do not all ripen at the same time. There will be flushes of ripening spaced over several weeks during the harvest. As the berries turn red and ripen, they become swollen with water during times of heavy, pro-longed rains. Under such conditions the berries rupture and within two or three days after this they fall from the branches to the ground. Early tradition held that coffee pickers would recover any berries which had fallen, picking these up from among the leaves and litter on the ground. However, in time this tradition ceded to the tedium and slow labor involved in such work, and little such recovery of fallen coffee is made today.

By noon low clouds close over the *cafetal* where our family has been working; it begins to rain, and the mother and one pregnant daughter and the smaller children hurry off to the shack, there to make a fire in the hearth and attempt to dry some of the clothes in the wood smoke and to wash some of the clothes in a tub on a wooden stool near one wall. The older boys and the father, as well as one pregnant daughter, remain in the *cafetal*. All are wearing plastic capes. Yet the water runs down and into these as hands and arms are raised to reach for the higher branches and their clusters of berries in the coffee trees. Under sodden hats hair is straggled; faces become pale, drawn. This same pattern has been repeated now for several days: it has rained just after noon, and the picking has continued under the rain. A light breeze comes up, and from all parts in the *cafetal* where the pickers are working, the same complaint is made: "It is cold!" Indeed, it is cold now that all are wet. The pregnant daughter goes into the shack, and the boys shiver and look hopefully at the father. At length, the picking is stopped; the rain has become too heavy. All the harvested coffee must be carried to a central measuring location where the oxen and carts are waiting.

Throwing off the plastic, which is awkward now, the men help each other lift the sacks of berries onto shoulders and carry the sacks to the measuring place, an open area bordering a muddy lane. The men pour the berries from the sacks into the *cajuela,* a metal, cubical measuring box with handles, measuring exactly twenty liters when full. The pickers will be paid according to the number of *cajuelas* they have picked. The owner of the *finca,* the coffee farm, is here now, trying to encourage the pickers with light comments and jokes about the bad weather. He and his wife may have brought hot coffee and cups for the pickers to warm them under the rain; often the owner and his family will have been in the *cafetal* with the pickers, harvesting too, working with them throughout the day. All are aware that if this rain continues the coffee berries will start to fall to the ground, having become overswollen and waterlogged. There is a risk that part of the year's harvest will be lost. This sometimes does happen, but usually, by working longer hours and ignoring the rain, the harvest is brought in.

The story of the coffee harvest is not only a story of lightless afternoons and weariness and rain. There comes a time when, one night, the stars dance in a cloudless sky, the air grows chill, and those envoys of the transition of the seasons, the northeast trade winds, break over the silent and rain-quenched earth. In the morning the world awakens to a crystalline sky, and the dry season has begun. Now there is a song in the *cafetal;* the voices are merry. In the afternoon, late at the end of a dry day, the sound of the berries falling as they are poured into the *cajuela* carries music on the wind.

Throughout Coto Brus there are fiestas on the weekends. Firecrackers explode into the night as the Christmas and New Year holidays approach. At the fiestas in the plazas of the villages the families of pickers wear new clothes. The harvest is nearing its end, and there is money now, for a short time at least. People dance into the late hours.

But for eighteen years the price of coffee on the international markets was so low that producers in Coto Brus and elsewhere in Costa Rica and the rest of the world were brought to a point of failure. During the years when I participated in the management of the coffee growers' cooperative in Agua Buena, the cooperative was always near the point of bankruptcy. The co-op did not go bankrupt and it continues to operate today, but it shared in a long period of critically low coffee prices. Those of us who were coffee producers at that time understood that worldwide overproduction of coffee was at the root of the problems we were facing.

In Coto Brus this condition, which lasted from the mid-1950s until a little before the middle of the 1970s, could be considered as one of general poverty. Those investors who had come to the South Frontier to acquire land and invest in coffee growing gradually saw their capital exhausted with no adequate return on its outlay. The poor who had come to the South Frontier grew poorer. Eventually, a time came when any crop planted on the farms in Coto Brus would fetch a better price, in terms of adding to the value of the farm, than coffee. But there were no alternative crops to add value to the farms or land. Indeed, it was clear that no profit could be made with coffee, but then nothing else had turned out to be successful, either.

The region which had been the South Frontier and had eventually become Coto Brus presented at this time, the end of the 1960s, an aspect of broken endeavor. Everywhere roads alternated between impassable quagmires in the wet season and bumpy, partly rock-strewn tracks in the dry season. Farms along these roads showed a condition of general degradation. The coffee plantations were badly cared for; few growers could afford to buy fertilizer. The homes were frequently built of rough siding with dirt floors, with no glass in the windows, no electricity or plumbing. Children were barefoot, often naked from the waist down. Parents seldom could afford to see a dentist—had there even been a dentist in Coto Brus—so their teeth were decayed or completely lost. Intestinal parasites caused bloated stomachs in both children and parents. The forest mostly had disappeared; nowhere was there evidence of justification for its demise.

Those of the early settlers who had the means to do so left Coto Brus. The Italian colonization had not succeeded in meeting its broad objectives. A colony had been started; a settlement had been made in the rain forest; but financial well-being and a decent living from the land had come to no one. From the time of its initiation to a point twenty years later, the settlement of this frontier had demonstrated only many aspects of the inability of the people to meet the requirements of successful settlement. Although twenty years is not a long time in nature's scheme of life relationships, this period's end seemed an Armageddon reached by a road of exhausted expectations. Ultimately, the expectations were to be replaced by something akin to acceptance of inevitable poverty.

Over a region of mountainous terrain once clothed in primary rain forest a story had been written. Its pages could be seen in denuded hillsides, pastures sparsely grazed by cattle, abandoned or poorly cared for *cafetales,* successional forest returning natural systems to the land. No one wished to be known as an author of this story. There was a quiet sense of impotence on the face of this community. How defiantly had been lifted the arm in the presence of nature's challenge; how spent had become its blow.

Then a strange thing happened which no one had expected and none might have guessed. There were major freezes in the coffee-growing areas of Brazil. The price of coffee doubled for the producer in Coto Brus, then tripled. Like the wind which swept over the land at the end of the wet season, bringing with it the clarity of a fresh vision, a new day had come to Coto Brus.

This day could be seen during the dry seasons on many playgrounds, by churches and schools, on the plazas, on a Sunday. Toward midafternoon a jeep would appear on the plaza, driven by a boy in his teens. By the jeep would be walking a family, the father and the mother dressed in pressed, Sunday clothes, the brothers and sisters all attired for this day at the plaza. All in the family were intent on the boy in the jeep, this oldest son and oldest brother. The jeep would come to a stop in the plaza and the family would cluster around it, commenting, as though holding a critical, evaluating, conference. There would be an exchange of views between the father and the sons. The boy at the wheel would nod his head, and the family would move away from the car. Then the car would move several meters in reverse and stop. It would drive forward and make a turn and stop. Then the driver would execute several more turns, starting, backing.

None of the family would ride in this car. First, the son must learn how to operate it. The father and mother would know less about this than the son, and the younger brothers would look longingly at the son behind the wheel. On the faces of the sisters was a radiance of pride. The sky yawned over this plaza now, a vast, infinite blue. All to the east and west and north and south the land of Coto Brus expanded. There were no limits to this horizon. The sound of the engine of this car—indeed! that was an engine sound; had ever engine sounded such as this?—this car with its lights and spare wheel and bright red paint! The car moved forward and the boy at the wheel drove it with a growing confidence—and yet a certain disbelief—and the family watched as the clouds in the azure sky sailed on the wind over Coto Brus.

What was being seen that afternoon here at the school plaza in Cañas Gordas was, as I have said, being repeated in many villages in Coto Brus at the end of the decade of the 1970s. Families who had never entertained such a vision were acquiring their first car; and someone in the family, an older boy, was learning to drive.

That afternoon on the plaza at the school in Cañas Gordas after the practice session of an hour and a half, the jeep drove off the plaza and onto the road and, at a walking pace—for the boy would not shift out of first gear yet—returned to the home and the farm. And the rest of the family walked beside the jeep, for as yet none would ride in it until the son had thoroughly mastered all of the mystery of driving. On the face of the father as he walked with the mother and the other children home beside the jeep was a wistful expression, lost perhaps in the clouds and the sky, the expression of the years and the sun and the rain and the dark shadows and this family and the enigma of a strange land.

Along the roads now, leading through the various farming districts of Coto Brus, on the farms, homes began to appear with glass windows, flooring, interior siding, finished doors, and paint. Where there had been mud in the wet season and dust in the dry season, flower gardens began to take root. The coffee plantings were now relucent with meticulous care. Pruning was comprehensive, and replanting with new varieties was being carried out; the farms began to take on a neat, well-tended appearance.

The schools, which had been plain structures of rough lumber, were being replaced by well-designed buildings of concrete with ample eaves around the roof and large, airy classrooms. The children no longer went to school barefoot, and in the schools there were lunches planned for nutrition. The people of Coto Brus began to see themselves in a new light: they were not poor, they were able to reach into a world which, earlier, had been unavailable to them. And with this knowledge came a self-confidence and an ability to meet the responsibilities of civic and community growth.

The villages themselves began to grow. Banks extended their agencies from San José to Coto Brus. Stores began to stock more diverse and sophisticated merchandise. With more cars, there was more emphasis on improving the roads. Even electricity began to be thought of as a public service. More was expected of the national government. And the local municipal government found itself empowered to administer the public business on the footing of a viable economy. The people began to consider themselves the administrators of a collective treasury, the treasury of the bounty of this place and the industry of its residents.

Had all this been done by coffee, by the grain of gold?

In some respects, the answer to this question must be yes, for there is no substitute for a viable income; either people will make a decent living or they will not succeed. The increase in the value of coffee had indeed brought about most of these changes. But, once the changes had been set in motion, the matter of self-confidence, of trust in one's ability to meet the unknown aspects of the future and measure them by what had already been accomplished, took control.

There is more to the emergence of success here than the upswing in the value of coffee. We have looked at the forest and the new environment issuing from it in terms of its complexity of systems. It is no surprise to us, then, that the complexity of life, our own as a group or a community, goes well beyond this forest and its now modified, resulting environment. We live in a world where we do not only compete with the natural life systems of our particular segment of earth, but also with each other across great distances, in remote ways. This world is one in which we must achieve relative advantage: the coffee pickers with the coffee growers, the coffee growers with the *beneficio* management, the *beneficios* with the exporters and the roasters, and these with the retailers. The windfall for the coffee growers of Coto Brus, and elsewhere in some coffee-growing regions, was the misfortune, perhaps the failure, of coffee growers in Brazil, a country whose coffee production is so large that it has vast influence on world markets and the trade in coffee.

The life systems which govern our environment are not confined to the former domain of the rain forest; they are tied to the economies of coffee-consuming nations all around the world and with the intricacies of modern merchandising and trade.

If we go a step beyond this point in our outlook on interrelationships and their supporting or associative structures, we will see that global weather, conditions in the atmosphere, the seas and the sunlight and the wind affect us, sometimes in ways much more direct than we suspect. No one could have predicted the frost and low temperatures in Brazil. But these, combined with the mechanisms of international marketing, brought about an entire new outlook in a small part of Costa Rica.

We touch and mold. We may be either delighted or appalled at the work of our hands. We have seen in the tiniest granules of earth a mystery beyond recognition, and then, as though transformed by some magic in the moment, this mystery grows to encompass a universe. Is it no more than this, a few grains of earth in the palm of a hand, or did we, perhaps, touch a secret of our being?

We have been given an opportunity now to move ahead. There is momentum again in the settlement of this frontier. We must pick up the tools at our disposal and with these build something for tomorrow.

EIGHT

Children
of the
Settlers

*I*n Costa Rica a woman schoolteacher for the elementary grades is called a "child." She is called this by her pupils, but when these pupils have grown to adulthood many of them will still affectionately refer to their former teacher as *la niña*. Although these teachers may move on to teach at the university level, they will still be remembered by their former students as *la niña Emma* or *la niña Cecilia*.

The term sounds strange to our unaccustomed ears; indeed, there is no appropriate translation in English. This is an instance of the inadequacy of translation, for we are translating not a word but an aspect of culture.

La niña, the teacher, is a "child" because she is in some senses identifiable with her "children." The teacher is not a person who stands apart; she is one of a larger family, the community of Costa Rican children.

The term does not have a counterpart for a male teacher. There is no such thing as *el niño* for a man who teaches the elementary grades. Such a teacher is called *maestro* or by the title *don* and his first name. But here too there is no imposed separation between teacher and pupils. The teachers are respected; they are recognized as occupying advanced positions in learning, but they are also part of a group sharing equally in cultural values.

My daughters went to elementary school in Costa Rica. Since that time, there have been many groups from the elementary schools around Cañas Gordas who have come on outings and picnics to Finca Loma Linda. For such outings, there are always games, and always the teachers are as much a part of the games as the children.

There is a sense of unity with the children in these relationships— and I am describing the rural culture I know here in Coto Brus without supposing that this means that my knowledge is applicable everywhere—a sense of children being a central and orienting rationale of life. A main motive force in the life of adults is to care for and be with children. Much in community and adult life is interpreted as it relates to children. In this respect children are a strong link between and among families, *between* and *among* because these are links which tie a community together. *Within* families the same relationship holds true; the children are a reason for doing much that is done in the home over the years; they are a mortar cementing the adults' equilibrium.

In a community such as Coto Brus, recently emerged from its origin in settlement, such ties, with their emphasis on children, might be expected. Emergent communities with similar backgrounds have, in other places and other times, evidenced such capabilities. Rural life in the United States once did. These attitude of closeness within the family, with children, continue to prevail here.

However, the children of the settlers also live in a present molded by forces alien to and divisive of those ties of unity which characterized the family life created by their parents. What are the profiles of this first or second "native" generation following in the whispers of the rain forest? How will these children deal with the legacy of the forest and their parents' management of it?

Few generations will bridge such different worlds. As I noted at the beginning of this book, the South Frontier was actually an anachronism, even in its own time. It existed by virtue of its inaccessibility. Although for those settlers who bore the limitations of this isolation through two or three decades this did indeed seem like a long time, the same sense of prolonged deprivation of the comforts and attributes of the modern world did not affect the children in the same way. Once having left behind its roots of seemingly remote detachment, Coto Brus moved quickly into an association with all that its many windows on the larger world offered. Television and other media of communication, travel, education—all these and others became part of the life of the children of the settlers.

This generation needed also its own rationale—its own expressed attitudes—to articulate its relationship with the emergent present. Education—formal education—that very element whose absence had so acted as a limiting factor in the parents' lives, became a driving force of change in the children's expectations of the future.

How was this future to be interpreted? In many respects its definition was never clear. It is one thing to recognize the vacuous effects of the absence of a quality in life, another to interpret how that quality, in application, might operate to change and improve life. By this I mean that the children could well identify education as being a goal while also having no clear idea of just how that goal, upon its realization, might apply in their future. They emerged in a time of young adulthood when it was apparent that the bounds of limited professional training had been a handicap in the lives of the parents. It remained for them to define how they might overcome such a handicap through education in their own lives.

First, and practically, how much formal education could actually be applied in Coto Brus?—i.e., was there an economic infrastructure in this young community to support specialized training and knowledge? If not, then did education mean that the children would have to move away from family and community and look for employment and professional status in one of the cities?

Most of the children would remain at home if it were possible. The generation of children who came to early adulthood during the years following the freezes in Brazil while coffee prices remained high in Coto Brus could stay at home. The parents' land was subdivided or additional land bought. These lands were distributed among the sons and daughters. In all such instances coffee became the fulcrum upon which success was to balance. For several years these new landowners could enjoy a life of some financial success. Early on they built their homes, might even have bought a truck or jeep. It could well have seemed that this stability, security perhaps, would go on indefinitely.

But the price of coffee did not remain high for more than a few years; increased world production eventually brought the price down. With this, security and stability became what they always had been—transitory. Those children of the settlers coming to adulthood a little later than these more fortunate first ones found themselves viewing a different prospect with coffee. Now the perspectives projected through education became a dimension with no relevancy to the present condition of life. There seemed to be no workable means by which this education could be applied successfully at home.

All generations face their frontiers. Let's look at the frontier as seen by the first generation of native *Coto Bruceños,* the name by which residents and natives of Coto Brus call themselves.

It is unlikely that these native-born *Coto Bruceños* will regret the passing of the hardships, isolation, and inaccessibility that characterized the early years of settlement. But they will from time to time regret the passing of the "simplicity" of that earlier time. They may characterize this simplicity in terms of what they will interpret as a time of freedom from acquired problems, those problems that one generation passes on to another. The freedom of those rains and winds which fell over Coto Brus when the land had received the imprint of no human hand is gone now, irretrievably part of the past. And, as we have noted, that which is yet untried, the opening of a frontier, poses the promise of many possibilities which do not seem to be part of "land" that has been worked over by others' hands.

Such feelings, which do influence life from time to time, are probably more romantic than practical. And the people of Coto Brus are preeminently practical in their thinking and planning. Because of this, the children of the settlers do recognize the value of the work done by their parents. The home farm represents a concrete and solid value, and, generally, the children will remain here if the home farm can be subdivided and there is land enough to go around. They will do this if it is possible to make a living.

This brings us to a point of the merging of many of the elements characterizing this "new" frontier. It is a condition in which romance has recently been replaced by many established and unromantic exigencies. It is a condition in which education has suggested a hundred other modes of life without yet enabling aspirants to touch and experience them. It is a condition in which what is known and experienced is fraught with uncountable recognized problems, most of them highly complex in nature. Here then will surface once more the desire for an unknown frontier, where the placement of some specialized ability or training may cause the future to take on a personal imprint.

Some of the children of the settlers will study to become physicians, attorneys, engineers, veterinarians. Such students will usually have relatives in San José who can help with residence and study there. Other young *Coto Bruceños* will study for professions in electricity, building, mechanics. A large number would like to be employed in one of the government agencies or social services institutions. Some will study agriculture but, here again, with a view to obtaining a post with some government service or employment with a private business firm. The high schools, located at different parts of Coto Brus, will be offering courses in these many fields. And there are university extension courses and professional trade extension courses. In fact, it is not hard *not* to be educated in Costa Rica.

There are the dynamics of an emergent society, emergent in an unusual context. We had at the beginning of this story a highly complex and incomprehensible structure of natural systems represented by the rain forest. We have seen that this structure of systems, having been changed by the elimination of the forest, remains probably equally complex and certainly as incomprehensible after the forest has been removed. We have looked at the attitudes characterizing the life of the early settlers. Indeed, many of their straightforward confrontations with the forest and unsettled land do seem now rather "simple," less enmeshed in recognized tedium than life today. We now see a very complex human society taking up residence in this same environment, and, by virtue of number of persons and education and expectations, this society is more complex than that of the earlier generation.

Those who must now launch themselves from this infrastructure face a prospect in which new ingredients in the society of human relationships are active. Where to go with a background of study in teaching, medicine, law, agronomy, the trades? How to preserve those values of family and community synthesis so fundamentally a part of childhood? With more and more people aiming for positions in these professional fields, the number of positions may be, and probably is, limited. Fortunate indeed were the parents and grandparents who found their purpose in life to be setting the foundations for the growth of a new era.

This new era, for it marked a change from the rain forest to a settled society—still as complicated as the earlier one in its natural systems, yet much more complicated in its human systems—is, nonetheless, yet a frontier. This is what must be recognized.

Already in Costa Rica there are many doctors, many teachers, many lawyers. From a national planning point of view, there may already be enough people in these professions, in some instances too many. Yet the need for learning, for further education, is acutely apparent. We need to learn more, do more, become more competent in managing our environment, and this can be seen nowhere more clearly than right here at home, in Coto Brus. As a perspective on the horizon of this new frontier, this opportunity to apply education and specialized training at home, where problems are so familiar—and hence tiresome and seemingly unresponsive—is disconcerting. It is more comfortable to propose the solution of problems in prospect than to apply what is known today in an effort to overcome a lassitude of uncertainty.

There is really no difference between the old frontier and the new frontier in terms of their demands on our resources and abilities; the requirement to meet challenges is undiminished. We still must learn how to live well on the face of the earth; we must learn how to do this now in the presence of more people.

If the generation of the children of the settlers were to define its challenge in this way, what would be the result of such a definition? To approach this question—there is no "answer" to this question, only information leading to further questions—I'd like to describe an experiment we conducted some years ago at Finca Loma Linda.

Before the experiment is laid out, let's look at some of the conditions that called it into being. In most places in Coto Brus in the past—and even at present—where a row crop is planted of ten meters or so in length, its performance and yield will vary greatly along the length of ten meters. Such variation may not be uncommon in other parts of the world, but here it is exaggerated, often being the difference between stunted, arrested plants and others a few meters away that are growing well, even flourishing. This happens with all crops: coffee, vegetables, fruit trees, pasture grass. This apparent disparity in the soil is seen in extremes in row crops, such as vegetables, and less so in pasture, but everywhere it affects what is planted. The differences in crop performance often are so striking as to be hardly credible within a framework of farming experience. The conditions I am describing exist on this farm and all farms in Coto Brus. They may exist in many other parts of the tropical world too.

From a landowner's point of view (that of the farmer), this divergence in crop growth means that there are many—very many—farms on a single farm. In fact, no small segment of land seems to be quite like another. All are different; all are separate, small worlds to themselves. It is hard to farm this land because much of it falls on the very low side of crop performance. No planter remains without a wish to see all of the land come up to the level of that small portion which yields best.

The straightforward solution to this problem should be, it appears, to take soil samples from the good sections and the bad sections, see what the good sections have that the bad sections don't have, or, if the bad sections have something that is toxic, identify this and see what can be done to correct the problem, either way the results of such testing may fall. In principle this, in fact, is what we do attempt to do. But many farmers and all scientists know that the simplicity of this "solution" does not work out in soils such as these of Coto

Brus. It does not work because our knowledge of soil analysis and the evaluation of nutrient sustainability within the soil for crop growth is too limited to provide comprehensive answers to the questions we are asking.

We have seen earlier in this book that the soil is not a place where a storehouse of plant foods are to be found, it being necessary only to keep up the proper quantities of these "foods" for good crop growth. Rather, the soil is a living system; the atmosphere around it supports a living system; the moisture and solar energy entering it become integrated in living systems; the microbiota inhabiting it constitute living systems; and these—and more—continually combine and recombine, changing from instant to instant. It is not within our ability to arrest this process, disassemble it, and see how it works. We must observe these processes as dynamic, acting systems and address them in their entirety. Within the context of technology and scientific methodology this is not easy to do. As farmers we have even less in terms of methods of analysis at our disposal. But we can learn many things by taking soil and other samples, by inserting different testing probes within this continuum.

Scientists will follow such methods; farmers will have recourse to fertilizers, soil manipulation, different cropping systems, sprays, and other technologies. Many large pieces of land will fall completely within the low-yield conditions for all crops planted, with perhaps a few square meters here and there showing remarkably good crop performance. Time itself will become a factor in which farmers will be compelled to lay their faith. When all the quick remedies which can possibly come to mind have been tried and have all become disappointments, then hope is pinned upon the eventual—over a period of many years—"mellowing" of the soil so recently released from bondage to the rain forest. However, although four decades seems a reasonable time for "mellowing," in four decades this mellowing has not really produced the results we had hoped for.

One reason this has not taken place is that it is not going to fit our expectations. We do not recognize what changes are taking place in the soil because we do not understand what we are seeing or what should be happening in this environment, even with this elapsed time after the elimination of the forest, because this mellowing is an assumption, having little relevance to the lifetime of a generation or two of people.

For the settlers and their children this soil disparity is a discouraging circumstance. Seemingly, all possible additives of fertilizer, lime, foliar sprays, and the like have been tried without bringing about a solution to the problem or even a recognition of its nature.

At earlier times in the settlement of this earth, farmers would have moved on to other lands. Now this option of finding solutions on other land, at least hoping to do so, is gone; for there is no more new land available. An alternative is to limit the use of the land to those few crops which can succeed on it, even though these will be far from uniform in their growth and production. Coffee and pasture grass are two such crops. In any given field planted to either, there will be differences in the way the two crops grow from one segment within the field to another; still, taken as a whole, coffee and pasture will succeed.

The children of the settlers know this as well as their parents. Farming in Coto Brus has meant growing coffee or working with pasture. Some vegetables are planted, but the methods of production here in this rainy climate must be so exaggerated that even the growers concede that it is only by dint of excessive labor that vegetables are made to grow.

Farming, as it is carried out in most parts of Costa Rica, is not just a business; it is a way of life, a home, a family. It also is the land. But when the land is unpredictable, so is all which is dependent on it.

In Coto Brus an objective of many of the children of the settlers would be to remain on the land, make homes, raise families. A further objective would be to make the farm a little better each year so that in time the kids, the next generation, would have an opportunity to live here too. It is in the interest of the people and the country, many countries, that these objectives be met. Substitute the word *environment* for *land,* for the land is never just the surface of the earth, and we have the new frontier. We stand at its threshold.

We are going to apply those same attributes celebrated in an earlier time — resourcefulness, initiative, individual endeavor — to the task of this challenge, and we will enlist the procedures, discipline, and objectivity of science. Our task with the experiment we are about to set in motion is to learn how to build a better environment. We must do this not academically; we must make this environment work today, under present economic and social conditions, in the face of much that we may believe to be politically wrong. Research is not only a formal inquiry, conducted in a conventional context; it is also the daily search, by trial and error, by insight and introspection, made by every individual who touches the environment and hopes thereby to elucidate a collective understanding. But in all such quests there must be a specific focus on what is being looked for. Let's determine how we will lay out this experiment.

It must have complete relevancy to the rain. What is this rain? It is a force that displaces, in conjunction with other forces, huge, or smaller, segments of land, causing them to collapse and move, so that at this point in our life in Coto Brus, we see that the entire surface of the earth has been altered by the rain. The land is so steep, so scooped out, so sunken that we recognize that even while we are managing our farm it may quite literally fall out from under us and become new, even more accentuated and extreme.

The rain also is the force that drives with the tremendous power of hydrology through the layers of the soil. While it does so, it alters both the chemistry and the physics of the soil. The rain saturates the air and the ground for days on end, giving rise to different forms of disease. All that we do in this experiment will have to be relative to the rain.

This experiment must enhance our understanding of how to harness the forces of biodiversity and direct them toward the ends of uniformity. The very nature of biodiversity is alien to uniformity, but we must make an attempt in this direction. Perhaps we should substitute the word *stability* for uniformity, or even go beyond this and state as our objective *sustainability*. When we have done this we acknowledge that we do not honestly know how to define the specifics of our objective, other than that we must bring about some greater degree of *control* in our management of this environment. We must study the principles of biodiversity in order to approach farming management systems which go beyond simplistic mono-cultures. When we contemplate biodiversity we are looking at life systems and their supporting substrates; our experiment must be founded on these. Just as we have recognized that the forces in rain must be compassed in our experiment, so too must those of the sun, the air, its temperature, the forces of gravity, those of the wind, the multitude of interactions we know as chemistry, our own natures as individuals and as a society, the accumulation of what we have come to acquire as working knowledge.

In this experiment we must address the matter of soil disparity in crop production systems, the genetics of new strains and cultivars, the husbandry of animals upon the land. We will begin, of course, with the soil, because we manage this with more facility than we do many other things in our environment, but we will expect the soil to lead us to some understanding of these others too. In other words, we are trying to put together what we and others have taken apart and make it work for us, as we have seen that it works when we do not meddle with it. Do we have the ability to do this? We may have, at least, the humility to try. For in reality what we are doing is setting up a framework which enables us to understand our questions. This is the first step in our experiment: the gradual development of an awareness of what we don't know. Only when this becomes clear to us do we have any opportunity to learn. Interestingly, in the degree that we elaborate our uncertainties, such is the response to our understanding.

During several years prior to this point in our research, various experiments have been carried out at the farm; these have been con-ducted by faculty and graduate students from different universities in the United States, and there have been visiting graduate students from Latin America and the United States who have received orien-tation courses based on these experiments. From this earlier research and these courses in biology, environmental sciences, and agricul-ture, we will draw information as well as practical knowledge from our work in the field for the present inquiry. Many years, many sea-sons of experience are behind us. This experiment, to be laid out now, must synthesize much of what we have been learning.

Better than most people, we know the importance of planning this experiment well; it must yield the most comprehensive, the most relevant information. There has been a review of literature relative to this inquiry; the earlier research on this farm has been consulted. We don't have unlimited time to come to grips with these immediate problems; each day farmers are making decisions which compromise the environment. This experiment must meet these issues. It will be a preliminary trial; it must indicate the direction for future research on the farm; many experiments will ramify from it and investigate more thoroughly the information this present test will bring to light.

The experiment is to be laid out on a new piece of land which has just been graded and leveled. We are looking for soil uniformity on this site. The grading has been carried to a depth of subsoil, thereby eliminating some of the problems in the surface soil, such as nematodes, white grubs, and soil-borne diseases. Too, we will have reduced the conditions of soil disparity, we have reason to believe, by grading to the subsoil depth. On this site, which we call El Noga-lito, we are going to lay out rows of concrete building blocks, standing these on edge. The rows will be laid out so that we can make compartments 40 centimeters wide and 84 centimeters long. There will be 385 compartments, each 20 centimeters deep. Solar exposure and rainwater drainage are provided for in our planning.

We will include twenty-two treatments in the experiment with twenty-one replicates. (A treatment is a method to test a certain hypothesis; a replicate is a repetition of a treatment.) The treatments are designed to supply information on the response of test crops to different levels of chemical fertilizer applied to the soil as well as to the foliage; their response to soil-applied limestone; their response to additions to the soil of organic matter, in the form of compost; and their responses to different combinations of these treatments. We will have, of course, what is referred to as a "control" within this experiment, i.e., a treatment which is composed only of the soil used in all of the other treatments with nothing added.

The soil we will select as the base soil must be uniform and homo-geneous; it cannot have the same properties of disparity which are, after all, among the very concerns we are investigating. If we allow these conditions of disparity to enter this trial, much of what we interpret in the resulting data will be confused because we will not know to what extent natural soil conditions influenced the results of the experiment and to what extent these results were the outcome of our treatments.

To overcome this problem of difference in the composition of the base soil, we have taken a representative controlled quantity of soil from a single, small site where farming has not been carried out and where there have been no inputs of fertilizers, pesticides, and the like. We also selected this soil for low nematode or soil-borne disease population. This soil will be mixed thoroughly so that it is as homogeneous and uniform as we can make it. We will measure lots of the soil by volume, following careful methodology in all measurements, and then add precise amounts of the fertilizer, lime, or organic matter to the respective lots, mixing these well.

So that each test plant will be growing in exactly the same amount of earth and the additives called for by our treatments, there will be a measure of soil for each plant, again by volume, and each plant is to grow in an individual plastic bag, thus, again, providing for uniformity in the methodology. These plastic bags will then be placed in the concrete block compartments at El Nogalito, twenty-one bags per compartment. These will comprise the twenty-one replicates. We know at this point that scientific procedure requires that twenty-one bags be randomly scattered among the many compartments used in the experiment, but to do so would make it impossible to carry out some of the subsequent steps in the experiment, and this is a trial, a bellwether, which must break ground quickly. It will not impair the initial data in our experiment to "block" the replicates in single compartments.

The test crops we will be planting will be two cultivars of kidney, or field, beans, lettuce, mustard, carrots, and other vegetables. We have taken steps to ensure the uniformity of the seed; we will plant, or thin to, the same number of seedlings in each bag, establishing, after germination and emergence, one plant per bag.

Let's move ahead now to look at the results of our experiment. What did all this effort bring to light? From the moment the seedlings, lettuce or beans, emerged from the ground, it was apparent that they were responsive to their environment. We are accustomed to understand that seeds bring with them a reserve of food to help get the young plant started. Yet these seedlings, from the earliest leaflets which broke the surface of the soil, expressed a response to the soil in which they were planted. All of the seeds planted in the control treatment failed to grow and develop. Once having emerged, the seedlings remained stunted, unable to sustain development. As the days went on, the seedlings remained small green fragments, each of the twenty-one bags in the control compartment supporting its single seedling, these changing very little from day to day or week to week.

The soil used in this experiment had been dug to a depth of 60 centimeters; this meant that about half of the soil was composed of the dark, surface Andisol; the other half, the subsoil, composed of a weathered Andisol with characteristics similar to an Ultisol. The latter soil is a highly weathered soil found in the humid tropics, the former a soil of volcanic origin, often quite fertile. Had the seedlings in the control treatment been planted only in the top soil, the Andisol, they might have grown rather well; with the subsoil and topsoil mixed, as they were, these seedlings were arrested at emergence and did not recover from this condition.

A further consideration enters here. There was no surface, no litter, layer to the soil in the bags in the control treatment. The earth had been turned topsy-turvy when it was mixed. What might have been under natural conditions a thin surface layer of rootlets, decaying plant material, and other organic constituents was nonexistent in this control soil.

Other treatments used different application rates of a commercial fertilizer high in phosphorus, a 10–30–10 formula, ranging from a low rate of application to a high rate with intermediate stages. The beans and the vegetables did not grow well in these treatments. Mostly, they remained stunted. Only at the highest fertilizer application rate did they show some growth, but never complete development or good yield. So far we were seeing here in El Nogalito what we had seen repeatedly over the years in our field plantings. Commercial fertilizers could not overcome such soil limitation problems.

A PLACE IN THE RAIN FOREST

The lime application in this experiment gave astonishing results. The literature and our experience in farming indicated that this lime—ground limestone, calcium carbonate—should act very slowly in bringing about soil improvement conditions. Yet here in this experiment, within weeks, there was positive, statistically significant response in crop performance in the lime treatments. One needed only a glance to see outstanding differences in crop growth in the lime treatments as compared to the control or fertilizer treatments.

Foliar fertilization also showed marked improvement over control and soil fertilizer. There was also a positive response in the treatments where a complete liquid fertilizer had been applied in solution to the roots of the plants.

But nowhere was there a response such as that produced by the addition of organic matter. The difference in crop performance in the treatments with organic matter as compared with those without organic matter was stunning. Lettuce growing in a treatment with organic matter produced at time of harvest 732 times more fresh weight per plant than did the lettuce growing in the control.

What the El Nogalito experiment was showing us must be interpreted as many things. First, and foremost, it was saying, "Yes, we would have answered long ago, had only you known how to ask." As I walked through the experiment during those days when these many responses were forming a comprehensive "answer," I thought again and again of this single aspect of the experiment: Had only one known how to ask. Had it taken four decades to learn only this? Of course, knowing how to ask was not just knowing how to set up the experiment. El Nogalito was a good experiment, but it might have been carried out by other investigators working with similar principles. The experiment was not simply knowing how to put the treatments and replicates together; it was the recognition of the entire context of what these combinations represented.

That organic matter supports good crop growth is known the world over. Composting, work with organic matter in gardens, has been practiced from early history. But what took place in El Nogalito was part of what had constituted the sustainability of life systems in the rain forest; it was an indicator of all that that world represented. And for a brief interval of time, during those days at the end of the wet season and the beginning of the dry season at the end of 1989, a now vanished rain forest had returned to speak through this experiment and convey these meanings.

A new horizon would now have to be viewed for humid, tropical areas such as Coto Brus. All that we had learned and thought we knew from farming experience in other parts of the world would have to be modified—indeed, relinquished in some measure— in light of these quiet mornings and afternoons under the clear, windswept skies over El Nogalito. Now there would be a focus on the successional forest, on the legacy of the rain forest, on all the rich diversity of plant life and other life which nature had been waiting to have recognized as a basis for an entire new agriculture in the wet tropics.

Many ghosts walked upon the land during those days at El Nogalito; they spoke in a thousand tongues. It would take us decades—more—to begin to be able to differentiate among their meanings. Rarely would a single experiment synthesize as much as this one had.

From this point research has continued at El Nogalito and on many other parts of the farm and in other locations in Coto Brus. El Nogalito did not initiate this research; as I have said, it was built on earlier research. Nor is it responsible for all of the research which has followed. But it synthesized an entire area of principles in the management of tropical ecosystems. And from this synthesis we are taking fresh initiatives.

We are not well equipped today to solve the kinds of problems the experiment at El Nogalito addressed. As I review past research and current research here at Finca Loma Linda, I frequently find that, at best, our methods for understanding the natural systems of which we ourselves are part are restricted, tediously slow, and fragmented. It may be that we have lost an ability, which possibly in a remote past might have been ours, to interpret natural systems more intuitively. This, of course, is merely a guess. What does come to light, however, is that our methods today in research seem scarcely adequate to meet the task at hand.

Our frontier has many aspects. As we advance it opens upon broader and more extensive unexplored horizons. Perhaps we err in looking for that which is precise and definitive. We may mistake our desire for assured understanding for an absence of the courage to live habitually with uncertainty.

The settlers of the South Frontier came to the new land by an act of will. In other words, they were *acting*. Their children were born on this land; they inherited their place on it. In such a condition, they became accustomed to its status of limitations. To break such a status requires again an act of will. The El Nogalito experiment, like most well-designed experiments, challenges a position of acquired perspectives. The challenge may have to be met with slow and rudimentary procedures. But at least the problems will be addressed.

Uncertainty is a useful condition in experimentation. We must always be meeting horizons in the knowledge that we do not know where our next steps will lead but that they must be taken without reliance on artificial reassurance. In some respects the education being acquired by the children of the settlers in Coto Brus today derives from a desire for such reassurance. To address the actual and recognized conditions of agricultural and rural life in Coto Brus poses more uncertainty than to pursue the established trade or profession which has a conventional aspect of dependability. To confront the horizon of ecological considerations in the management of an environment is to face all of our doubts about how to understand and act. But the frontier must be met. That we can recognize it is evidence that it is already part of our lives; tomorrow we will recognize more, and we will have to meet this also.

The El Nogalito experiment, in conjunction with other research work, points the way to many things which must be further explored and which can, and will, lead to much that will be useful in tropical agriculture in the future. In the next chapter I will show where some of these research findings will lead.

We are proceeding on responsive ground. Our knowledge is forever being challenged by these discoveries. We move forward to find that this step ahead did not transport us but, in effect, expanded the vista around us. When we recognize that the horizon is, in fact, a part of ourselves, we will be better prepared to define its relationship with us. We are not as separate from what we study as we are inclined to believe; much in these natural systems is an extension of our growing awareness of ourselves. Partly, this is what the experiment at El Nogalito communicated. What it brought forward is what already had been touched upon during earlier work. The pieces of the components of earlier experience—and I am not referring to what is strictly personal—had been rearranged in a manner to make them more clearly identifiable.

The children of the settlers, and these are not just here in Coto Brus, have this option: they may address the challenges of the ecological frontier and feel that they are not strangers in so doing.

In this we will have to proceed with the tools we have, certain applications of our scientific methodology, which, in truth, at times are clumsy; better ways will occur to us at length. Such an improvement in our methodologies will ultimately be a reassessment of ourselves relative to what we see at present as external to our personal experience. These two conditions, what we define as us and what we define as around us, may eventually share a common ground. The initiative to act is up to us.

Many of the steps being taken by the second generation of farmers in Coto Brus at this time—and by their fathers who, in fact, started them—may lead to a compromised future. By its nature, Coto Brus is not a versatile farming region. It is like many other parts of the highland, wet tropics: limited in what can be done at this point in our understanding of agriculture. In Coto Brus and similar areas, yields in crop production and livestock management are extracted at high cost. For instance, sometimes it is cheaper to import a harvest of the same crop from halfway around the world than it is to grow it on the home farm. The meaning of such economics is sobering to young farmers. There seems to be no way by which the shortcomings of the home farm can be overcome, for they are based on topography, climate, geographic position in the world—conditions beyond the control of the individual or the community.

Facing these limits, the young farmers rely heavily on the products of the chemical industry to keep themselves in business. The conditions in Coto Brus are probably not much different from those in other parts of the world, except in degree—all farmers are engaged in battles with crop pests, diseases, soil problems, fertility depletion—but in the tropics the intensity of these battles is greater.

I have spent most of my life as a farmer, as have my neighbors, involved in such battles. In order to bring in successful crops, I have spent years spraying plantings with different products, exterminating weeds with herbicides, manipulating fertilizer applications. Such practice has been and continues to be a way of life for most farmers here. The outcome of what we have done, or are doing, is beyond us. I have applied certain spray products over the years only to find that, two or more decades after their recommended use by government agencies in the United States and Costa Rica, they are banned and prohibited from use because they have been found to be harmful to health and the environment. Twelve years ago I stopped application of all pesticides on Finca Loma Linda, but before that time I had been as heavily dependent on their use as other farmers here. It is not reassuring to work for many years with products which have been recommended by qualified agencies to find at some point later that they may have been causing long-term environmental harm. This is particularly true in an area so recently free of these residues, such as Coto Brus. In this part of the world we have moved in less than a half century from a condition of natural adjustments in the rain forest to one in which almost nothing in the way of food or farm products is produced in a sustained manner without being subject to frequent and continued application of pesticides.

This picture is not good from the viewpoint of those of us who settled the new land. As a farmer I am as aware as others that the use of these pesticides, and the many products related to them, is necessary in order to maintain food production in a world of expanding human population. There have been many times when I have been both grateful and appreciative for the resourcefulness behind the development and manufacture of these products. But also as a farmer I have been impressed repeatedly with how awkward and almost unmanageable most of these pesticides are. It is not good to don your protective clothing, goggles, respirator, gloves, boots, and a knapsack sprayer and pretend you can work with these on steep terrain hour after hour, day after day, week after week. To keep the powders and liquids off of yourself, to keep them away from places they should not reach, to see to it that foodstuffs are not contaminated, to preserve the resources of air, soil, and water from such contamination — none of this is as workable as the labeling on the various pesticide products would make it appear.

These problems are faced by young farmers in Coto Brus, those who would like to see themselves as permanent residents on the land, the producers of good and useful things from the earth. Yet as time goes on the difficulty of accomplishing this becomes greater, and the attraction of getting away from the problems and becoming an electrician, an accountant, a lawyer, or a physician becomes stronger.

We have transmitted a strange legacy to our children. Are we responsible? Collectively and individually we are, of course, responsible. We are always responsible for our tenure on the earth, regardless of how we might wish to see the responsibility shifted elsewhere.

What is this condition that has overtaken us so soon on this frontier? Have those earlier steps we took so burgeoned as to have transformed themselves beyond recognition? Has the rain forest returned to us now the burden of what we failed to learn?

In some respects this may be true; the key to better management of our environment, better ways of producing food, might have been found in the rain forest. Our current methods of producing foods rely too heavily on technologies which show little sensitivity to relationships we group under the name *ecology*. For those of use who have worked for many years in Coto Brus applying fungicides, insecticides, and herbicides, there is reason to believe that this is not the right way to overcome the problems we are encountering in crop production and livestock raising. Applications which worked several years ago are working less well today. The tendency is to increase the strength of concentrations of pesticides and shorten intervals between applications. It requires only a few years' experience to convince most farmers that this road is leading to an unmanageable outcome. Food production systems may be maintained, but they will be maintained at an increasing risk of discovering in the future that the cost of such production will go far beyond what at present can be foreseen.

A simple answer to these problems of increasing pesticide applications in crop production and related livestock raising would be
to blame some group or an established economic framework. In
other words, as people we would tend to blame other people for our
troubles. This might be the case, but my years on the land and background from the frontier leave me less prone to single out certain
groups of economic interests as being responsible for what essentially
we do not know today. We may well know which are the abuses and
who are committing them. But it is unlikely that knowing this will
be an adequate answer. We have proceeded quickly—and I am
making specific reference to our experience in Coto Brus—from
an integral forest frontier to a kind of management of the environment which we recognize as being badly out of adjustment in many
respects. It is one thing not to understand the intricacies of natural
arrangements; it is another to see that the arrangements we are producing are leading to much we suspect is not in our best interest.
Our technology is divorced from the results of its application.

These results are too often neglected by science, while the primary
objective of the technologies that produce them is simplified and
designated merely as the production of food. The production of
food and what more? It is not the fault of any particular industry
that we do not have an answer to this question, because no industry
is in a position to answer it. Nor is it the fault of an economic system
that we do not have an answer. Groups and systems may contribute
to complicating the search for an answer, but they are not the principal cause for its absence.

Let's return to a farm in Coto Brus. It is morning, the morning of
a new day. The rain forest is almost all gone, but there are still some
patches of it visible from where our young farmer stands. Birds sing,
insects are active, the land itself is teeming and vital with life. This
young farmer, one of the children of the settlers, is remarkably free.
At home in the little house on this farm is a young wife and the first
of the children who will come in a growing family. The vitality that
is a reality in this earth, that which the farmer feels at this moment
under his feet, also wells within him. He knows that he is strong,
capable, intelligent. Every moment for him is a new opportunity, a
beginning. The answers to problems and questions begin now, here,

with him. He may not know where the next step on this little farm will lead, but he has confidence in taking it. As long as he can place his feet on the earth, his hands on his tools, his heart and his mind in his wife and his home and their family and this land, he is well; he is strong. He does not want this land to be ruined; he does not want his children's future here to be compromised. From this huge, incomprehensible mesh of interrelated life systems around him, he will take his spiritual, intellectual, and practical nourishment. Daily, he will receive what this environment has to give. And he has yet enough of humility to be receptive. He will learn from others' experience; he will not assume that others don't know.

This is an accurate picture of many young farmers in Coto Brus. They are indeed surrounded by an infinity of problems; they recognize the limitations these impose; but they have the vitality, the confidence, and the courage to act. On such elements we must build.

The "answers," the "solutions," start here, now, with *me*. It is no good looking somewhere else for someone to blame. It is true that none of us is a paragon of right and blameless conduct in environmental management. But if we are to find the answers and the solutions, we will have to start at home, here, today. I think we will. Each generation is endowed with an opportunity to try.

NINE

By This
We Stand

*T*he Percheron draft
horses could be seen in the predominantly gray and black colors of
this breed on an afternoon in the dry season under the shade of the
tall *amarillón* trees standing in the pasture at the edge of the rain
forest. The big animals were quiet on such an afternoon, long tails
swishing the flies, powerful legs stamping from time to time, hooves
thudding down on the dry, packed earth at the place where the horses
were accustomed to drowse at this hour, having grazed earlier in the
open segments of grass.

The logs, stumps, branches were diminished now; time had
gradually reduced the bulk of the fallen forest, decay speaking its
message of slow release and integration with the fecund ground.
Fences ran along the edge of the forest, at one point dropping
within it where a trail dipped to a stream. The horses walked here
to a watering drum located on the bank, the liquid, slow murmurs
of the stream lost in the folds of brown, moldered leaves and the
languidly playing shadows.

The cry of a laughing falcon rose upon a breath of wind, the air moving briefly, then subsiding, the cry, majestic, exultant, hovering in the distance.

All during that morning under the seamless sky, distant and cloudless, the sun had burned with its intense brightness and heat; all during that morning there had been this whisper of the wind, the air, drying now, the distance over the land, the message in the cry of the falcon, reaching its freedom, its airy grandeur.

The horses had been at work, the clink of the chains in the traces, the heavy hoof tramp upon the land; bent into the collars, the dust rising, deep in the nostrils, the fragrance of the ground. Like a ribbon of orange and tans, the road had wound along through the green tapestry of the foliage of the successional growth, finding its way through this undulating yawning of green, and the teams had tramped back and forth, drawing the equipment, building the road. And behind the sweat and the smell of the horses, of the chains and the leather of harness and collar, the boots treading in the loose earth, reins over the right shoulder and under the left armpit, a hand on the handle of the fresno, came the footsteps in the weeks and the months and the years; the road stretched in a ribbon, segmenting the green.

By evening the heat wore out of the air; a chill instilled itself with the coming of night, a pause and then a spoken whisper of wind, darkness and the liquid, distant, infinitely sad descending notes of the tinamous. The dew fell upon the road, emergent, lengthening along the land; the dew formed droplets on the handle and blade of the fresno, left here by a mound of loosened earth, glinting in little droplets in moonlight, the dew freshening the grass where the horses grazed.

A road, a farm, a pasture, and horses; the night; a home upon the land; candlelight by the window, the glow of the kerosene lamp; the battery-operated record player, Beethoven's Pastoral Symphony; and a story, a legend and literature in the hours of evening. Then the stillness and the stars and the deep murmur of vast, infinite time and place receding, the hours along a track of remembrance.

A thousand minutes make an hour in time in a life in this ever resurgent solitude.

There came the days upon the days, searching, hungering in the ground. In a morning the air sprang, quickened to the sound of the building of a barn. Timber upon timber, the strength in planks of the bone of the land, this longevity of wood, plank upon plank, the nails singing by the blows of the hammer, valid in the rain and the sun; this day of our building.

No fragment can exist here lest it be something brought from this union, some worthy segment of all the past of this forest, retained and preserved in this wood; now with the hammer and the song in the wind of the barn.

All manner of animals, all creatures to be and become, will dwell here. By the light of electricity now, the rumble of the diesel plant hovering in the strange, evasive night; the moths aflutter in the quick light, the barn, the secret of its purview. The rabbits, the geese, the guinea fowl, the chickens, the goats, the quail—dogs and cats; a rhythm of life, a single quick beating in many breasts, this empathy of barn, all eyes longing at feeding time.

And the squirt of milk in the bucket and the froth on the pail, in the morning and the evening by the stanchion.

We stand by these things. No man or woman tills the earth without planting therein and receiving therefrom something of this: the years of our strange tenure. It is in the interest of our society and our future that men and women persevere and endure upon the face of the earth—that this be urged onward by the labor of my hand. No hand sows which does not return to the grain replenished by the gift of fertility. For there may be a time of desire and a time of restoration, but these grow upon the soil, like seeds upon the land.

We learned many things during those years of the morning of our planting. Now the day lengthens and the shadows reach across the fallen marks where my footsteps and theirs walked in seasons.

Many generations brought us to this point in our understanding. The intimacy of tillers with their livestock, with soil which supported these, brought about a companionship which closed a cycle of fertility on the earth. Feed was collected for the animals and brought to the community of people and livestock, and, in time, the possibility of permanency upon this place, a residence, arose and gave way to the establishment of farms. It is an old principle, that of maintaining the fertility of the land through livestock husbandry and the bringing in of feed for the stock from sources off the farm; and it was basic in my decision to work with the draft horses and begin a diversified livestock program in the barn. The principle, however, is dependent for its success on the transport of fertility from other sources to one's own farm. With livestock programs this happens when feed is bought and brought to the farm. The manure, the bedding, the litter from stables remain on the farm and are returned to the earth. Meat, milk, eggs leave the farm. With draft horses, less of this "imported" fertility is taken off the farm.

Principles such as this are relative: their successful application is dependent on many associated conditions. There is a tendency for us all to espouse a principle which is appealing and allow it to dominate our planning beyond its actual worth. This happens frequently when farming systems are being tried in new land areas or areas of settlement. In the absence of a background of experience in such areas, principles are adhered to and rationalized in lieu of practical working knowledge. Let's watch the way this particular principle, that of maintaining and returning fertility to the land through livestock raising, actually applies to farming in Coto Brus.

These skies, overflowing with clouds, seem often to hover over the land. During the wet season there is an envelope over the earth; it is an envelope of moisture, unseen but felt, the regression of the rain to the atmosphere in tiny droplets drawn up from the ground, in the mist hovering over the foliage, droplets in play in solar energy among the leaves of grass in pastures, the circulation of air and moisture between the sky and earth. Impregnated as it has been, the earth is a great reservoir of the water of the rain. This immense reservoir rises and recedes within the earth, subject to a multitude of dynamics, of countless expressions of energy.

We might think of this as pulsations, the pulsations of life, or lifelike processes within the earth and atmosphere. Indeed, these two are one in their interrelated processes of regeneration. There comes a shadow over the darkening forest; the mist of low clouds blows upon the surface of the ground; moisture collects and drips from the tips of leaves; there is a reluctant quality in the overreach of water upon the grass in the pasture, a stillness, and the slow action of the drops of fallen rain upon the leaves.

Across the veils of clouds, fallen in shreds and lengthening in gaunt specters prostrate among the trees—these seen now as shadowed phantoms within the mist—come the horses and the cattle on the pasture. This earth is fragile, this relationship established here among the atmosphere, the sky, the earth, the water; the action of air and moisture, of energy and rain is in vibrant balance. And there comes the heavy passage of the horses across the ground.

Many of our passages upon the earth are overlaid with insensitivity. We fail too often to appreciate that life is a suspended cognizance, held in a web of interconnected statements of conditions which we hold to be not life but which are so closely associated and essential to life as to be inseparable from it.

The heavy passage of the horses or cattle across this pasture during the wet season, thus creating mud on the trails where the livestock has walked, is not wrong, for we are not concerned here with what is "right" or "wrong" in the sense of an imposition of judgments; it is, however, *incorrect,* not in the best interests of our management of this environment. The environment probably has the ability to adjust and recover from mismanagement, but we, as farmers, may not have the time to so recover or to correct our misapplications. Where the terrain is steep, the rainfall high, the soil light and open to the passage of air and water, the grazing of livestock is a difficult system to accommodate.

Bringing the livestock into the barn, cutting the feed and carrying it to them, protects the soil from the effects of heavy grazing. But it is well known to economists and farmers that such a program of livestock raising requires special market conditions for its success; in other words, there must be a market within practical, working reach of the farm which will enable the livestock raiser to meet his production costs when marketing what is produced. Frontiers, newly settled areas, rarely meet such requirements. Some of the principles we have been looking at in livestock management have been appealing; their application, however, has been out of time and out of place.

But there are many principles. We saw earlier in this book how the tillage of the soil with teams of Percherons and the disk harrow brought about an apparent condition of degradation in the tilth, aeration, and possibly the chemical relationships, following heavy rains. The subject of tillage as a system of crop production came into question on Finca Loma Linda. There was no application for tillage in coffee production. As the land on the farm became cleared, mostly through natural decay of the forest obstructions, there was no well-defined plan for tillage with the horses. There was much I didn't know about this matter of tillage, and eventually I sold the entire herd of Percheron horses and devoted myself entirely to coffee.

Many years later the farm acquired a new, four-wheel-drive, fifty-two-horsepower tractor with a disk harrow, a rear-mounted scraper blade, and some other implements. Conditions had changed with respect to the farm's access to markets; roads were not good, but they were passable during most of the year. The possibility of selling produce to markets in the lowland banana plantations held a prospect of some income for the farm. Again, I was ready to look at the workability of tillage.

During those years the mornings were starlit, a bright star on the eastern horizon, low against a silhouette of a high point of land, in the hour before sunrise. There was no electric light; the day began by flashlight. It was cold, damp, yet fresh with the prospect of a certain mystery in the fading darkness following the hours of rain during the preceding afternoon and evening. My truck was loaded with produce, *El Mercado Móvil* lettered in black on its orange, fiberglass cabin over the bed, this Mobile Market linking the farm with its lowland market in the banana plantations. Twice a week, on Tuesdays and Fridays, the Mobile Market traveled over these roads.

In the wet season it was about the same for the truck as it was for the oxen and carts. The carts had advantages over the truck: their wheels and axle clearance were higher, and, of course, the carts never did more than local hauling, mostly with coffee. The quagmires were the same at the end of the wet season, when the coffee was ripening; there were times when it was impossible to get over the road with the truck.

I had made heavy tire chains for all four wheels—conventional chains were far too light—and they made all the difference in the world, gripping the solid clay under the mud. Those chains on these starlit mornings leaving the farm during the wettest months were an extension of eyes and hands, the shift lever, the pedals. Every turn of the truck's wheels was a sixth sense, this sense of metal and tissue going out in the headlights, the swaying of the truck body, its quiet engine sound, in the glint of the light on the surface of the puddled water, a sixth sense remembering how it was on the last trip, how it would be now.

Each trip wore a little more away of the road; each time an oxcart slipped, its wheels slicing deeper in a hole filled with mud, there was less purchase at the edges of that hole. It was the purchase that the chains and wheels and lights searched out; every nuance of balance in the truck was dependent on momentum, weight distribution, the surface below the mud. Contrary to what might be supposed, such driving seldom involved a rush, a burst of power; it was a combination of positioning and the forward flow of momentum, each moment feeding its message to the wheels and the engine.

It would do no good to use the winch if a miscalculation caused the chains to miss the point of purchase on the clay at the edge of a deep hole; trucks had gone in sidewise, skewed across the road, and by the time they extricated themselves precious time had been lost, the market still a little under two hours off.

Each of these journeys to market during the hardest part of the wet seasons took place at night, in the early hours before dawn— a night when the rain spoke in a wakened anticipation; black, so dark in the bedroom, the thoughts then, the quagmires on the road, thoughts stealing in the stillness and the steady raindrops, pressing to know the secrets of the extension where the starlight lay in liquid shadows.

And the whisper, the whisper in aloneness; the headlights bolting in the shadows; the forward leaning; sensing in a search for purchase; a path, a whisper in this night; how cold; how deep the mud; oh night upon the day—how long this journey!

By starlight and flashlight I unclasped the chains from the wheels. Three kilometers beyond the farm the mud met the rock-surfaced road. Here the chains came off. There would be twelve hours of work in the plantations and I could not reach them with muddy clothes. But it was only necessary to reach in over the tire and find the clasp on the chain, wet and cold, loosen it and let it drop, and drive off it. The chains went into a sack; later they would have to be washed in a river before being put back on for the return to the farm.

Still the world was asleep; there was not another soul on the road; indeed why would anyone want work such as this?

But Finca Loma Linda could be a supplier of food. This was valid work, this produce harvested from the earth; there was something in that earth. This Mobile Market was an extension of much that had been accumulated, of much that had been planted in the expectancy of this morning come now upon the trek to market.

Each rock, each cliff edge along this road by dawn was a segment in this work. There, by dawn, spread out the panoply of the coastal flood plains, banked by green; the rivers, tropical, sultry; the small clusters of laborers' houses in the banana plantations; seen well below the road, dropping vertically from its edge down over this rock path, the cliffs above the lowlands. In the distance were the low coastal mountains, somber with hideaway purple in inert shadow; beyond these the haze of the Pacific, seen more clearly beyond the land; and once and again the bright arrow, caught in the rising sun, of one of the steamers of the United Fruit Company's Great White Fleet putting in to port at Golfito to load bananas.

I wonder if they ever thought about this small truck clinging to the edges of the cliffs on the road, this Market leading down from the mountains above the panorama of flood plains and sea, this orange, black-lettered venture coming from the mountains to the sea.

How clear were the sunlit skies of those days over the plantations, when a wishing, a desire to know, would reach over that tropical lowland in the distance, the torch of the lowland sun, the place and the hour and the people and the fragmented separateness here on the cliffs which spoke such a sense of loneliness and detachment.

By midday the heat was intense, and the orange Mobile Market would stand by the bananas in the plantations or move slowly through the tapestry of laborers' barracks and railroad spurs, stems of bananas strung along cable conveyors, canals carrying the excess water in the flood plains to the rivers.

Coriander, cabbage, radishes, peppers, squash, cucumbers, tomatoes . . . — by hand I carried these in baskets from the truck to the plantation workers' houses, selling from door to door.

The sun at midday; the airless heat; the languid, lazy hammocks along the corridors of the barracks; the red, corrugated metal roofs above green, two-story houses; the trudge across the grass in the plaza at midday; the masonry floors, the rude kitchens and showers; dark faces, dark hallways in the tropic torpor.

The mountains were a bulwark then, a high, precipitous escarpment, for that thread of road, clinging to the limestone cliffs. It could be seen from any point in the plantations, the road leading to Coto Brus. It rose like a series of loops, vertically ascending in switchbacks, the rampart overlooking the plains. The clouds grew out of the day, high there along the mountains. With baskets in hand and from door to door I went in the shadow of the mountains and home.

By afternoon the Mobile Market moved through the flood plains to the port of Golfito. There was the steamer seen as a dart upon the gulf that morning from the vantage on the cliffs, seen that morning when the day had spread its light upon the ocean; how far had been the steamer!

Golfito, in its laborers' district, was a cluster upon the shore, a cluster drawn out in a string of shanties and brothels and bars all backed by the tropical forest by the edge of the sea. And ever and again came the long strings of railroad cars, pulled by the diesel engines, rumbling out on the wharf; the transport of bananas to the sea; the sea beyond the gulf beckoning to the west coast markets in the United States or through the Panama Canal to the eastern seaboard.

That horizon had been mine in the morning when the truck crept along the cliffs by the road leading down from the highlands to the flood plains and the sea. The sea and this steamer had been mine in the morning when there was a link between the farm and the port:

the Mobile Market coming down, caught in the intricacies of the port and the squalor, the romance of distance; the smell of the sea.

And from store to store with the produce from the highland.

By late afternoon the clouds had fallen. Paths of lightning threaded through the dark over the mountains, a storm filling the rivers, the rivers filling with the flood of the rains, falling from the mountains, from the highlands.

And there was the road, losing itself in darkness, the long thread along the cliffs in the distance, seen from the flood plains. Now the Mobile Market was empty; now began the trip home. The windshield wipers played on the vacant glass where the drops splattered; veils of rain came slanting; and night came over the plantations.

Always there was the Caño Seco River, a curious combination of characters: a dry channel by the dry season, a torrent sometimes after heavy rain. A truck could be swept and overturned by its surge, rains filling the ford with turbulence, cataracts tumbling in the mountain canyons. Now by the headlights of the truck there was the piled push of water, shaped like the back of some aquatic creature, convoluted across the ford. In midriver there was a high point, a rock in the mound of water, muddy, rapid in the light of the headlights; rain on the windshield. Gingerly I drove, with acceleration and slack, feeling the surface of the bottom, the pickup rocking and rocking and the water rising, rising, pounding against the door with the spray reaching the window, the lights gripping and bouncing in the turbulence, the ford a mismatched crosscurrent of sections. What unsurety by night, this ford in flood; and the Mobile Market, orange and water-crested, marking a way.

To wash the tire chains by the bank of the river now, the ford one more memory of a lengthening past; a moment in the midday sun by the edge of the sea, in the rainstorm home by the bank of the river.

And now by night to the highland, home to the farm. To think, thoughts alone on this road, days of planting; the candlelight and the children in their beds; my wife, possibly enduring far more than I in waiting so many hours upon the days into the evenings when the rain spoke of such distance and isolation.

Then came the end of the rock-surfaced road, again the chains, quickly laid out, the truck driven forward and the tires positioned just at the chain ends, clasped to grip, tight; each small section of road a renewed test of grip and purchase.

These days went on for several years. I cannot speak for my wife and our girls, waiting at home as they did each Tuesday and Friday; each trip during these severe months of the wet seasons was a view beyond the empty window where the rain fell and the darkness and the sound of the years were lost in waiting and stillness.

Out of such experience arose a knowledge of meeting the food requirements of a local market. This knowledge marked also a commitment, one which found expression at this time in flowing contours which traced their lines across the slopes on Finca Loma Linda. I made these contours with our new tractor and its rear-mounted, grading blade. The earth was turned and spread and leveled. A wide range of forward and reverse speeds on the tractor made the work efficient.

What I was building were bench terraces cut across the more gentle gradients. The work marked a permanent decision in farming management; it would determine the direction of land management on this farm for the future. There are few steps more fundamental in land-use planning than a major reconfiguration of the surface of the farm. Much of this decision had been influenced by the marketing work. The production objectives on Finca Loma Linda were still those of diversity, some mechanization, and environmental balance.

One day in a section of the farm which came to be known as the Central Tillage, I stood on a group of newly made terraces and watched under a heavy rain as the runoff water sluiced and tumbled over the terrace banks, carrying away with it the loosened soil. Nowhere in my experience had there been a heavier moment. No error is as unforgivable for the farmer as that of losing the soil to erosion. The purpose of these terraces had been to control excess water, to protect the soil from the rain.

I walked that afternoon alone in the rain forest. Here was the answer; here was the answer to so much. If only I could understand. What was it that I was seeing? As always the stillness, the eloquent

voices of ages. What was it here in the soft play of light and shadow—
this shimmering containment of the rainwater across the litter on
the forest floor?

Immediately, we set about planting grass hedges on the terrace
banks. We worked from dawn to evening, day after day. Fortunately,
the heavy rains subsided, and after two days of hard rains, there
were weeks when the rains were only moderate or light. We were not
planting grass seed in the hedges but rather rooted grass segments.
The grass, an erect, nonspreading species (*Axonopus scoparius L.*),
grew quickly, and in less than a year each terrace was bordered by a
strong bulwark of grass hedge. Since then, regardless of the severity
of the rains, there has been no detrimental erosion on these terraces.

But the lesson of the rain forest was not yet complete. It was
not enough to protect the edges of the terraces from runoff water
there; the surface of the soil itself needed protection. And so the
grass hedges fulfilled their second purpose. We cut them by machete
and spread the grass over the surface of the terrace. Thus the soil was
not exposed to the action of the rain or the intensity of the sun; soil
temperatures were moderated; a microflora and microclimate were
created.

A further major benefit of these hedges was the addition of their
organic matter to the ground. As often as the hedges were cut and
the grass spread on the ground, fresh organic matter was being
supplied to the terraces.

Each terrace had its own management record. In this record notes
were—and continue to be—kept on planting, fertilization, hedge
management, soil amendments such as liming, and crop production
history. No two terraces were the same; in fact, no two terraces have
ever been the same.

I believed during those hard years of marketing in the banana
plantations, when only enough money was being earned to meet
the farm's payrolls and very little else, that this system of land management, the terraces and their hedges, their detailed, individual
records, was a means of meeting the requirements of high-rainfall,
tropical agriculture where some mechanization must be practiced
on gradients. I continue to believe this. But as is the case with

all systems with which I am acquainted in tropical agriculture, this, the terrace, the grass hedge system, is only one step in a journey which has no resting place, no final point of arrival or destination. This, as all other systems, must continually be modified, be made to meet new requirements, be ever flexible and adaptable to the changing circumstances within a never fixed or halted environment. However, each day that I spent in the sometimes overwhelming heat and limited market finance of the banana plantations confirmed my faith in what I was doing on Finca Loma Linda in this management.

If we return now to those earlier experiences with the draft horses and the disk harrowing—experiences in which it appeared that this work had broken down the physical condition of the soil, making it much less fit for planting and successful crop production under heavy rain—it becomes apparent that the terraces, even under tillage, with their grass hedges, go far to overcome this problem. During many successive years I have carried out tillage on the terraces with good crop response.

As with almost all else in farming, and especially with farming here in Coto Brus, there are few, if any, hard and fixed rules. To state flatly that tillage is wrong and never should be followed in the wet tropics does not agree with my experience as a farmer on Finca Loma Linda. There have been many instances when it has been wrong, or would have been wrong; but there have been many others when it has worked well. Tillage is associated with a multitude of other environmental dynamics; if a farmer has acquired enough experience and ability to accurately evaluate these, tillage can often be productive.

However, the ability to make such an evaluation is not easily earned nor is it acquired soon. The principles of accumulating fertility in the soil and concentrating it, such as we saw in an earlier part of this book in reviewing how seedbeds and coffee nurseries were built up by using the broad-bladed *pala,* are relevant to tillage. But there are many other principles too; one of our most important areas of work is to recognize and study them. We have been doing this for several years on Finca Loma Linda. The work is strict scientific investigation, but, wherever possible, we try to make this also applicable to the farming needs of this community.

To understand how this is done, I'd like to make reference to some of the most skillful farmers I know, those from whom I have learned most, my Costa Rican neighbors. Let's join them in a system of agriculture which dates back to pre-Columbian times.

In its successor the grace and beauty of the rain forest have perished; the successional forest holds no resemblance to its primary forebears. There is, in fact, no progeny here; the seeds of the primary forest are not to be found as direct offspring in the successional growth which naturally follows the elimination of the rain forest. This successional growth, in time a successional forest, seems nothing more than a tangle of weeds, none of which strikes the eye immediately as beauty or elegance; maybe we cannot overcome our revulsion at the destruction of the primary forest, and this faint shadow which follows in its place seems a sorry outcome—a just statement on those who have taken up the axe and machete against the majesty which once occupied the land.

In some parts of the world this successional forest might be called the "bush," a tangle, something which obstructs any informed use of the land. Certainly the tool to deal with the "bush," the machete, is primitive, a limited recourse, the restricted means of an unsophisticated people. So easily is nature's offering, so readily is the accumulated wisdom of a culture, dispensed with.

This "bush," the successional forest, occupies a large part of Finca Loma Linda today. It is the subject at the present time of intensive scientific study. It will be, without the slightest doubt, one of the keys to important discoveries leading to better systems in humid, tropical agriculture.

It is interesting to see how closely this secondary forest and the machete actually are associated; for the former cannot practically be worked with any other tool, and the tool itself is a means of transforming and creating yet unexplored combinations and delicate adjustments in this successional growth. In this regard the machete may be the most versatile tool in tropical farming management.

But the tool relies for its employment, and in fact the artistry of

A PLACE IN THE RAIN FOREST

its employment, on the skill and experience of those who use it. Here in Coto Brus it is always used with the *garabato,* the hooked stick I described earlier in this book. For generations in Costa Rica and elsewhere in Latin America, the machete has been the only tool used for the planting of beans in a system known as *tapado,* "covered," in successional growth.

In this system bean seed, the common kidney bean (*Phaseolus vulgaris L.*), is broadcast — cast by hand — in the standing successional growth. This successional growth is a dense tangle of vegetation ranging from a meter to three or four meters high and composed, as we see it today on Finca Loma Linda, of about thirty principal species of plants. (Our work is yet preliminary.) These plants are annual and perennial; none of them is a "tree" in the sense that we connect with the primary rain forest. All of these successional plants grow quickly; given a little time in areas not already dominated by other vegetation, such as pasture grass, they will quickly cover the land if the soil there has not been degraded by erosion or misuse. The successional growth is a habitat for many birds and animals; it is not, however, the same habitat the primary forest was.

As I have said, the bean seed is thrown in the "weeds." It is not thrown haphazardly; much skill is required to broadcast this seed evenly, and such skill has been passed on from father to son in generations of accumulated experience. In order to broadcast the bean seed evenly, narrow trails have been cut with the machete through the successional growth in parallel; these trails cross the entire area of the vegetation where the beans are to be planted.

Immediately following the broadcasting of the seed, the successional growth is cut with the machete and *garabato.* For those persons who have never used the tool — and certainly people living outside the tropics are unfamiliar with it — the impression of cutting vegetation with a machete is that one just swings the blade and sees that everything is cut. The slash of the successional vegetation is, of course, more than this. This is so because each separate "weed" is just this: a separate, different kind of life, a different plant, about which culture and working experience over time have transmitted a knowledge. These are not merely weeds; they are components of a finely interconnected, remarkably diverse system of food production which involves one of the closest approximations to an ecologically balanced use of the land in the tropics that we will encounter. In the hands of the farmers of Coto Brus, the machete is used in a variety of ways to bring about planned growing conditions in the cutting of successional growth.

Following this slash, there is a second phase of the work with the machete called the *repica*. This is a recutting of the slashed vegetation and a redistribution of its mass over the surface of the ground. In this work the *garabato* is of equal importance with the machete, for both tools, in the hands of the workers, quickly and efficiently spread the cut vegetation on the ground, leaving it neither too thickly massed nor too thin.

The bean seed, then, is covered by the chopped weeds; it is not planted in the soil nor covered by the soil. It has come to rest on the decomposing litter that is always present on the earth under successional growth; thus the bean seed seldom actually comes in direct contact with the mineral soil.

The principles involved here—just in this first phase of the work— are abundant. There is enough here in this method of planting in the bean *tapado* system to keep scientists busy for years learning what is taking place in this traditional "primitive" food production. For we are not dealing only with the planting and production of beans; we are in touch with an entire frontier of planting, land management, and environmental sustainability. At some point in our contact with *tapado* planting we become aware that nature has been constantly tapping at the door of our consciousness, prepared to reveal much that is in our interest to learn.

Following the *repica*, this recutting and distribution of the chopped weeds with machete and *garabato*, there is no further work in *tapado* planting. No fertilizer has been used; no sprays are applied. Nothing is done here now until it is time to harvest the beans. A little less than three months after planting, the beans are harvested, pulled by hand, bunched in the field, later flailed with sticks, winnowed by hand on a windy day. The beans must be planted at the end of the wet season so they can be harvested during the beginning of the dry weather. All of this seems rather prosaic, hardly a matter of general interest; one more instance of a local method of food production requiring a lot of slow, manual work and not adding up to any large-scale production. The world is not going to be fed with such systems.

This is certainly true; *tapado* bean planting as compared with mechanized production methods does not appear to have much of a future beyond its traditional, small-scale practice. In the search for better ways to feed growing human populations and more efficient ways to obtain higher yields from the land, *tapado* planting is not likely to attract much attention as a farming system of the future.

It is because of its reliance on hand work that it has not attracted much attention until now. But what we should be seeing is not a system of producing beans but systems of nutrient cycling, active biodiversity, reduced pesticide inputs, and greater natural control of crop pests and diseases.

We must look more closely now at the graceless, inelegant successional forest.

Here in Coto Brus, as elsewhere in farming communities, farmers have learned to recognize certain plants—weeds—as indicators of the fertility of the land where they are growing. To a Costa Rican farmer, successional growth will reveal a lot about the prospect of carrying out planting. There is the story about the blind merchant who was led to a certain site and asked to advance money for a proposed crop to be planted there. The sightless businessman asked several questions about the weeds on the land, naming several specific species. In learning that none of these was present in any significant number, he declined to make the loan, adding that the crop being planned would fail. The story is an engaging illustration for young farmers, but its meaning is rooted in generations of careful observations.

We may recognize today that some species of plants are to be found on soils with good physical and nutrient characteristics, whereas other plants indicate many of the opposite conditions. We might ask: Are these "good" species here because they only grow on better land, or do these plants themselves contribute to making the land better? Would the same "good" species, for instance, nurtured and assisted over a period of time, help to reinstate and restore the impoverished land where now only the "bad" species are to be found? Would the successional growth accomplish this land restoration unassisted, and, if so, what amount of time would be needed?

Such questions are familiar to scientists and investigators. They also are familiar to farmers. Given enough time, nature does tend to restore the intercessions made by people. But humanity is an anticipated state of expectations; our needs and wants don't await a passive submission to natural processes. We are concerned with how to manipulate these processes in order to introduce haste in meeting our objectives.

In the *tapado* bean planting our manipulation with the machete appears to be quite successful. Let's look more closely at the conditions we are working with. First, here in this tangle of weeds, the successional growth, we are impressed with its diversity. The number of different species may or may not be greater than we have seen on a similar piece of land in another environment (this will depend on what comparisons are made), but all here in this successional growth is mixed; there is an evident contention for space and light, the resources of the soil and the air, each family and species adapting itself to the circumstances of its particular relative status on this land. If we reflect, we will recognize that here, naturally, are the processes which provide increment in populations and dominant individual traits to the strong. The establishment of different kinds of life, their multiplication and increase in this environment, is something we are concerned with, for we too must build our farming systems on traits and characteristics which have such strengths.

Were we to go into an experimental field and test conditions of "strength" in our planted crops, we could not, however we might try, equal the testing ground here at our beck in the successional growth or, for that matter, our recollection of that immense testing ground represented by the primary rain forest. But here in the successional growth, nature is at work in those same processes which led to the climax forest. The degree of culmination is obviously far less complete, but in the secondary forest the same processes of incrementing strength are at work. We might spend decades trying to introduce one or more of our chosen crops in an environment, only to find eventually that it did not adapt well, while here in the successional forest the intensity of the test of fitness has already made a selection beyond our means. We have good evidence to postulate that the many species growing well here from year to year are able to contend with plant parasitic nematodes, with the effects of high-volume, leaching rains, with the diseases and pests prevalent in this environment, with the soil nutrient deficiencies which so limit our crops. All of this is suggested to us because the successional growth thrives and continues to grow well.

But a distinction must be made: we are referring to the successional growth in its entirety, as an overall system of life and supporting relationships. In other words, we are recognizing that, having destroyed the rain forest, we are meeting its processes anew in this successional regeneration; we do have a second chance. Nature has not abandoned its quest for life, diversity, an expression of a million different impulses. Nor have we been abandoned in our opportunity to learn. Any given species within this successional growth may meet with temporary or long-term adversity; there are no guarantees of survival in these natural systems. But always, like a great natural barometer, the successional forest itself will adapt its integrated life systems, modify its nature, fit changing conditions of climate and soil — the natural circumstances of its environment. Is this important? Is there something we can do with this successional forest beyond a laborious, manually limited system of planting beans? There are many things we can do, but we have to recognize them.

From a high point of land, the summit of a hill here on Finca Loma Linda, the Pacific coast can be seen in the distance to the southwest, some four thousand feet below the farm. The hill is backed on the northeast by a section of primary rain forest, and coming up from the west is a spur of land, also in primary forest, a route followed by white-faced monkeys who come here from time to time to visit. The hilltop itself is cleared, relatively flat, and has been used during recent years for experimental work. Looking out over much of the rest of the farm from this vantage, in the near distance and also to the west, one can see the mountains rising above Agua Buena, painting their tapestry of coffee farms and pastures against the sky. We call the hilltop Windmer, and in 1986 we began some experiments there with a scientist from the University of California, Martha E. Rosemeyer.

In preparing the site for several tests with crops being studied for their root association with a fungus (vesicular-arbuscular mycorrhizae) thought to be involved in systems of phosphorus assimilation, we had cleared the land surface at Windmer using the tractor and the blade, pushing away the successional forest and some of its litter. We carefully laid out the experiment and planted. Soil fertility on the site seemed to disappear overnight. Our plantings failed; commercial fertilizers, applied as parts of the experimental treatments, did not help.

Windmer, as I have said, is bordered on two sides by sections of rain forest. The successional forest occupying the planting site before we cleared with the tractor also had been well developed, robust, vigorous. What had gone amiss over this period of only a few days? A great diversity of plant life had been thriving here; now the land seemed unfit to grow anything. Had the little seedlings themselves, our test crops, which never developed beyond a stunted, arrested condition, been able to speak, they could not have spoken more eloquently of their plight. We were baffled. This was not at all what we had foreseen for the experiment. The days went on; the vistas of the sea and the mountains and the sky maintained their disinvolved enchantment. The monkeys came and went as before in the adjoining sections of rain forest. But we had been halted in our work; our machinery, our carefully drawn-up plans coming to no successful outcome. Our objectives in the experiment would not be met.

As often happens in research, nature, life, the environment were trying to communicate with us.

Several months later on the same land, natural systems had restored a new carpet to the soil; Windmer had received a new coat of verdure. Martha's earlier experiment had run its course; we were preparing to make a second test.

This planting, with beans, produced beautiful yields with flourishing growth. We were still using the same location; only a few months had intervened between the first and second tests. What had changed?

Many things had. The surface of the ground had been restored from our earlier scraping and displacement of the successional growth and its litter. So quickly had life systems returned to endow the earth with their vitality. Also, we had planted these beans in season. The climate now was what these beans, genetically, had been looking for. There were many other things which had changed which we did not recognize and could not recognize then but which, at a later time, we would recall and understand.

In this period of months, embracing a crop failure and a crop success, the environment had been poised to reveal to us one of the principles I have referred to in this book. It is this: In wet, tropical areas such as Coto Brus, fertility is a condition of life; it is not something that is deposited in the ground. In eliminating the successional forest at Windmer with the tractor and blade, we had destroyed—just as I had destroyed by cutting the rain forest many years earlier—the life-sustaining mechanisms which are, in effect, fertility. Fertility had vanished in a matter of days. It would take us many years to understand this. There would be numerous other experiments; other investigators would join in the work; but gradually the pieces of this puzzle would fit together.

Subsequent experiments at a site adjacent to Windmer, called El Naciente, broadened our understanding about what was happening with the successional growth and its decomposing litter. We compared *tapado* planting with clean culture, simulating what might be the case where weed growth had been eliminated with herbicides. These tests, which have continued over subsequent years, also involved different levels of commercial fertilizer applications. The experiment at El Naciente has spoken clearly of the dynamics of fertility and associated plant and related life. Martha has published some of her findings and will be publishing more. What we have been seeing and continue to see is the potential for improved cropping systems in what has come to be called "mulch agriculture." Shorn of its research complexity, this term means an agriculture which relies on mulches, the residues of plants and other biota, to bring together a responsive, life-giving layer of fertility on the very surface of the ground.

A few years after the experiment at Windmer, I carried out the independent experiment at El Nogalito I described earlier. This experiment, along with another experiment planted for Martha and her former professor, Stephen R. Gliessman, director of the agroecology program at the University of California at Santa Cruz, brought us closer to understanding the mechanisms of mulch agriculture, the importance of organic matter in fertility transfer in the tropics, and the potential in these for environmental management. Steve Gliessman had worked with me here before going on to take up his position with the University of California. We had talked about many of these research prospects during our work together.

As groups of graduate students from U.S. and Latin American universities visited Finca Loma Linda through courses in agroecology, which Martha eventually directed for the Organization for Tropical Studies, we found our thinking being challenged and developed by these students' questions about this work and where it was leading. One student, James Kettler, from the Institute of Ecology at the University of Georgia, joined us in the research with a three-year, doctoral dissertation project. He set up a resourceful alley-cropping experiment with four species of trees in an experimental area on the farm called Los Arcos. Again, further information about the principles embraced in *tapado* planting were investigated.

Jim was joined shortly after he got started with his project in Los Arcos by Kenneth Schlather, a scientist from Cornell University who was also working on his doctoral dissertation. Ken brought a dedication to his research interests that impressed us all. Early in his contact with our work he recognized the opportunities for groundbreaking experimentation in an area which could have meaningful implications in tropical soils research and farming. Setting up several of his own experiments, he joined Martha and worked with Jim to uncover more information about the interaction of phosphorus and soil organic matter in crop nutrition. The work returned to the basic principles observed in *tapado* planting. Here, indeed, in this joint work, we were on the threshold of discoveries relating to overall nutrient uptake under vegetative covers. Finding himself close to the research goals he believed might involve an important phase of his life, Ken carried out a marathon of testing and analyses of soils and plant tissues in the laboratory at the University of Costa Rica to consolidate his own research goals and demonstrate where such work could lead.

While we were seeing momentum develop in all this work, a scientist and member of the faculty of the University of California at Irvine, Frances Lynn Carpenter, began her own research program at a location near Finca Loma Linda, where she bought a neglected and impoverished farm with the intention of restoring it through reforestation with native, primary forest tree species and several treatments with interplanted cover crops. *Tapado* planting was among the experimental treatments she was testing, and there soon grew up a close coordination between work at her farm and the research being carried out on Finca Loma Linda.

At an earlier time, a professor on the faculty of the University of California at Santa Cruz, Deborah K. Letourneau, had directed a six-year research project in the rain forest here at the farm to explore the relationship in a little universe within a fragment of forest, a relationship between ants and their host plant. The project challenged the resources of investigation with all of the elements of mystery, like a puzzle to be solved. Over the years the meaning of the interactions of these diminutive forms of life became clear to us, and Deborah went on to publish her findings in several journals and explain them at international conferences. She also taught me my first lessons in scientific methodology and helped enable me to train my farm personnel to do qualified scientific work.

These employees, all part of the generation of the children of the settlers, confirmed what I believed—that from our local community here in Coto Brus could be recruited outstanding research personnel. Lorena Lobo; Román and Leonel Gómez, brothers who made some of the critical breakthroughs in months and months of work in the rain forest for Deborah; José Castro; Sandra Méndez, who worked on the research projects with us in recent years; and my secretary and research assistant, Julieta Méndez, on whom I rely to correct so many of my professional shortcomings, are among the people who have carried our research forward with their hands and their hearts and minds in the work from day to day.

Where will this lead? Each of the scientists working on this project, and those who are becoming associated and will become associated with it, will make his or her findings known through conventional scientific means. Their work will focus on separate parts of an overall picture. I'd like to delineate some of the dimensions of this picture and how it looks from my perspective.

We have now in Coto Brus an opportunity to trace with closer proximity the origins of much that has been transmitted from a point of initiation of settlement. We have also an opportunity to recreate and reconstruct much that was dismantled in the recent past without becoming disinvolved from that past by a long interval of time. This is a rather unique opportunity.

Our research is going to lead us into the area of restoration and rebuilding. And it is going to broaden our horizons so that we will recognize that tropical agriculture, like agriculture anywhere, is not merely the cultivation of the land for a particular profit, but rather an overall management of the environment for a better way of life for people on the earth and their counterparts, other living things. We have this opportunity particularly here today in Coto Brus. Our environment is still young, our generations of farmers and residents on the land still resilient and imaginative.

As we encounter this frontier, the frontier of this fresh horizon, we must not narrow our focus in our different pursuits to a point where we fail to remember that that earlier frontier, the frontier of the rain forest, was always an integrated system of many splendors. It will not be possible to till the land without remembering too that the climate is part of it, to look at the earth and neglect to understand that the sky, the air, the moisture, the solar energy, are part of it. We will, of course, have to look closely at the element phosphorus; at symbiotic, fungi-root associations; at the role of leguminous trees in maintaining soil productivity; at the possibility of restoring degraded land through reforestation; and at the secrets of ants and their host plants in the darkened forest.

But what will distinguish the research to be carried out here in Coto Brus will be an integration of these many insights. It will also be an integration at the scientific level with the farmers in whose hands the future of the environment so closely rests.

We will see new, specific farming systems emerge from this work. Where disease problems so affect all of our crop production and these diseases become so entrenched in the very land on which the crops are to be sustained, we will see a transfer of the properties of soil productivity through plants' tissues and thence to litter or compost to constitute a separate growing medium divorced from some of the site-specific problems which, under crop production, would eventually overtake any long-term use of a given piece of land. This matter is critical; it is the ability to transfer and concentrate the means of sustaining land use by conveying the resources from one piece of land to another.

Here the successional forest can become a classroom, as the rain forest before it might have been. As we study the different components of this successional growth, its interacting systems, we will have an opportunity to learn how natural processes function, are established, and are maintained. This information will help us plan and maintain farming systems. The successional forest is made up of many species. At present we are studying these to learn their individual characteristics. We will find that these species are indeed different in their adaptability to changing environmental circumstances, and in learning more about these differing traits, we will become better informed about how to relieve some of the stress and environmental tensions inherent in our production monocultures. When we have learned more about these natural systems—those seeming to rise spontaneously without any deliberate culture from us—we will be in a better position to introduce new crops, combine them with the existing successional growth, and manage them for productive and commercial purposes.

Manage weeds for productive purposes? The idea does seem strange. What we will come to see, however, is that these weeds are part of the long shadow cast by the rain forest. In them that forest still may be known. The day will come when we will harvest these weeds—we are doing this now on Finca Loma Linda—and convert them into a growing medium for plants and improvement of the soil. As we do this we will find that fertility in the successional forest is spatial, having a vertical dimension above the surface of the ground in the stature of the vegetation growing there as well as below the ground surface where roots have created an as-yet-unexplored world.

As we learn to think in terms of this spatial fertility, we will recognize too that the rainfall, the sunlight, and the moderate temperatures here in the tropics can be harnessed through the plant and microbiota systems crowding over the earth to create new concepts in farming, in which part of the land will be used to support production on other portions, and these will be rotated and become supporting areas in their turn. We will learn how to obtain more "yield" from the nutrient inputs in commercial fertilizers, by incorporating their nutrients in the organic matrix of growing plants and other life associated with these, and how to keep these added nutrients in sustained circulation in cropping systems, thereby reducing the requirement for frequent application or high fertilizer inputs.

In wet, tropical areas such as Coto Brus, we will also come to cultivate many of our plantings in the mulch and litter at the very surface of the ground, finding in this layer under adequate moisture conditions a special dimension in our agriculture, where cultivation will be redefined as our ability to develop and maintain this litter layer with as little physical and disruptive intervention as possible.

Some of this is well beyond our present understanding, but we cannot accept that what we know is a stopping point, a place beyond which we need not pursue what we have begun. Our presence here enjoins that we learn and act upon an expanding horizon of learning. That the horizon may be formidable is only a measure of what we can attain.

We have this opportunity. We probably are not as far removed from its partial realization as we may suppose. Our record upon this earth is a record neither of triumphs nor of concessions; we are not yet so wise as to know with certainty which character in reality is ours. What we must do is stand equally by our errors even though we may wish to be known only by our achievements. For there cannot be the one without the other. And we cannot advance forever in the shadow of apprehension. Few people are more responsible to themselves, to something within themselves, to a past and to a hope and a wish for a future, than we who have taken up the blade against the rain forest. Yet, we have this injunction to go on.

By these things we stand.

The Green Mantle

*S*everal days ago I was returning in the afternoon from Windmer, where I had been looking in at an experiment we are just beginning at El Naciente for scientists at Cornell University, and as I came to the brow of the hill looking down at the rest of the farm, I paused to look out at the mountains beyond Agua Buena, clear on that afternoon, with some wisps of clouds blowing across the summits. The wet season was ending; the air was at once lucid and moist, moisture actually saturating everything. This is a green land, but, seen on an afternoon like this, much of the green landscape in the distance has tones of deep blue and purple, shadows, deep saturation of rain.

I also had been at the experimental site at El Naciente that morning, and, looking down over the Pacific coast, I watched the long shadow of a storm there, very dark and extended all along the horizon. The volcano, Barú, in Panama was also somber that morning, yet the sky above it was open under high, metallically gray clouds.

The experiment would be looking at plant pathogens, particularly nematodes affecting the roots, and the scientists involved would be visiting the farm later in the season. Before their arrival there were several things we needed to do with this new trial, an experiment that would be linked closely with other research at the site.

But as I paused at the crest of the hill at Windmer, my thoughts were only partly on the experiment. As a boy I had wanted to go to sea and spend a good part of my life traveling. Had anyone asked me when I was in high school what part of the earth I might most have liked to explore, it would probably have been Canada and Alaska. I had no thought at that time of my life about remaining long in one place, much less the tropics.

The clouds were moving steadily across the slopes and a little above the summits of the mountains beyond Agua Buena; I must have seen them so a thousand times. Always, of course, they were different; a different character, truly, with each changing moment. Yet, how many characters could you imbue or explore in a scene that had been imprinted over decades upon the mind? Still, there was always something almost spoken in these moments, as though the clouds were bearers of some ageless message, all conveyed in silence, the grand voice of some unlettered past.

Those farms on the mountains now would be experiencing some increased well-being; the price of coffee was up again, after seven very bad years. Families would be returning to their land; people would be cautiously optimistic—but then farmers always are cautious, rarely admitting that they are hopeful about the market's future.

This indeed was a green land, a million different aspects of this color flowering and bursting into form and light.

How might it have been, I wondered, if I had gone to sea? Those same clouds that now skirted the slopes of the Agua Buena mountains would have been the companions of a distant, azure horizon. No mountains there; no teeming, almost suffocating, green—just the endless sway and motion of the orb of sky and the blue, unmeasured expanse of ocean. But even in my lifetime that world too had changed. In reality, my longing for the sea had been a longing for freedom, expanse, distance, that illimitable place always just beyond the day—a world to be explored and won.

I might go down to the sea; I had spent many summers at the ocean when I was a boy. Down to the sea.

But here was all the green and the expanse of the land and the sky, and the deep, dark purple of the secrets in the shadows.

Generation upon generation would flower upon the earth, availing themselves of this capacity for life and diversity. There had come a storm in the morning out over the coast at sea. The clouds spoke now in wordless austerity above the farms and the homes at Agua Buena.

Would it have really mattered whether it had been the land or the sea—a life of adventure, always moving, always breaking new horizons in some distant travel? Would it have led to any other outcome?

There, here now, it was, always as it had been from the first—clouds crossing the distance in the mountains, spilling down in dark memories. Still, we had the work to be done in the experiments, in a thousand ways to search and ask. The clouds were falling along the river channels in the mountains above Agua Buena, faint wisps in the mantle of green. There wasn't any difference, really, the sea or these mountains; they were part of an unknown horizon, an expanding future. That time is behind me now, I thought. Then that age-old message spoke in the silence, the distance, the mountains: I had been lucky to know them when all the vista of this future was young.

CPSIA information can be obtained at www.ICGtesting.com
Printed in the USA
BVOW04s0039130314

347517BV00001B/46/P